MW01259870

WOMEN AND WEALTH

WOMEN AND AND WEALTH

A PLAYBOOK TO EMPOWER CLIENTS AND UNLOCK THEIR FORTUNE

CARY CARBONARO

WILEY

Copyright © 2025 by John Wiley & Sons, Inc. All rights reserved, including rights for text and data mining and training of artificial intelligence technologies or similar technologies.

Published by John Wiley & Sons, Inc., Hoboken, New Jersey.

Published simultaneously in Canada.

No part of this publication may be reproduced, stored in a retrieval system, or transmitted in any form or by any means, electronic, mechanical, photocopying, recording, scanning, or otherwise, except as permitted under Section 107 or 108 of the 1976 United States Copyright Act, without either the prior written permission of the Publisher, or authorization through payment of the appropriate per-copy fee to the Copyright Clearance Center, Inc., 222 Rosewood Drive, Danvers, MA 01923, (978) 750-8400, fax (978) 750-4470, or on the web at www.copyright.com. Requests to the Publisher for permission should be addressed to the Permissions Department, John Wiley & Sons, Inc., 111 River Street, Hoboken, NJ 07030, (201) 748-6011, fax (201) 748-6008, or online at http://www.wiley.com/go/permission.

The manufacturer's authorized representative according to the EU General Product Safety Regulation is Wiley-VCH GmbH, Boschstr. 12, 69469 Weinheim, Germany, e-mail: Product_Safety@wiley.com.

Trademarks: Wiley and the Wiley logo are trademarks or registered trademarks of John Wiley & Sons, Inc. and/or its affiliates in the United States and other countries and may not be used without written permission. All other trademarks are the property of their respective owners. John Wiley & Sons, Inc. is not associated with any product or vendor mentioned in this book.

Limit of Liability/Disclaimer of Warranty: While the publisher and author have used their best efforts in preparing this book, they make no representations or warranties with respect to the accuracy or completeness of the contents of this book and specifically disclaim any implied warranties of merchantability or fitness for a particular purpose. No warranty may be created or extended by sales representatives or written sales materials. The advice and strategies contained herein may not be suitable for your situation. You should consult with a professional where appropriate. Further, readers should be aware that websites listed in this work may have changed or disappeared between when this work was written and when it is read. Neither the publisher nor authors shall be liable for any loss of profit or any other commercial damages, including but not limited to special, incidental, consequential, or other damages.

For general information on our other products and services or for technical support, please contact our Customer Care Department within the United States at (800) 762-2974, outside the United States at (317) 572-3993 or fax (317) 572-4002.

Wiley also publishes its books in a variety of electronic formats. Some content that appears in print may not be available in electronic formats. For more information about Wiley products, visit our web site at www.wiley.com.

Library of Congress Cataloging-in-Publication Data:

Names: Carbonaro, Cary, author.
Title: Women and wealth : a playbook to empower clients and unlock
    their fortune / Cary Carbonaro, FL, US.
Description: Hoboken, NJ : John Wiley & Sons Inc., 2025. | Includes
    bibliographical references and index.
Identifiers: LCCN 2024060024 (print) | LCCN 2024060025 (ebook) | ISBN
    9781394300273 (hardback) | ISBN 9781394300297 (pdf) | ISBN 9781394300280
    (epub)
Subjects: LCSH: Women–Finance, Personal. | Finance, Personal. | Investment
    advisor-client relationships. | Customer relations. | Financial planners.
Classification: LCC HG179.5 .C362 2025 (print) | LCC HG179.5 (ebook) |
    DDC 332.024/01082–dc23/eng/20250218
LC record available at https://lccn.loc.gov/2024060024
LC ebook record available at https://lccn.loc.gov/2024060025

Cover Image: © Zen Rial/Getty Images
Author Photo: Courtesy of the Author
Cover Design: Wiley

SKY10099444_030725

Dedicated to my Dad in heaven, whose wisdom and passion for finance inspired my journey into wealth management and taught me everything I know about money. To my incredible husband, Steve, whose unwavering support allows me to pursue my life's calling. And to all the remarkable women who inspire me daily—you are my motivation and my mission.

CONTENTS

CONTENTS

Contents

Dear Readers,

Welcome to *Women and Wealth: A Playbook to Empower Clients and Unlock Their Fortune*. I'm so glad you've picked up this book, and I want to share a few thoughts about how best to use it to maximize the value you get from it.

This book is designed as a guide to help you navigate the unique financial challenges women face while empowering you to build stronger relationships with your female clients. Whether you're a financial advisor, a professional working with women on financial matters, or a woman looking to take control of your financial future, this book will provide you with tools, strategies, and real-world insights to move forward with confidence.

Here's how I suggest you use it:

1. **Read with Intention**

   Each chapter covers a specific aspect of women and wealth, from understanding the female psyche to effective communication, planning for long-term care, and even how to make the financial industry more female-friendly. You'll get the most out of this book if you approach it with a mindset of learning, reflection, and action. Take notes, highlight key points, and jot down any ideas or strategies that resonate with you.

2. **Use the Case Studies**

   The case studies in this book are included to show real-life examples of how certain financial strategies and practices can work with female clients. Study them carefully. Think about how they might apply to your own clients or financial situation, and use them as models to guide your decision-making.

3. **Pause and Reflect on the Questions**

   Throughout the book, you'll find questions designed to encourage self-reflection and discussion. If you're an advisor, these questions can help you assess your current practices and identify opportunities for improvement. If you're a woman navigating your own financial journey, use these questions to think critically about your financial goals, concerns, and the type of advisor relationship you want.

4. **Tailor the Advice to Your Situation**

   While this book provides comprehensive insights, each client's or reader's financial situation is unique. Don't hesitate to adapt the advice and strategies presented here to your own circumstances. Customize the solutions to fit your needs or those of your clients.

5. **Take Action**

   Knowledge is powerful, but it only makes an impact when it's put into action. Whether it's rethinking how you approach women clients, changing the way you communicate, or revising your financial plan, commit to taking at least one action step from each chapter. Implementing these changes will not only benefit you but also help you build stronger, more trusting relationships with your clients or partners.

6. **Use It as a Resource for Collaboration**

   If you're part of a team, this book can be a valuable tool for team discussions and improvements. Consider hosting a workshop or roundtable discussion using the content from this book to help foster better collaboration around female-centric financial planning.

7. **Rethink Your Client Experience**

   A major theme in this book is understanding women's financial needs and creating an experience that serves them fully. As you read, consider how your business or your personal approach could evolve to be more inclusive, holistic, and empowering. Small changes, like active listening and empathetic communication, can have a huge impact.

8. **Keep It as a Long-term Resource**

   This isn't just a book to read once and set aside. Refer back to it often. As new challenges and opportunities arise, revisit certain chapters, questions, and strategies. It's meant to be a playbook— something you can come back to as you evolve in your role, as a woman or as an advisor.

Finally, my hope is that this book will not only help you grow financially but also encourage you to become an advocate for women's wealth, empowering others to do the same. Together, we can reshape the financial industry and ensure that women are not just participants but leaders in creating their financial future.

Thank you for joining me on this journey toward financial empowerment for women.

With gratitude,
Cary Carbonaro

CHAPTER ONE

MY STORY

Be yourself; everyone else is already taken.

-Oscar Wilde

INDEPENDENT WOMAN

I was born in Brooklyn, New York, and raised in Long Island. Like many women, I came from a very traditional household. In witnessing the dynamic between my mom and dad, I decided I wanted to be more like my dad: I wanted to be the one who made the money. I learned at an early age that money equals power. I was brought up with the notion I could be anything I wanted to be–even president. I never felt like I had to compromise or that a profession like finance was too male. It never even occurred to me. My dad worked in finance, and I wanted to follow in his footsteps.

I'm human, just like everyone else. I've had some great successes, great failures, and I've had to rechart my financial life in the face of change more than once. I built a successful business, got married, experienced a painful and financially damaging divorce, and then had to rebuild. My firm was sold, I almost lost my career, and I have had to rebuild again. But I've also followed my passions. One of those passions is financial planning. As a child, my banker father exposed me early on to the financial world. He taught me strong money values, the importance of working hard, and gave me my love for being smart with money. He took me to work with him before there was a "Take your Daughter to Work" day. My mother was a big part of that passion too. She is a certified public accountant (CPA), and she also went back to school later in life, when I was 13. After graduating from college, my career moved quickly up the corporate ladder, including eight years on Wall Street at JP Morgan Chase, three years as a vice president at Citibank, and two years as a director at Lord Abbett Investments. By the time I turned 30, I was earning $500,000 a year. I thought I had it made! I had met and exceeded so many goals in life. I was financially independent and confident in my ability to support myself. I refused to learn normal domestic duties because I had determined that would not be for me. I thought: If I make the money, then I will be safe, be able to make my own decisions, and have freedom. What could possibly go wrong?

This line of thinking is nearly always a preamble for disaster. As women, we can often set ourselves up for failure. Life takes us to unexpected places all the time. In my case, it led me into a marriage that, in the end, severely compromised my happiness, my confidence, and my financial bottom line. I made the wrong choice in my life because of my unhealthy emotional state. It wasn't for lack of intellect or knowledge. In fact, bad decisions are often fueled by either conscious or unconscious emotional responses.

MONEY CAN'T BUY ME LOVE

When I got married, I had no idea what I was in for. I was vulnerable and trusting, which made me the perfect victim. Sounds familiar, doesn't it? All the while, I carried the bulk of our shared financial burden. I had come into the marriage as the primary breadwinner, and that showed no signs of changing any time soon. We never had a joint account. He had his money, and I had mine. I thought that would protect me. I always paid my own bills, so at first, I didn't realize I was paying for nearly everything. Bills came in, and my income went out. My husband had his own reasons for not chipping in. He referred to himself as a "serial entrepreneur," who would never work for anyone other than himself. He was stubborn, unwilling to undertake traditional work, and dependent on my financial support.

He said he was an ex-hedge fund manager who had retired twice by the time he was 30. His money was his and was "unavailable" for paying bills. I soon realized that his finances were a mess. On the surface, he was successful and well-to-do, but scratch the surface, and he had terrible credit. He'd never paid back his undergraduate or law school student loans. He had accounts under his control in his father's, his mother's, and even an old girlfriend's name, in which he would sock money away. He had more than a dozen companies set up in his name, creating such a quagmire around tax time that his files would arrive in a box nearly as tall as my 5 foot 5 inches. It was impossible for me to figure out what was going on with his money, but he always seemed to know what was going on with mine. I simply accepted his lies and wrote the checks because I was taught to always be responsible and pay the bills on time. My stellar credit rating was very important to me, and he knew it.

Three years into this unhealthy relationship, my father passed away. The ground slipped out from under my feet, and I was spinning out of control. Looking back, I can say with some certainty that this time in my life was my rock bottom. And then one day, I was surprised with a marital separation agreement that my husband had drafted completely on his own. When I arrived at home, I was ambushed by six witnesses waiting for me to sign a 100-page document that I'd never seen before. After reading only six pages, I realized the agreement stipulated I hand over 50% of my business...the only thing I knew I had control over was 100% my own.

The rest of the day turned into a blur as I was bullied into signing the document through verbal abuse and threats. My professional side knew something was very wrong, but the emotional toll of the situation was just too much for me to take. I signed the agreement under duress. I literally gave away half of what I earned and half of what I had worked tirelessly to build. Through my signature, it was his.

When the divorce began, money was literally flying out the window as quick as it came in the door. Ultimately, I found myself on a long, lonely road to divorce. It was a process that lasted for years and included countless contract negotiations and financial red tape that threatened not just my earnings to date, but my future earnings as well. Once the relationship ended, the financial conundrum began. My ex-husband felt he was entitled to much of what I earned and almost all that I built. Never mind that I made most of the money and paid the bills. That was not enough. He wanted it all. And worst of all, he felt that it was his right. He told the divorce attorneys and the judge the financial planning practice was his and he was suing me for it.

It was an arduous, six-figure-plus divorce with emotionally driven decisions affecting me at every turn. I owned two houses, but while the titles of those homes were in both our names, the mortgages were in my name alone. This meant that, for a long time, my ex was living in one of those homes while I paid the mortgage, bills, and car payments. He was living the dream while I was trapped in an emotional and financial nightmare. Relief was nowhere to be found.

Anyone who knew me asked, "Why would you do that?" The short answer is that emotions were fueling my decisions. Of course, it's never as simple as that—emotions never are. For one, I had fabulous credit and, as taught by my parents, felt driven to pay every bill for which I was responsible, fair or not. I knew that in the long run, I would be punished if I didn't pay the bills. One of my biggest reasons for staying as long as I did was *FEAR*. It wasn't just the threats my husband levied against me, but I was afraid of losing everything I'd built. The only thing I still had control over was my business. I'd created it and watched it start to thrive despite everything that was happening in my personal life. It became my lifeboat, so I started to think that if I could get to a certain benchmark in my career, I could make things start to happen in my personal life. "When I make X," I'd reason with myself, "I'll walk away."

For weeks, he and his staff refused to provide me with a copy of the marital separation agreement. When I finally received a copy of the agreement, I went to see a dear trusted friend, who is also a family law attorney. We reviewed the entire agreement and found that not only did it ask me to sacrifice half of my business, but it also appointed my ex-husband as executor of my estate–he was to receive 50% of my future inheritances and get to use my credit for the rest of his life and many more stipulations that, in hindsight, were crazy. If I violated any stipulation, including moving my business, the "agreement" stated I would owe him five million dollars in a "liquidated damages clause." On top of everything else, as soon as divorce proceedings started, I was sued for alimony and temporary support. It was literally a one-sided financial catastrophe.

After endless tears, my friend offered a glimmer of hope. She said the document was so egregious that she didn't believe it would hold up in court. It was clear to any unbiased bystander that I was manipulated and coerced into signing the agreement. I hired an attorney and prepared for battle. During the divorce, I was bleeding cash. I could not make money fast enough, and I was in the red every month for the first time in my entire life. I was fortunate to have an emergency fund, something I advise all my clients to have, and it allowed me to get through the almost four years of negative cash flow. I remember one month my attorney bill was $50,000. I was paying it by credit card at the attorney's office and crying. I was not my best self! I pay off my credit cards in full at the end of the month. Then I thought of a quote from one of my favorite movies, *It's a Wonderful Life*. Annie, the Bailey's housekeeper, gives George some of her hard-earned cash at the close of the film and says, "I've been savin' this money for a divorce, if ever I got a husband!" But I was determined to put my head down, suck it up, and stand strong to ensure I stood for what I believed. It was time I fought hard to protect what I built over the first half of my life. I was a powerful woman, and I would not let this man try to take everything away from me. I fought to regain my power, freedom, and life.

I WILL SURVIVE

If you are a financial advisor, you will appreciate this story. I started to receive calls from my clients saying, "I just got a call from an SEC attorney asking me if I lost money in 2008." This was 2009. The global financial crisis was from 2008 to 2009. If you lived through it, you remember. Everyone lost money no matter what you were invested in. My ex-husband hired an SEC attorney to start a class action lawsuit against me and started contacting my clients asking if they lost money in 2008 and if they wanted to be part of a class action lawsuit. First, everyone knew that was ridiculous. It was the global financial crisis and markets melted down all over the world. By 2009 my client accounts were all back up. At the time it was enough to send me off a cliff. It was embarrassing, dragged my clients into the divorce, and cost me more money with the attorney to force him to stop. Throughout my personal struggles, financial planning remained a professional endeavor and a safe haven that brought me joy. It was as if I was living vicariously through the intelligent financial decisions of others. I was paying for my mistakes, but at least I was helping others. It all felt worth it. So, I refocused on my job and found new aspects of the industry that made me happy. After years of struggle, as well as personal development, I was ready to take my life to its highest and best use. My personal trials and tribulations could only be fantastic examples and learning experiences for others.

Many of my bad decisions came in the form of my taste in men. My Achilles' heel was intimate relationships. I was simply attracted to the wrong type of guy. I had a wonderful role model in my dad. Why should I keep making poor decisions in this area of my life? I explored this for years in therapy. When I first started, my therapist asked me, "What do you feel?" I didn't even understand the question. I was so out of touch with my emotional being, which I deemed to be too female, that I didn't know what I didn't know. How could I choose the right partner when I didn't even know how to emotionally relate? This took years of peeling back the onion, layer after layer. It was hard work, and I always wanted to quit. My therapist would say, "Cary, I am committed to you; you have to be committed to me. This is your life we are saving." I had already been burned badly. I was still trying to put the pieces of my life back together. My life and my business were damaged.

And then came a glimmer of light at the end of the dark tunnel. I was at the Orlando airport one Monday morning in late 2009 when I struck up a conversation with a man in the security line. This wasn't unusual. I often start conversations with people around me and don't think much of it. But by the end of the line, I knew he was from Long Island just like me and lived in Central Florida, just like me. He worked in both states and was a professional in the pharmaceutical industry. He also had experienced a very difficult and contentious divorce.

After talking for a long time, we exchanged contact info. He emailed me the next day and asked if I wanted to go out for coffee, lunch, or dinner in Florida or New York. He said it was my choice. He wanted to give me options! I really wasn't sure if I should accept; I didn't think I was ready to let another man into my life. To be completely cautious and not rush into another relationship, I kept my distance and allowed our friendship to grow.

We communicated via email over the next few months. He had such a positive outlook on life, with an amazing spirit, and a genuine smile that reached his eyes. He was very confident in himself, and he knew who he was. It was extremely refreshing. When I told my therapist I wasn't sure

I was ready to date, he told me to give him his number so he could reach out and speak with my new interest. I was terrified, but I did it. They spoke for an hour and a half. My therapist called me afterward and told me, "This is the man I have always wanted for you–a true partner. You can give and receive love to each other." I felt relieved and was excited that I was able to filter through the crap and find a man that could potentially be a healthy fit in my life. I was seeing spots after my last relationship, so I was unsure if I could ever focus again. So, it was with great enthusiasm that I began the process of opening my life to this man.

As our life blossomed together, I began to take a very reflective and strong look at my life up to that point. I quickly began to recognize that many, if not all, of my poor financial decisions were directly related to the opposite sex. My relationships led directly to much of the financial hardships I experienced.

That may be the first and most important lesson I can impart on my clients: *Don't allow your emotions to control your financial decisions*. It is a recipe for disaster. I lost hundreds of thousands of dollars because I couldn't see that my emotional relationship was manifesting bad financial practices in my monetary relationship. This could have all been avoided if I simply opened my eyes. This is a common story for many women. We are emotional beings, and we often lead with our emotions, allowing us to trust people we otherwise would not. And the result can be debilitating.

Inevitably, at some point in your life the line between personal decisions and financial decisions is going to blur; this was a blurry time for me. The emotions were heavy and real, and they made it that much more difficult to see the forest from the trees, as the saying goes. This dichotomy of the head and the heart is the root cause of many poor financial decisions, and I was not immune. I lived it, and the silver lining is that I have learned to use those experiences to help others now that I've made it through the worst. This is so important for financial professionals to understand and understand what women are going through.

I was not your typical woman who was worried about ending up penniless. I was an educated, successful, self-sufficient woman of means who had designer bags, shoes, etc. My therapist said it was a dichotomy he thought was funny. He called me the Designer Bag Lady. I loved the name, and so it stuck. I knew I was not alone when in 2006, Allianz published a study, "Women, Power and Money" indicating that 27% of women who made over $200K had the same issue.[1] Thus, I gave birth to the term "Designer Bag Ladies." My clients love to say aloud, "I am the Designer Bag Lady." They call me and ask me if they can afford a new car or house. They admit their fear keeps them from being able to spend money even though they are successful and have more than enough. They quickly become their own worst enemy. More about this later.

WOMEN EMPOWERING WOMEN

So, where do we go from here? To start, women should be empowered and uplifted to begin the process of saving at an early age. It is not just about avoiding financial landmines as you age. It is also about being able to recover if you do step on one. My financial landmine was marrying a man and allowing him to siphon off much of what I worked hard to build. He was not entitled to it and did not deserve it. But I was manipulated and could not get out of the way of my own emotions. The important thing is to understand that if you counsel your clients to save and invest, they will be positioned to absorb whatever life throws their way. I recovered and made it out of that relationship in one piece because I had the padding (emergency fund) we all should have. In the end, I had to *pay* my ex to get out and was emotionally and financially devastated. He had more money than me but was hiding it offshore and in other names. He appeared to be a pauper on paper. It was not a fair outcome, but I needed to move my life forward. I needed to pay for my freedom.

THE RAINBOW AFTER THE STORM

I was a solo practitioner as a fee-only registered investment advisor (RIA). I wanted a large, independent fee-only RIA to join. I just couldn't handle everyone on my own anymore. It was me and one staff member Rich Westhelle, who is still with me today. We've been together for 15 years and counting.

After the divorce was final, I moved my firm to United Capital. It is a very different model from the big banks and brokerage firms. It is also more difficult to work this way because you don't have the branding and marketing of a big name. It is only you. The clients have to buy into you, not the firm. I self-sourced every client I ever got. I was never handed clients or leads from a retiring advisor. I was always a fiduciary and put my clients first. It was a great move for me. I wanted the resources and camaraderie of a large firm. I really loved the other advisors and founders of the firm. It was a great decision. Their client experience was very female-friendly because of our behavioral finance tools. We were growing organically and inorganically. I was on the advisory council that helped to shape the decisions of the firm. I wrote a business case to the chief executive officer (CEO) of the firm about how important women were to the future of the industry. I included many of the stats you will find in this book, and it was approved. I, along with Emily Sanders, ran Women's Leadership at United Capital. I felt like I was moving the needle for women and wealth there. We were big enough that I had a platform and a voice to affect change. My practice went from $50 million, which was small mainly because of my protracted divorce, to more than $200 million assets under management (AUM) as a solo practitioner while I was there. According to Michael Kitces, financial planner and commentator, at $200 million plus AUM, I should have a staff of seven, not just me and Rich. I wrote my book (*The Money Queen's Guide: For Women Who Want to Build Wealth and Banish Fear*), spoke everywhere, and again was doing my one thing, helping women in a meaningful way.

UNITED CAPITAL SALE

It was 2019, and I was right where I wanted to be! I had many roles: head of Women's Leadership, the Voice of the Women, which the head of the firm asked me to represent the firm in the media, TV, etc. I was FinLife Coach for other advisors, and last but most important, I had a Diamond Winning Office and Practice at United Capital, which means I was one of the best of the best at United Capital. We were ranked by seven key performance indicators (KPIs): organic growth, net promoter scores, retention, revenue per employee to name a few. Every year we had an annual partners meeting. In 2019 it was in Arizona at the upscale Phoenician. It was the first time my firm offered a prize that actually came with something. A 20% increase in pay for a year! It was like winning the lottery. I was sure I was winning it. Of the seven KPIs, I knew I had at least six of the seven. We did this only one year, and out of 100 offices only six offices won. What I highlighted and found most remarkable was that four of the six, or 66%, were women-led offices. I remember highlighting that on social media, and it went viral. I was also voted no. 4 in financial advisors in the United States as ranked by Investopedia in 2019. Life was good! I was making a difference for women and wealth and the profession by making it more female-friendly!

United Capital 2019 Diamond Office Winners, 75% Women-Led Firms

My life philosophy is not about getting new clients; it is about speaking the truth. I know this makes me different. It has never been about the money for me as much as it has been about helping women and making the world better than when I got here.

CALL ME²

I was at an Invest in Women's conference in 2019 where I was speaking and running two panels. Soon after, I was on a conference call with everyone–all the managing directors, executive team, and our charismatic

CEO, Walter. I loved him; he is why I went to the firm. He informed us that we just got an offer from the most prestigious investment bank on Wall Street to buy us. I sat on the phone in awe. What did he just say? How could that be? We were a national RIA firm, but we are quite small to any of the broker dealers. All of those are household names. I am a sassy New Yorker. I tell it like it is, I am very direct, and I don't hide my feelings. Under normal circumstances I am also very *confident*. Sometimes it scares people, depending on the situation.

This firm was the white glove untouchable firm I knew from my early career. I was in the JP Morgan Chase at the time in the Chemical Bank Management Training program. I took care of a bunch of these bankers because I worked with select or private banking clients. I was always calling them to tell them they have too much cash in their checking account that was not even interest bearing. How could they leave free money on the table? I offered to convert it or sweep something at least into a savings or money market paying much more. I loved doing it and helping people make more money or maximizing what they had. I liked the people I worked with from there. This was in the early 90s before it went public in May of 1999. I never thought about working there, but I remember they made *a lot* of money!

How could this firm want to buy us? Why would they? They were 150 years old, and we were just over 10 years old. This was a big deal.

It was exciting, and I was optimistic about my future and the future of my firm with the weight and resources of a giant firm. I knew they had a class action lawsuit with women employees ongoing for 10 years. I imagined all the ways I could help. I am a known advocate for women. This could be a win-win. It could give me a large platform (the largest investment bank in the world), and I in turn could make it more female-friendly like I was doing at United Capital.

GIRL INTERRUPTED

The next few weeks no one had any idea what happened, what it was going to look like, or when it was going to be announced to the public, and we weren't allowed to tell anyone.

My husband and I had a trip planned for the end of May 2019, around Memorial Day, to go to Japan. We were going to Tokyo and Kyoto. Japan is 14 hours ahead of New York. The deal was announced while we were in Japan. My phone started ringing off the hook, and it was such a time disparity that it was almost impossible to speak to my clients. I said we have to cut the trip short and not go to Kyoto. We will have to come back. Little did we know the world would shut down months later and my life as I knew it was going to drastically change.

Upon returning from my trip things moved very fast!. It was announced at the end of May 2019, and we would be closing and becoming their employees by July 15, 2019. That is some sort of a record. We were told there was going to be a large amount of money granted in stock options to the partners and executive team. Our current shares of stock would also be converted into their firm's shares, and we would not have an unexpected tax event. We are financial planners by trade and this came out of the blue. To go over and be paid, we all signed new contracts. We also had to do background checks, fingerprints, etc. and keep running our business with clients who had more questions than we could answer.

A week before the sale, we found out we were not getting the promised stock; they were just giving us cash for our shares. This of course caused a large and unplanned capital gain, but no one seemed to care. Then a few days before we were starting, we got the ironclad contract, which was also wrapped into stock options. I had been hearing on all the calls how much money it was, and when I received mine, I just was in shock. First, I cried, then I scheduled a meeting to find out how this was calculated. I was told by Joe, Walter's right-hand guy, it was a formula based on what you brought to the table. I got on the phone and pleaded my case. I just won the Diamond award for the Top Office. I was head of Women's Leadership. I was cementing my role as Voice of the Women. I was a speaker, writer, influencer, and social media expert for the firm. I was also a coach to outside advisors who licensed our tools and technology. I had a massive footprint for the firm and went above and beyond with everything I did for the firm. I was once told at an industry event that I am the embodiment of United Capital. We were not supposed to know what anyone got, but we all talked. I got less than half of what any man I spoke with received. I asked all the women, and all but one were *not* happy. When I pressed them for the formula they said, "We ran out of money. You are lucky you got anything." I thought, do they not want me to come? The contract being ironclad was to force all ex-partners into staying with a two-year noncompete, nonsolicit, non-acceptance. It has the most unilateral language, and it was their way or the highway. There was *no* negotiating with them. We were just chattel.

DAY ONE AND SOCIAL MEDIA

We shared our merger on social media. I then shared it on my social media pages: LinkedIn, Facebook, Twitter, and Instagram. I got an email immediately from someone I didn't know at Compliance to "take it down." I asked why. I saw all the other ex-managing directors (males) who posted it and none of them were told to take it down. I had more followers, audience, and influence. Why wouldn't they want me to post it? That was the start of them trying to break me. I was watched like a hawk. I was under different scrutiny than anyone else at my firm because I had a voice, and that would be taken away. For the next two years if I posted anything (and I mean anything) on social media, within two minutes I would get an email to "take it down or else." I saw Walter and dozens of guys from the firm posting every day. I would ask Marketing and Compliance why they could post and I couldn't. I never got an answer. Then they said I could post if I use their new system. It would be a unilateral post. That meant I could only post but not interact or reply to anyone who commented or reached out. I said it's called "social" media, not "unilateral" media. This made no sense. I said it is like someone calling you and you can't return the call. I refused to play the game this way and was not able to communicate for three years.

DEMOTED!

We were eventually told that we (all managing directors/partners/owners) were being demoted to vice presidents. I was a vice president at a bank in the 1990s. This was like going back 25 years in my career. I know I am a competent professional but coming into a hierarchical work environment where I am now what I was 25 years ago was quite deflating. The only people who got to keep their titles were Walter, who was a managing partner and four people on the executive committee at United Capital. They made one concession to call us Head of Office so we would be a little elevated over the 20-something vice presidents but still under the 20-something managing directors.

WINNING MY AWARD AND ANTI-BRIBERY

Two weeks after we arrived, the Top 100 Advisors as ranked by Investopedia was released. I was in it for 2017 and 2018. It is an honor to get on the list, but to be in the Top 10 is like hitting the lottery. It is based on numerous criteria. The Investopedia 100 celebrates financial advisors who are making significant contributions to critical conversations about financial literacy, investing strategies, life-stage planning, and wealth management. They influence the practice of financial advice and help educate millions of investors. I was ranked no. 4 in the United States. I was at the top of my game and the top of my profession. I was making an impact in the world but trying to change the world of wealth management for women. I immediately fired it over to the entire ex-executive team from United Capital and marketing. Nothing, no response, crickets. I justified it to myself: They are busy; I will give them a week or so. I sent another message saying this is a big deal, and we should be leveraging this for all of us! I waited another two weeks, and I got back, *"You can't share this, post this on social media, tell your clients or anyone."* I said they are doing press releases; it will be all over the media. When it came out, I got offers to go on multiple TV shows, podcasts, radio, and news publications. They were all turned down. I just could not wrap my head around this. This is all great free press. I have seen other advisors double their business within a year from this. Little did I know they hate all press and don't understand how to leverage this for a win-win. Nor was I ever going to represent them in the media or speak or write or go on TV again until I got out. It was so demoralizing to be recognized for this honor and I wasn't allowed to tell anyone. Then I was told if I did their culture training, I would know they don't recognize people, only the firm. I reasoned that *PEOPLE* make up the firm. Isn't their success your success? What happened next, I couldn't have imagined in my wildest dreams. I got an email from the anti-bribery team. They questioned me on how and why I won this award and what I did to get it, implying something nefarious. I couldn't believe this. Then they forced me to go through anti-bribery training for an hour. So, I won this award, and I was punished. I never got to share it or tell anyone. I was afraid if I sent it to my clients I would be fired on the spot. Some of my friends put it out in the world, but it didn't really go far. I have the crystal award on my desk. In 2020 I was still on the list but fell out of the coveted Top 10 spot. By 2021,

I was off the list. They had succeeded in dimming my light and taking my career, influence, and life's purpose away from me. My business contracted over the next three years.

TOO MANY PEOPLE WILL SEE IT

I was asked to do a TV segment on a 6 p.m. nightly news show with a famous New York anchor. He even has a street named for him. It was going to be on helping people retire. I had been on the show before but never with this anchor. His producer reached out to me, and we planned it a few weeks in advance. That is a large lead time for live TV. A day prior is standard. I never imagined this would ever be turned down in my wildest dreams. It took a long time to get this approved. I wrote up the segment and sent it out for review. I was then asked to include all my past TV segments, why I should go on TV, and what the benefit was. The benefit was that "people would see it and we could get revenue and clients from this." My current clients also enjoyed seeing me on TV. It was free advertising highlighting how we could help people retire. The day before I was to go in, the request came back with, and I quote, "The answer is no because too many people will see it." I couldn't even wrap my head around this response. Now not only could I not do it, I left the producer with no segment at the last minute. It was a lose-lose situation. I was still not deterred; I would just have to keep asking.

SEXIST TROPES

My favorite word in the English language is Freedom and I had none of it. I am a Certified Financial Planner (CFP) Board Ambassador. I had to get this approved. It was an honor to be appointed by the CFP Board. I had been at this company for more than a year and had not been able to write, speak, do social media, or have an opinion on anything. I kept asking anyway, even though the answer was always, "No." I asked more than 116 times, and then I asked, "Should I stop asking?" and that was the only "Yes" I ever received. The CFP Board said you have to write a blog; it's been over a year. They said to write about the mistakes women make with money. I was so excited, I wrote it in less than a day and said give me six months to get it approved. When I first sent it out with excitement, since I was already approved to be a CFP Board Ambassador, they said, "We didn't approve you to write." Here we go again. Over the next few weeks, I received emails from a host of people who said, "Why am I reviewing this? Who is Cary Carbonaro? What is this? This is a waste of time." I kept following up and after a few months, I received an email saying, "The Executive Office is uncomfortable with this blog post; it is filled with sexist tropes and has no value." I literally cried for two days. This is my life's work. How could anything I say be considered sexist? Then it occurred to me, they think I am a man. They don't know me, and I have a unisex name. At least that's what I told myself.

MY BIO

I had a long bio with a list of accomplishments like my book, awards, experience, education, speaking, TV, etc. I received an email from someone from a firm I didn't know with my new bio. It was one sentence: "Cary is a CFP with a decade of experience, and she likes to volunteer." Who wrote this? Where is my book? Where are my awards? Where is my MBA? I have been working for almost three decades. They came back with, "Everyone's the same. You are no better than anyone else. We want everyone to look alike." I showed it to a client, and they said but this and what you've done and who you are is why we hired you. The company said they did not want me to profit from any book sales because of them. I never got answers why my entire career was reduced to one sentence. My professional identity vanished.

RESENTMENT AND RESTITUTION

I did not sit on the sidelines. I kept reaching out to my old executive team and asking for help. I scheduled meetings and set agendas. I even tried to incorporate my Women's Leadership group within the firm. They almost laughed at us and said they already had their own group. They didn't need anything from me. I would always ask what I was doing wrong? Why can't I help or add value like I did before? Why am I not in any growth programs? I was a Diamond Winner when we came over. I was ranked no. 4 in Investopedia in the United States. Then they would say they don't want women to fail. They even said they want to prioritize happy employees. I guess I wasn't the only one unhappy, but I was one of the ones trying to address it. I asked if I was being forced out. A colleague told me to just leave and retire. He was a Have and I was a Have Not. They actually labeled us as such.

THE HAVE AND THE HAVE NOTS

I had a website, carycarbonaro.com, featuring my first book and 20 years of media content, which I used for business. Initially, I was told I couldn't keep it. After pushing back, they allowed it but required compliance wording changes. I agreed, but they insisted only a firm-approved vendor could make the changes. My web designer went through the approval process for months but was denied. I asked marketing and compliance for an approved vendor but got no help. Eventually, I found out that only internal teams could make the changes, leaving me stuck.

During my time there, I wasn't receiving client leads, unlike a colleague at my level who was overwhelmed with leads. I relied on my website for outside marketing to attract clients. Compliance then informed me that I couldn't participate in lead programs because my website wasn't compliant. Despite my efforts to resolve this, I was caught in a bureaucratic loop.

In frustration, I took my website down, losing 20 years of content, hoping to get on the "Haves" list for lead distribution. I never did. They openly referred to us as the "Haves" and "Have Nots," clearly discriminating. My inability to market myself or bring in new clients left me feeling helpless and unable to fulfill my mission of helping women.

REVIEW TIME!

When working with a large Fortune 100 firm, it is standard practice to receive regular performance reviews. At United Capital, this was not done at my level, but I expected it to be different there. However, while everyone else received their reviews, I did not. One year passed with no review. Then two years. I started to suspect this might violate some Human Resources (HR) policies.

By the third year, I was desperate to leave. I even offered to buy my business back and negotiated for six months to be released from my contract. They initially agreed but later went back on their word. During this period, when I thought, I was paying to leave, I finally received a performance review. To my shock, they failed me for "not waving the One Goldman flag."

Why did it take three years to give me a review only to penalize me on my way out? Furthermore, I was willing to pay to leave because the environment was unworkable for me, and I was marked down for that. Throughout my career, spanning decades, I had never received a negative review. A friend described the situation perfectly: It felt like being on Mars, unable to breathe.

YOU ARE A LIABILITY, NOT AN ASSET

My friend Jamie Fiore Higgins, who wrote the book *Bully Market: My Story of Money and Misogyny at Goldman Sachs*, said there was no way they were going to let me be Cary Carbonaro there. They were going to do everything to cut you down. They only want women who are nothing without them. I was a problem because I arrived already successful. I was told that I was a liability to them, *not* an asset. Who could work under those soul-crushing conditions?

DON'T BE A HERO TO YOUR CLIENTS

After two years under worsening conditions, I decided to leave. My lawyer advised that the only way out of my contract was to have a negotiated exit and pay to leave; we are talking seven figures plus legal fees. It took me about six months to come to terms with paying to get out. Just like my divorce, I had to pay to get out. After an agreed-upon price they came back and said, "We've lost the taste for these deals." Just like that it was taken away from me. Now I had to quit and run out of noncompete to get my freedom. I asked my handler what I could do to be successful there, and he said, "Don't be a hero to your clients." Yes, that is correct. Too late! I already was! No wonder I was such a miserable failure.

RESIGNATION

They decided to lower pay for the ex-managing directors of United, and with it came a new contract with a six-month noncompete versus the previous two-year noncompete. This was my way out. I preferred to buy my way out, but when that door closed, I said, "I will take the six-month option." I was refused an exit interview and that was that.

For the second time in my life, I had to jump out a window without a net. I had no idea what was on the other side. Would I have any clients? Would they sue me? I felt very strongly they would not touch me because I had called them out on discrimination since I was the only one who could not buy their way out. My ex-attorney disagreed and said they were going to make an example out of me. The uncertainty of what was coming kept me up many nights. In the end, I was correct! They left me alone. But I also abided by all my contract stuff like the nonsolicit and ran out my noncompete.

CLASS ACTION LAWSUIT

In 2010, I was one of 2,800 women who worked for the firm as an associate or vice president in the United States in the investment banking, investment management, or securities divisions who filed a class action gender discrimination lawsuit against Goldman Sachs.

The lawsuit accused Goldman Sachs of hindering women's career advancement and paying them less than their male colleagues. Goldman

Sachs agreed on May 8, 2023, and settled for $215 million. After attorney fees, each woman received approximately $50,000. This is what some of them made in a month, not exactly restitution for clear and blatant discrimination.

Beyond the payout, the settlement stipulates that Goldman Sachs will hire independent experts to study its performance review process and conduct pay-equity studies for three years and it would change how it presents the case for career advancement with vice presidents.

After the lawsuit was settled, I received an email from the attorney representing us. He informed me that United Capital employees were specifically excluded from this payout. To my knowledge I was the only one, which meant that I was specifically excluded. Sadly, I expected it. The perfect ending to my story here.

LIVING IN A BOX

We now know why they bought United Capital. They didn't buy us for who we were: smart out-of-the-box thinking world changers in wealth management. Au contraire, they bought us to fit into their box. It was very small.

They admitted later they made big mistakes with us, and they were not satisfied with their purchase. Trying to fit entrepreneurs in a box is like herding cats. In summer 2023, they announced we are selling off United Capital. My phone buzzed for a month from reporters and recruiters as well as ex-partners and colleagues. My colleagues were all scrambling to get out. They kept saying I was right about all of it, and they should have left when I did. Only one person from United Capital's executive team was left. At that point, maybe 25% to 30% of advisors had quit, been fired, or retired. Then another 60% left from the time the sale was announced to when it closed with Creative Planning on October 22. Goldman Sachs paid $750 million for United Capital and sold it for $100 million. At the time of the first sale, United Capital had $35 billion AUM; by the time it was sold, and everything transferred over, it had $7 billion AUM. I said they should study this case in business school as a horrible failure and what not to do. Of course, Goldman Sachs never admitted blame, and said we were a rounding error. All 600 employees, thousands of clients, and billions of dollars, we were nothing to them.

"It does not make sense to hire smart people and tell them what to do! It makes sense to hire smart people and let them tell us what to do," Steve Jobs.

COMEBACK

After my noncompete period ended, I had one firm willing to take me. They would not support me if I got sued and gave me a poor contract. They also didn't have open architecture for investments. I figured I could deal with it on the other side; I just had to get there.

When I came back to work, I was like someone who got out of jail. I could not write or speak or share my opinion fast enough. Words were pouring out of me. I started writing for Rethinking 65 for advisors. I started blogging, writing for MarketWatch, and got my beloved social media back. I even got back on TV, which was a total shocker. My practice started to grow again after four years of contracting under Goldman Sachs. I still had to find a home. I wasn't in the right spot. I kept beating myself up. I talked to my clients and said the options are I retire or you have to Docusign again. They all said Docusign again. This time I was in a position of strength. I owned my clients, 100% self-sourced, and most had been with me through most of my ups and downs. I was getting my mojo back slowly. Then I got asked to be on the Nasdaq Advisory Council as the sole female.

It was an incredible honor. Next up, Ashton Thomas. This is my last firm move with my clients. Believe me, I evaluated just doing it on my own again with just Rich and I, but at this stage, it was just too much work. I wanted a platform I could leverage just like what I had at United Capital. I was super excited for the next chapter.

NOTES

1. Allianz Life Insurance Company. (2006). *Discoveries for women, money, and power* [white paper]. New York: Author. Available at: https://www.allianzlife.com/-/media/files/allianz/documents/ent_277_n_wmp_2006_white_paper.pdf.
2. The names have been changed in this section.

CHAPTER TWO

WHAT IS THE TRILLION DOLLAR OPPORTUNITY?

I skate to where the puck is going to be, not to where it has been.
–Wayne Gretzky

Wayne Gretzky's strategy for becoming one of the greatest hockey players in history was anticipating what comes next. This principle of looking forward, not just reacting to the present or the past, is critical in financial services, especially now as we stand on the brink of a significant wealth shift from the silent generation and baby boomers to Generation X and millennials.

PROBLEM

The chapter highlights a significant challenge in the financial services industry: the need to adapt to an unprecedented wealth transfer to women, particularly as baby boomers pass on their wealth. Historically, women have been underserved and often disrespected by financial institutions, leading to a gender wealth gap and dissatisfaction among female clients.

Financial services have traditionally been male dominated, with only a small percentage of women in advisory roles, which can limit the quality of services provided to female clients. Additionally, societal and systemic issues like the wage gap, lack of representation, and unique financial challenges faced by women of color compound the problem.

A wise woman once told me that most decisions in financial services come down to three things: ego, economics, or power. It is a profession where guiding, teaching, and consulting people about their money is not just beneficial but noble, as we help turn dreams into actions and realities.

I initially wanted to title this book, *Compel Her, Don't Sell Her!* Why compel? It may seem neutral, but in my story, it's positive. If you feel compelled to do something, you feel you must do it because it's the right thing to do. Women taking care of their financial future is always the right thing to do. Notice the word "feel"–women need to attach emotion and connection to why they buy. They don't want to be sold, told, or forced into anything!

THE UNPRECEDENTED WEALTH SHIFT

Women make great clients! This is a great place to start!

For decades, we've heard that women are the next wave of growth in US wealth management. An unprecedented amount of assets will shift into the hands of US women over the next three to five years, representing a $30 trillion opportunity by the end of the decade. According to a 2020 McKinsey white paper, recent research on affluent consumers, which included surveying more than 10,000 affluent investors, nearly 3,000 of whom were female financial decision-makers, and leveraging analysis from McKinsey's proprietary PriceMetrix solution, highlights a rich view into affluent women as investors. Women are set to inherit $28.7 trillion in intergenerational wealth transfers over the next 40 years.[1]

Women are a formidable force. They represent 50.8% of the US population, have surpassed men in college education rates, and are increasingly climbing to the highest corporate leadership positions. As their financial power grows, so does the importance of understanding how to serve their unique needs.

Women as Financial Decision-makers

According to McKinsey, in approximately two-thirds of affluent households in the United States, men are the key financial decision-makers. For decades, wealth management has been a male-dominated field. Most financial advisers are men (female representation is just 15% across channels). But this is about to change. By 2030, American women are expected to control much of the $30 trillion in financial assets that baby boomers currently possess, a potential wealth transfer of such magnitude that it approaches the annual gross domestic product (GDP) of the United States. It is a fantastic profession to help guide, teach, and consult with people and their money. Today, roughly 70% of US affluent-household investable assets are controlled by baby boomers.[2] Furthermore, two-thirds of baby-boomer assets are currently held by joint households (where a female is present but not actively involved in financial decisions), meaning that roughly $11 trillion in assets are likely to be put into play. As men pass, many will cede control of these assets to their female spouses, who tend to be both younger and longer lived. In the United States, women outlive men by an average of five years, and heterosexual women marry partners roughly two years older than they are. After years of playing second fiddle to men, women are poised to take center stage.[2, 3, 4, 5, 6]

Preparing for the Shift in Wealth Management

As more wealth transitions into the hands of women, firms must take a strategic and holistic approach to transforming their business models. The future of wealth management requires a deliberate shift to acquire, retain, and support women as long-term investors. Like the automotive and real estate industries, which evolved to cater to women's preferences, wealth management must also adapt. For example, the real estate industry acknowledged the rise of single female buyers–outpacing their male counterparts–by shifting from a focus on married couples to developing unique value propositions for women purchasing homes.

Wealth management is now facing a similar inflection point. Firms that fail to act risk missing out on the next wave of growth. Women, as decision-makers, influence a significant portion of purchasing power, accounting for 94% of home furnishings, 92% of vacations, 91% of homes, 60% of automobiles, and 51% of consumer electronics.[7] This dynamic means that financial advice will increasingly blend financial expertise with empathy, education, and empowerment, fostering a collaborative client relationship.

Affluent Women's Approach to Wealth Management

Affluent women approach wealth management differently from their male counterparts. They are more inclined to seek professional advice but may feel less confident in their financial decision-making abilities. Women often prioritize long-term life goals over short-term gains and are generally more risk-averse. When choosing an advisor, they emphasize personal connection and are more likely to seek guidance after a significant life event. This shift means that wealth managers must align their services with the emotional and financial needs of female clients, delivering advice that goes beyond numbers to provide real-life support and solutions.

The Winning Playbook

The winning playbook involves a multiyear approach incorporating several distinct modules that firms can roll out over three sequential phases:

1. **Adapt:** Meet the needs of current female clients better, with a sharpened value proposition across distinct segments.
2. **Evolve:** Client service and business models put women's needs front and center, with aligned pricing and compensation models.
3. **Leap:** Transform the value proposition and fundamentally rethink how the firm creates value for the women they serve, while extending the footprint into new areas via business builds and digital extensions.

Financial services wins the prize as the industry least sympathetic to women–and one in which companies stand to gain the most if they can change their approach.

In a 2009 *Harvard Business Review* study,[8] survey respondents were scathing in their comments about financial institutions. They cited a lack of respect, poor advice, contradictory policies, one-size-fits-all forms, and a seemingly endless tangle of red tape that leaves them exhausted and annoyed. Consider just a few quotations from their interviews:

- "I hate being stereotyped because of my gender and age, and I don't appreciate being treated like an infant."
- "As a single woman, I often feel that financial services institutions aren't looking for my business."

- "Financial service reps talk down to women as if we cannot understand more than just the basics."
- "I'm earning close to $1 million a year and should retire with $20 million plus in assets, so I'm not right for a cookie-cutter discount broker, nor qualified for high-end wealth management services."

An unhappy customer with $20 million plus to invest represents a golden opportunity. Overall, the markets for investment services and life insurance for women are wide open. (For three of the largest opportunities, see Figure 2.1.)

Figure 2.1   Financial Categories Where Untapped Sales to Women Are Worth Trillions.

	Investments & Financial Advisory	Life Insurance	Payments
UNMET NEEDS	• Financial education • Advisers that understand and cater to female life events • Equal treatment with men	• Education about insuring entire household versus just the primary earner • Equitable coverage for working women and men • Valuations for "at-home" work	• Reward programs and payment plans that cater to women
POTENTIAL VALUE IN U.S.	• ~$2.1 trillion in wealth held by high-net-worth divorced or widowed women	• ~$2 trillion in incremental coverage	• ~$1.4 trillion in credit card purchases
GOALS	• Win market share • Grow market	• Grow market • Create new market	• Win market share • Grow market
KEY INFLECTION POINTS TO TARGET	• Divorce • Death of a spouse	• Marriage • First home purchase • Promotion • Birth of first child	• First credit card • College commencement • First job

Source: https://hbr.org/2009/09/the-female-economy

The financial services industry holds significant opportunities, especially during key life transitions such as marriage, divorce, childbirth, or career changes. These pivotal moments often prompt women to reevaluate their financial strategies, making them more likely to make critical investment decisions. Firms that can effectively engage women during these transitional periods stand to capture extraordinary growth and new client relationships.

Addressing the Gender Wealth Gap

Many people know about the gender wage gap, but do you know about the gender *wealth* gap? The wage gap has remained relatively stable in the United States over the past 20 years or so. On average, women earned 82% for every dollar men earned in 2022.[9] A woman working full time for 40 years will lose out on $470,000 due to the wage gap.[10] These losses are even worse when you specifically look at Black and Hispanic women.[11]

While many are aware of the gender wage gap, the gender wealth gap is less well known but equally significant. Women typically have lower net worth than men due to historical and ongoing factors like employment discrimination, lack of access to credit, and barriers to property ownership. Women also live longer and have higher medical expenses, which means they need more money in retirement. Moreover, women often prioritize caregiving, which affects their earnings, promotions, and Social Security wages.

The Path Forward

To address these disparities, women should work with a CFP® professional who can guide them and be their financial advocate. Many women are great planners but may not consider planning for retirement or know that growing their net worth is something they can actively manage. As women are poised to inherit $30 trillion in assets over the next decade, financial planning will become increasingly crucial. According to Starling Bank's #makemoneyequal campaign, nearly 90% percent of female-targeted financial articles advised women to "cut back" on their spending. You can see connections to diet culture here, with women constantly being told that they naturally tend toward excess and that they need to restrict and restrain themselves in order to "stay small" and be good. This needs to change just as one example.

Black and Latino women in the United States face significant financial disparities compared to their White counterparts, primarily due to wage gaps, job segregation, and systemic economic challenges.

Super Positive Stats
Growth of Women-owned Businesses

- Women-owned businesses represent *42% of all US businesses*–nearly 13 million businesses in 2019. This is a rise of 21% over five years, compared to 9% for all businesses.
- A whopping *1,800 new women-owned businesses* are started every day in the United States, with women of color leading the charge, starting 89% of these new businesses.

Revenue and Employment

- Women-owned businesses generate *$1.9 trillion in revenue annually.*
- However, women-owned businesses account for only *8% of the total private-sector workforce* and *4.3% of total private-sector revenues*, highlighting a gap in scale compared to male-owned businesses.

Global Representation

- Globally, women account for *one in three entrepreneurs*, according to the *Global Entrepreneurship Monitor (GEM)* report.

Venture Capital

- Women-owned businesses face challenges in raising capital. In 2022, female-founded startups raised *2% of total venture capital funding* in the United States.

Industries

- Women-owned businesses are most prevalent in the *healthcare, education, retail, and professional services* industries.

Black women are...

- 30% more likely to describe themselves as financially savvy,
- 37% more likely to be motivated by ambition for personal achievement, and
- four times more likely to have invested in a business they run themselves.

According to the same source, 58% of Black women are working with a financial advisor.

Affluent Black women and Latinas, according to research by JP Morgan, *are more confident* than their White counterparts about their financial future. More than half said they faced more challenges to investing, including financial advice that fits their needs.

Wage Disparities

In 2023, Black women lost $42.7 billion in wages compared to White men, while Hispanic women lost $53.3 billion. This disparity is largely due to job segregation, which places Black and Hispanic women in lower-paying jobs more frequently than White men. According to a March 2024 news release from the US Department of Labor, Black women earn 69 cents for every dollar earned by White men, and Hispanic women earn 57 cents.[12]

Employment and Earnings

Black and Hispanic women experience higher unemployment rates and lower earnings. In 2022, Black women had an unemployment rate nearly double that of White women. Furthermore, Black and Hispanic women are overrepresented in the service sector and underrepresented in higher-paying management and professional occupations.[13] According to Pew Research Center, Black women have a median wealth of just $6,000, and single Black women have even less, often only a few hundred dollars, highlighting a substantial wealth gap.[14]

Educational Attainment and Entrepreneurship

As of 2023, Black women-owned businesses (BWOBs) number 2,079,000, which is 14.8% of all women-owned businesses and 52.1% of all Black-owned businesses. BWOBs employ 528,000 people, which is 4.3% of all women-owned business employees, and generate $98.3 billion in revenue, which is 3.6% of women-owned businesses' revenue.

BWOBs have been growing, outpacing other types of businesses in recent years (2017–2020). The number of employer businesses owned by Black women increased by 1.41 percentage points, reaching 52,374 in 2020.[15]

FINANCIAL SECURITY

Approximately 71% of Black women report living paycheck to paycheck, and only about 36% have an emergency fund covering three months of expenses. This financial insecurity is compounded by higher rates of debt, including student loans and medical bills.[16, 17]

Health and Economic Impact

Health disparities also intersect with economic challenges for Black and Hispanic women. They experience higher rates of certain health issues, which can affect their economic stability. For example, Black women are more likely to suffer from conditions like hypertension and have higher maternal mortality rates, impacting their ability to work and accrue wealth.

Addressing these disparities requires concerted efforts in policy changes, education, and support for entrepreneurship to help close the wage gap and improve financial security for Black and Hispanic women. We are making strides within the area of African American advisors and Latino advisors. In 2024, the Association of African American Professionals had their first ever Women's Conference. I was fortunate to be able to attend and speak on a panel. It was there that it was highlighted that this great wealth shift may not be all women.

Fewer than 24% of certified financial planners are women, and only 2% identify as Black or African American.[18] Besides showing the slow pace of progress, the ongoing lack of representation is bad for clients; clients aren't receiving the best possible services from financial firms that don't hire and advance women.[19] And Black women, on average, face long odds when it comes to building investment portfolios and retirement nest eggs.[20] They earn 64 cents for every dollar made by White men and have about 90% less wealth, according to the Urban Institute.[21]

Women are set to control a significant portion of the nation's wealth, representing a monumental opportunity for the financial services industry. By understanding and addressing the unique needs and challenges of female clients, financial advisors can play a critical role in this wealth transfer, ensuring that women are not only prepared to manage their financial futures but empowered to thrive.

Key Questions and Considerations for Financial Advisors: Financial advisors must consider several key questions and strategies when working with female breadwinners.

1. **Leveraging Cultural Representation:** How can advisors leverage cultural representations and influential figures to support and empower female breadwinners in achieving their financial goals?
2. **Partner Dynamics in Financial Planning:** How do male partners typically react to their female partners becoming primary earners, and how does this dynamic impact financial planning discussions?
3. **Intersectionality and Inclusivity:** How can advisors address the intersectionality of gender, race, and socioeconomic status when advising female breadwinners, recognizing the diverse experiences and challenges faced by different groups?
4. **Unique Advantages of Female Breadwinners:** Have advisors encountered unique advantages or opportunities that female breadwinners bring to financial planning conversations?
5. **Gender Roles and Financial Decision-making:** Can advisors provide examples of how gender roles and societal expectations influence financial decision-making within families where the woman is the primary earner?

Solution

The "Million Dollar Opportunity" refers to the potential growth and client base expansion for financial firms that can effectively serve the unique needs of female clients. This opportunity is estimated at $30 trillion by 2030, representing a massive shift in financial control to women. The solution involves several key strategies:

1. **Understanding and Serving Women:** Financial firms must develop a deeper understanding of women's financial needs and preferences, focusing on life goals and risk tolerance. This includes recognizing the significant role women play in decision-making and creating services that respect their financial savvy.

2. **Transforming Business Models:** Firms need to adapt their business models to better cater to women, incorporating empathy, education, and empowerment into client relationships. This involves rethinking service delivery, pricing, and compensation models.

3. **Addressing Disparities:** There is a need to address the gender wealth gap and the specific challenges faced by women of color, such as lower wages, limited access to credit, and employment discrimination. This includes increasing representation of women and minorities in financial advisory roles to better serve diverse client bases.

4. **Leveraging Opportunities in Transitions:** Women are more likely to make financial decisions during life transitions, such as marriage, divorce, or career changes. Financial advisors should be prepared to engage with women during these times, offering tailored advice and support.

5. **Educational and Empowerment Initiatives:** Empowering women through financial education and advocating for their long-term financial planning can help bridge the wealth gap. This includes advising on investments, savings, and managing expenses effectively.

Questions for Financial Advisors to Ask Themselves

1. **Understanding Client Demographics**
   - How well do I understand the financial needs and preferences of my female clients, particularly those who may be newly empowered as financial decision-makers?
   - What steps have I taken to educate myself on the unique financial challenges faced by women, including the gender wealth gap and systemic biases?

2. **Adapting Service Models**
   - How can I adapt my service model to better meet the needs of female clients, including considerations for empathy, education, and empowerment?
   - Are my communication and advisory approaches inclusive and respectful of the financial savviness and goals of women?

3. **Addressing Wealth Transfer**
   - How prepared am I to guide clients through the upcoming wealth transfer, particularly women who may inherit significant assets?
   - How do I ensure that I provide value to clients during key life transitions (e.g. marriage, divorce, inheritance) where financial decisions are critical?

4. **Representation and Inclusivity**
   - How diverse is my client base, and what efforts am I making to include women of different backgrounds, including women of color?
   - Do I have strategies in place to address the specific financial needs and challenges of underrepresented groups?

5. **Client Relationship and Trust**
   - How can I build stronger, more trusting relationships with my female clients?
   - What feedback mechanisms do I have in place to ensure that I am meeting the needs and expectations of my female clients?

KEY TAKEAWAYS

1. **Anticipating Wealth Transfer:** The financial services industry faces a $30 trillion wealth transfer to women by 2030, making this a critical moment to adapt business models and better serve female clients.

2. **Women as Decision-makers:** Women are poised to take control of a significant portion of US wealth as baby boomers age, particularly in joint households where women may not have been primary financial decision-makers until now.

3. **Addressing Gender Disparities:** Women, especially women of color, face unique financial challenges due to the wage and wealth gaps. Financial firms must address these disparities to offer better service and representation.

4. **Life Transitions as Key Moments:** Women often make financial decisions during life transitions such as marriage, divorce, and inheritance. Advisors must be prepared to guide and support them during these pivotal moments.

5. **Adaptation and Inclusion:** Financial advisors need to create inclusive, empathetic, and educational client-service models that cater to women's specific financial goals and concerns, fostering long-term trust and success.

6. **Cultural and Systemic Change:** To fully capture this opportunity, the industry must transform both in how it serves women clients and how it represents women within advisory roles. This includes addressing the lack of diversity and ensuring the financial empowerment of all women.

NOTES

1. Baghai, P., Howard, O., Prakash, L. and Zucker, J. (2020). *Women as the next wave of growth in US wealth management* [online]. McKinsey. Available at: https://www.mckinsey.com/industries/financial-services/our-insights/women-as-the-next-wave-of-growth-in-us-wealth-management.

2. Fry, R., Aragão, C., Hurst, K., and Parker, K. (2023). In a growing share of US marriages, husbands and wives earn about the same. Pew Research Center. Available at: https://www.pewresearch.org/social-trends/2023/04/13/in-a-growing-share-of-u-s-marriages-husbands-and-wives-earn-about-the-same/.

3. Baghai, P., Howard, O., and Zucker, J. (2020). Women as the next wave of growth in US wealth management. McKinsey & Co. Available at: https://www.mckinsey.com/industries/financial-services/our-insights/women-as-the-next-wave-of-growth-in-us-wealth-management.

4. Shook, R.J. (2020). Women feel ignored by advisors, study says. *Forbes.* Available at: https://www.forbes.com/sites/rjshook/2020/08/07/woman-feel-ignored-by-advisors-study-says/.

5. Fidelity Investments. (2023). *Women's History Month 2023 survey.* Available at: https://preview.thenewsmarket.com/Previews/FINP/DocumentAssets/637610_v2.pdf.

6. CFP Board. (2024). *CFP® professional demographics.* Available at: https://www.cfp.net/knowledge/reports-and-statistics/professional-demographics [accessed November 8, 2024].

7. Baghai, P., Howard, O., Prakash, L. and Zucker, J. (2020). *Women as the next wave of growth in US wealth management* [online]. McKinsey. Available at: https://www.mckinsey.com/industries/financial-services/our-insights/women-as-the-next-wave-of-growth-in-us-wealth-management.

8. Silverstein, M.J. and Sayre, K. (2015). The female economy. *Harvard Business Review.* Available at: https://hbr.org/2009/09/the-female-economy.

9. Kochhar, R. (2023). *The enduring grip of the gender pay gap.* [online] Pew Research Center. Available at: https://www.pewresearch.org/social-trends/2023/03/01/the-enduring-grip-of-the-gender-pay-gap/.

10. Majumder, A. and Mason, J. (2024). *America's women and the wage gap.* National Partnership for Women and Families. Available at: https://nationalpartnership.org/wp-content/uploads/2023/02/americas-women-and-the-wage-gap.pdf.

11. Majumder, A. and Mason, J. (2024). *The wage gap #IRL (in real life) for women of color: Groceries, child care, and student loans.* National Partnership for Women and Families. Available at: https://nationalpartnership.org/wp-content/uploads/2023/02/quantifying-americas-gender-wage-gap.pdf.

12. US Department of Labor. (2024). *US Department of Labor releases research on continued economic effects of job segregation, pay disparities on Black, Hispanic women* [online]. Available at: https://www.dol.gov/newsroom/releases/wb/wb20240312.

13. Guerra, M. (2013). *Fact sheet: The state of African American women in the United States* [online]. Center for American Progress. Available at: https://www.americanprogress.org/article/fact-sheet-the-state-of-african-american-women-in-the-united-states/.

14. Edwards, K. (2022). *Most Black Americans say they can meet basic needs financially, but many still experience economic insecurity* [online]. Pew Research Center. Available at: https://www.pewresearch.org/short-reads/2022/02/23/most-black-americans-say-they-can-meet-basic-needs-financially-but-many-still-experience-economic-insecurity/.

15. NWBC. (2023). *NWBC 2023 annual report* [online]. Available at: https://www.nwbc.gov/annual-reports/2023/BytheNumbers.html#:~:text=The%20gratitude%20the%20Council%20has,women%2Downed%20businesses'%20revenue.

16. US Department of Labor. (2024). *US Department of Labor releases research on continued economic effects of job segregation, pay disparities on Black, Hispanic women* [online]. Available at: https://www.dol.gov/newsroom/releases/wb/wb20240312.

17. Edwards, K. (2022). *Most Black Americans say they can meet basic needs financially, but many still experience economic insecurity* [online]. Pew Research Center. Available at: https://www.pewresearch.org/short-reads/2022/02/23/most-black-americans-say-they-can-meet-basic-needs-financially-but-many-still-experience-economic-insecurity/.

18. CFP. (n.d.). *CFP® professional demographics* [online]. Available at: https://www.cfp.net/knowledge/reports-and-statistics/professional-demographics.

19. Peralta, P. (2024). *"An uphill battle": Lack of diversity in the financial industry is hurting women long-term* [online]. Financial Planning. Available at: https://www.financial-planning.com/news/a-lack-of-diversity-in-advisers-is-hurting-womens-financial-future.

20. Tanzi, A. (2024). *Unmarried Black and Hispanic women hold least wealth in U.S.* [online]. Financial Planning. Available at: https://www.financial-planning.com/articles/unmarried-black-women-hold-least-wealth-in-u-s.

21. Newton, T. and Colin, E. (2024). *How policymakers can close the wealth gap for Black women* [online]. Urban Institute. Available at: https://www.urban.org/urban-wire/how-policymakers-can-close-wealth-gap-black-women.

CHAPTER THREE

WHAT THE INDUSTRY IS DOING WRONG

The financial industry has been slow to recognize the different financial needs of women. This lack of understanding and adaptation can result in women not receiving the advice or products that best suit their unique situations.

–Mellody Hobson

The financial services industry has historically been male-dominated and often fails to address the unique needs and preferences of women. This chapter outlines the key issues and offers solutions for better serving women in the financial sector.

KEY ISSUES

1. **Lack of Representation**
   - **Leadership Underrepresentation:** Women are underrepresented in leadership roles, leading to products and services that don't fully address their needs.

- **Advisory Role Gaps:** Fewer women in financial advisory positions results in less personalized service for female clients.

2. **Gender Pay Gap**
   - **Slow Progress:** The industry has been sluggish in addressing pay disparities, impacting women's financial security and investment capacity. Lower lifetime earnings translate to fewer savings and investment opportunities.

3. **Marketing and Communication**
   - **Ineffective Strategies:** Financial products are often marketed using technical, intimidating, or condescending language that doesn't resonate with women.
   - **Lack of Targeted Education:** There's a scarcity of financial education programs tailored to women's specific financial goals and challenges.

4. **Product Design**
   - **Gender-blind Development:** Financial products often overlook women's distinct risk profiles, savings patterns, and investment goals.
   - **Life Events Consideration:** Products rarely account for life events like maternity leave or caring for aging parents, which disproportionately affect women.

5. **Service Experience**
   - **Patronizing Attitudes:** Many women feel patronized or dismissed by financial advisors, leading to distrust and reluctance to engage with financial services.
   - **Client Preferences:** The industry is slow to adapt to the preferred ways women interact with financial services, such as through digital platforms or personalized advice.

6. **Financial Literacy and Confidence**
   - **Lower Confidence:** Women often feel less confident about their financial knowledge, influenced by societal norms and conditioning rather than actual knowledge gaps.

- **Insufficient Literacy Programs:** Financial literacy programs are often not tailored to women's unique financial journeys, such as managing finances post-divorce or planning for longer life expectancy.

7. **Support for Entrepreneurs**
   - **Access to Capital:** Women entrepreneurs face significant challenges in accessing capital, with venture capital and funding networks favoring male-led businesses.

8. **Bro Culture**
   - **Toxic Masculinity:** The prevalence of toxic masculinity in the industry highlights the need for cultural change.

SOLUTIONS AND IMPROVEMENTS

1. **Increase Representation**
   - Promote women into leadership and advisory roles.

2. **Close the Gender Pay Gap**
   - Implement transparent pay practices and regular audits to ensure fair compensation for women.

3. **Tailor Marketing and Communication**
   - Develop marketing strategies that resonate with women using inclusive and empowering language.

4. **Innovative Product Design**
   - Design financial products that consider women's unique life circumstances and financial goals.

5. **Enhance Service Experience**
   - Train financial advisors to respect and understand women's financial needs and foster a more inclusive environment.

6. **Promote Financial Literacy**
   - Invest in educational programs that build women's financial confidence and literacy with practical, relatable advice.
7. **Support Women Entrepreneurs**
   - Create programs and networks to support women entrepreneurs in accessing capital and financial services.
8. **Change the Language**
   - Remove jargon and make the client experience more female-friendly.

By addressing these areas, the financial services industry can better meet the needs of women, fostering a more inclusive and supportive environment that benefits everyone.

NEW YORK LIFE WOMEN'S FOUNDATIONAL STUDY[1]

New York Life Investments conducted years of research to understand female clients. More than 3,000 women investors were polled from 2019 to 2023. Over that five-year period, not only was there no progress, but it actually got worse.

1. The percentage of financial professionals who are women differently increased from 40% in 2019 to 48% in 2023.
2. The percentage of women who feel patronized by financial advisors rose from 36% in 2019 to 48% in 2023.
3. The percentage of financial advisors who are less likely to listen to ideas from a women rose from 30% in 2019 to 40% in 2023.
4. The percentage of financial advisors (consciously or unconsciously) who push women out of financial conversations increased from 30% in 2019 to 40% in 2023.

5. The percentage of breadwinner women who felt patronized by financial advisors rose from 42% in 2019 to 57% in 2023.

EMPATHY AND TRUST

Empathy is crucial for working with women. Teaching empathy involves fostering an understanding of others' emotions and perspectives.

"Empathy is the most important skills necessary for working with women in my opinion," wrote Tara Schwegler, PhD, on LinkedIn in *The Empathy Gap in Financial Services*.[2] In many cases, empathy is something that needs to be taught.

Teaching empathy involves fostering an understanding of others' emotions, perspectives, and experiences. Here are several strategies and methods that can be used to teach empathy effectively.

1. **Modeling Empathy**
   - **Demonstrate Empathetic Behavior:** Show empathy in your interactions with others. This includes active listening, expressing understanding, and responding with compassion.
   - **Reflective Listening:** Teach the importance of listening carefully and reflecting what is heard to show understanding.
2. **Role-playing**
   - **Perspective-taking Activities:** Engage individuals in role-playing exercises where they must adopt another person's viewpoint. This can help them understand different perspectives and emotions.
   - **Dramatic Play:** Use scenarios that require students to act out different roles and consider how others might feel in various situations.
3. **Reading and Discussing Stories**
   - **Literature:** Use books and stories that highlight diverse characters and experiences. Discuss the characters' feelings and motives to deepen understanding.

- **Case Studies:** Present real-life case studies that involve complex emotional and social dynamics. Discuss the situations and explore the emotions and perspectives of all involved parties.

4. **Social-Emotional Learning (SEL) Programs**
   - **Structured Curriculum:** Implement SEL programs that focus on developing empathy, such as the "Roots of Empathy" program. What is SEL? It is the process of developing the self-awareness, self-control, and interpersonal skills that are vital for school, work, and life success.
   - **Regular Practice:** Integrate empathy-building activities into the regular curriculum, emphasizing its importance across all subjects.

5. **Encourage Emotional Literacy**
   - **Emotion Identification:** Teach individuals to recognize and label their own emotions and those of others. This can be done through emotion charts, discussions, and reflective exercises.
   - **Expressing Emotions:** Encourage open discussions about feelings and emotions in a safe and supportive environment.

6. **Service Learning and Community Involvement**
   - **Volunteering:** Encourage participation in community service projects, which can help individuals understand and appreciate the challenges faced by others.
   - **Empathy Projects:** Create projects that require students to research and present on social issues, focusing on the human impact and personal stories.

7. **Mindfulness and Reflection**
   - **Mindfulness Exercises:** Incorporate mindfulness practices that encourage individuals to be present and aware of their own and others' emotions.
   - **Reflection Journals:** Have individuals keep journals where they reflect on their interactions, focusing on moments when empathy was shown or could have been shown.

8. **Creating an Empathetic Environment**
   - **Positive Reinforcement:** Acknowledge and praise empathetic behavior when it occurs.
   - **Safe Spaces:** Create an environment where individuals feel safe to express their feelings and thoughts without judgment.
9. **Empathy Games and Activities**
   - **Empathy Games:** Use games designed to build empathy, such as "Empathy Bingo" or digital games like "Kind Words" that encourage positive and supportive interactions.
   - **Group Activities:** Engage in group activities that require teamwork and cooperation, emphasizing the importance of understanding and supporting each other.

FACTORS THAT DRIVE EMPATHY

- Based on the New York Life Women's Study, following are the most important factors for women when choosing a financial advisor:
  - Takes my concerns seriously
  - Treats me with the respect I deserve
  - Speaks in a language I understand
  - Takes time to understand my specific needs

WHO CAN'T LEARN EMPATHY?

- **Narcissistic Personality Disorder (NPD):** Those with NPD may have significant challenges with empathy due to an inflated sense of self-importance and a lack of consideration for others.

However, some therapy approaches can still help improve empathy over time.

- **Antisocial Personality Disorder (ASPD):** Individuals with ASPD, often associated with sociopathy or psychopathy, have significant impairments in empathy and may find it very difficult to understand or care about others' feelings. This group is typically the most resistant to developing empathy.

By incorporating these strategies into educational settings and daily interactions, empathy can be cultivated and strengthened, leading to more compassionate and understanding individuals. For more on this topic, you can refer to Roots of Empathy, Teaching Empathy, and How to Teach Empathy courses through Harvard's Graduate School of Education.

TRUST AND WOMEN

Trust is particularly significant for women in financial relationships. It is built through active listening, transparent communication, empathy, and personal connections. Trust fosters long-term client-advisor relationships and client loyalty, which is crucial for financial advisors.

Various studies and reports indicate that women tend to prioritize trust and relationship-building more heavily in their financial and professional engagements.

Why Trust Is More Important for Women

1. **Relational Orientation**
   - **Communication and Relationships:** Women often value the relational aspects of their interactions more than men do. Women

prefer to work with advisors who take the time to understand their personal and financial goals deeply. Trust forms the cornerstone of such relationships.

- **Holistic Approach:** Women generally favor a holistic approach to financial planning, where the advisor considers their broader life circumstances, which necessitates a higher degree of trust.

2. **Risk Aversion and Confidence**
   - **Financial Confidence:** Studies show that women often report lower financial confidence compared to men. Therefore, they tend to seek advisors they can trust to guide them effectively and reassure them in their financial decisions.
   - **Risk Aversion:** Women are typically more risk averse than men are, making women more likely to trust and value advisors who demonstrates understanding, reliability, and transparency in their advice.

3. **Long-term Relationships**
   - **Client Loyalty:** Women are more likely to remain loyal to an advisor they trust, leading to long-term client-advisor relationships. This loyalty is built on trust and the advisor's ability to consistently meet their needs and expectations.
   - **Referrals:** Women are strong referral sources when they trust their advisor, often sharing their positive experiences with friends and family, thus expanding the advisor's network. Remember women refer more than double what men do.

4. **Cultural and Social Influences**
   - **Social Support Networks:** Women often rely on social support networks and peer recommendations, making trust an essential component of their decision-making process when choosing financial advisors or professionals.
   - **Transparency and Authenticity:** Authentic communication and transparency are highly valued by women, enhancing the need for trust in professional relationships.

Supporting Research

- **The Center for Talent Innovation (2014):** This study found that women are more likely to seek out advisors they can trust, who understand their specific needs, and who provide holistic financial advice.[3]
- **McKinsey & Company (2020):** This report emphasizes that women expect their advisors to build trust through personalized and empathetic engagement, which significantly influences women's financial decision-making.
- **Fidelity Investments (2021):** Research from Fidelity indicates that women prioritize trust and loyalty in their relationships with financial advisors, leading to longer and more stable client-advisor partnerships.

Practical Implications

Financial advisors and professionals can enhance their relationships with female clients by focusing on the following:

- **Active Listening:** Take the time to understand clients' unique needs and goals.
- **Transparent Communication:** Clearly explain financial strategies and potential risks.
- **Empathy and Support:** Offer empathetic advice and support, especially during major life transitions.
- **Building Personal Connections:** Engage in meaningful conversations beyond just financial matters to build a deeper personal connection.

By emphasizing trust, advisors can better meet the needs of their female clients, fostering long-term, mutually beneficial relationships.

MYTHS ABOUT WOMEN AND WEALTH

1. **Women Are Not Good with Money.**
   - **Reality:** This stereotype suggests that women are incapable of handling finances or making sound financial decisions. Many women are skilled at managing money and have successful careers in finance.
   - **Myth Debunking:** Highlight stories of successful female financial professionals and provide data showing women's financial acumen.
2. **Women Are Afraid of the Stock Market.**
   - **Reality:** While women may have different investment preferences and strategies, many women take calculated risks and build significant wealth.
   - **Myth Debunking:** Discuss women's investment behaviors and provide examples of successful female investors.
3. **Women Are Dependent on Male Partners for Financial Security.**
   - **Reality:** Many women are financially independent and have achieved substantial wealth through their efforts. Currently, 16% of women outearn their male spouse; 50 years ago, it was 5%.
   - **Myth Debunking:** Present data on female breadwinners and their growing financial independence.
4. **Women Are Not Interested in Wealth Accumulation.**
   - **Reality:** Numerous successful female entrepreneurs, investors, and executives actively pursue wealth creation and financial independence.
   - **Myth Debunking:** Share stories of female wealth accumulators and the importance of financial goals to women.

5. **Women Are Not as Knowledgeable About Finance.**
   - **Reality:** Many women are well-informed about personal finance, investments, and wealth management.
   - **Myth Debunking:** Provide statistics and examples of women's financial knowledge and expertise.
6. **Cash Is King.**
   - **Reality:** While women may perceive cash as safer, they need to invest to keep pace with inflation and grow their money.
   - **Myth Debunking:** Explain the risks of holding too much cash and the benefits of diversified investments.
7. **You Can Lose All Your Money in the Stock Market.**
   - **Reality:** The myth that one can lose all their money in the stock market is often unfounded unless investing in a single stock that goes bankrupt or in a Ponzi scheme.
   - **Myth Debunking:** Educate clients on the importance of diversification and the historical performance of the stock market.

The financial services industry has traditionally fallen short in serving women effectively due to underrepresentation, gender pay gaps, ineffective marketing, and poorly designed products. To rectify these issues, the industry must promote women into leadership roles, close the gender pay gap, tailor marketing strategies, design innovative products that consider women's unique needs, enhance service experiences, promote financial literacy, support women entrepreneurs, and change the language to be more inclusive. It must teach empathy, foster trust, and debunk myths about women and wealth. These changes will foster a more inclusive and supportive environment, better serving the financial needs of women.

Solutions

1. **Increase Representation:** Promote women into leadership and advisory roles to ensure diverse perspectives are represented in decision-making processes.

2. **Close the Gender Pay Gap:** Implement transparent pay practices and conduct regular audits to ensure fair compensation for women in the industry.

3. **Tailor Marketing and Communication:** Develop marketing strategies that resonate with women, using inclusive and empowering language.

4. **Innovative Product Design:** Design financial products that account for women's unique life circumstances, risk profiles, and financial goals, including considerations for life events like maternity leave and caregiving responsibilities.

5. **Enhance Service Experience:** Train financial advisors to respect and understand women's financial needs, fostering a more inclusive environment that values women's input and experiences.

6. **Promote Financial Literacy:** Invest in educational programs that build women's financial confidence and literacy, providing practical, relatable advice.

7. **Support Women Entrepreneurs:** Create programs and networks to support women entrepreneurs in accessing capital and financial services.

8. **Change the Language:** Remove jargon and ensure the client experience is more welcoming and understandable, particularly for women.

Questions Financial Advisors Should Ask Themselves

1. **Representation and Leadership**
   - How diverse is my team, and do we have enough women in leadership and advisory roles?
   - How can we actively promote diversity and inclusion within our organization?

2. **Pay and Compensation**
   - Are our compensation practices transparent and fair? How often do we review and adjust them?

- What steps can we take to ensure equal pay for equal work within our team?

3. **Marketing and Communication**
   - Are our marketing materials and communication strategies inclusive and empowering for women?
   - How can we better tailor our messaging to resonate with female clients?

4. **Product Design**
   - Do our financial products consider the unique financial needs and life circumstances of women?
   - How can we involve women in the product development process to ensure their needs are met?

5. **Service and Client Interaction**
   - How do we ensure that women clients feel heard, respected, and valued in their interactions with us?
   - What training do we provide our staff to improve empathy and understanding toward female clients?

6. **Financial Literacy and Education**
   - What educational resources do we offer to help women increase their financial literacy and confidence?
   - How can we make our educational programs more accessible and relevant to women?

7. **Support for Women Entrepreneurs**
   - What specific services and support do we offer to women entrepreneurs?
   - How can we improve access to capital and financial advice for women-led businesses?

8. **Building Trust and Relationships**
   - How do we build and maintain trust with our female clients?
   - What can we do to foster long-term, loyal client-advisor relationships with women?

KEY TAKEAWAYS

1. **Underrepresentation of Women in Leadership:** The financial industry lacks female representation in leadership and advisory roles, resulting in products and services that don't fully address women's unique needs.

2. **Persistent Gender Pay Gap:** The gender pay gap remains a significant barrier to women's financial security, reducing their ability to save and invest for the future.

3. **Outdated Marketing and Communication:** Many financial firms use technical, condescending, or male-oriented language that alienates women. Marketing needs to be more inclusive and aligned with women's financial goals and values.

4. **Financial Products Ignoring Women's Needs:** Products are often designed without consideration for life events like maternity leave or caregiving responsibilities, which disproportionately affect women.

5. **Patronizing Service Experiences:** Many women report feeling dismissed or patronized by financial advisors, contributing to distrust and disconnection from the industry.

6. **Low Financial Confidence Among Women:** While women often feel less confident in their financial knowledge, this is not necessarily a reflection of actual skill gaps but rather a societal issue. Financial literacy programs need to address this confidence gap.

7. **Challenges for Women Entrepreneurs:** Women entrepreneurs face significant obstacles in accessing capital, as male-dominated networks tend to favor male-led businesses.

8. **Bro Culture and Toxic Masculinity:** The financial services industry's "bro culture" is still prevalent, fostering environments where women are excluded or pushed out of conversations.

9. **Need for Empathy and Trust:** Empathy is essential in working with female clients. Advisors need to actively listen and build trusting relationships by addressing women's unique financial concerns.

NOTES

1. New York Life. (2023). *Inspiring women by becoming a partner in their financial growth.* Available at: https://www.newyorklifeinvestments.com/assets/documents/lit/women-and-investing/women-investing-research-report-2023.pdf.
2. Schwegler, T. (2020). *The empathy gap in financial services* [online]. LinkedIn. Available at: https://www.linkedin.com/pulse/empathy-gap-financial-services-tara-schwegler-ph-d-/.
3. The Center for Talent and Innovation is now called Coqual (coqual.com).

CHAPTER FOUR

WHERE ARE THE WOMEN ADVISORS?

The 2008 crisis might never have happened if there had been more women in high-ranking positions to pull in the reins on the testosterone-tinged frenzy.
              –Christine Lagarde, Chairwoman of the International
                                                    Monetary Fund

PROBLEM

The financial advisory industry faces a significant gender disparity, with women being vastly underrepresented, particularly in client-facing and rainmaking roles. Despite substantial investment from organizations like the CFP Board's Center for Financial Planning and the American College of Financial Services, progress has been minimal in increasing the number of women advisors. Women in the industry often encounter systemic biases, including the male-dominated metrics for success (such as Assets Under Management [AUM] and Gross Dealer Concession [GDC]), which do not adequately reflect the value women bring through relationship-building and holistic client service. Additionally, women advisors face unique challenges in the workplace, such as safety concerns during business travel and networking events. Female clients also require a different approach, often seeking advisors during crises and valuing empathy and long-term relationships over transactional advice.

This was originally published in Rethinking 65, and it started a groundswell. I got so much feedback from this that I put together a mastermind group in response to it. Mastermind groups meet on a regular basis and offer a combination of brainstorming, problem-solving, and peer accountability to help members reach their goals more quickly. So many of us want to fix this problem. What is the problem with women advisors and wealth management? Where are all the women? Why do women get chewed up and spit out? Why do they start young and leave? What about the multimillions the CFP Board's Center for Financial Planning and the American College of Financial Services put into fixing this issue, and why has this barely moved the needle? I joined the Benefactors Circle for the CFP Board Center for Financial Planning specifically so I could help raise the number of women in the industry, and after more than 30 years in the industry, I have my own observations to help dig into these questions.

THE BATHROOM EPIPHANY

For my first couple of decades in this industry, I honestly never thought about how male-dominated the financial advisor business was. I had an epiphany about 10 years ago, when I was at a TD Ameritrade conference and the line was out the door for the men's bathroom. A female friend and I were able to just walk into the ladies' room, and we were the only ones there. This image, so opposite of what I was accustomed to, shocked me so much that I took a picture of it. I am not sure why it took me so long to see how outnumbered women are in the advisory world.

First, this is an industry that was built by men for men. The fact that we have more than 75% men and less than 25% women–based on the number of women certified financial planners (CFPs)–is not surprising. Many women in the financial advisory industry are in support roles, teaching roles, and client service roles–or not practicing.

The small percentage of women who are client facing are not necessarily the ones hunting and rainmaking to acquire the clients. Based on my years of experience, I know the number of women who are bringing in clients is very small. I would guess less than 5% of female advisors are rainmakers. I happen to be one of them. and once I was called a unicorn by a male advisor because of it!

BETTER METRICS CAN HELP

In most cases, women advisors get clients in nontraditional ways. We are often relationship based or consultative rather than transactional.

The industry's commonly used words of measurement–GDC, AUM, revenue, trailing 12, etc.–sound like a male measuring stick. And what about being called a "producer." Every time I hear that I think, "Wow, am I a cow?" Maybe a cash cow but still a cow.

I always use to say, "You can't tell what I make from my AUM." I get retainer fees and flat fees, and my business is not reflected in just my AUM. Some brokers have massive AUM on which they don't collect fees.

I believe there are far better ways to measure an advisor's contribution to a firm–and ways that would be more favorable to females. How many families does an advisor serve? How many relationships does an advisor have? Or how many lives has the advisor changed? How deep are the relationships? How many clients consider that advisor a VIP in their lives?

That feels impactful and important to me. Yet, advisors are rarely celebrated in trade publications unless big AUM numbers are next to their names. I believe this is changing but very slowly.

Women advisors can't go to the bar or out late socializing at conferences. We can't drink too much or at all. We have issues when we are traveling for work at hotels. We always have to be careful and not put ourselves in compromising positions. I am not sure if men even realize that.

WOMEN CLIENTS ARE DIFFERENT TOO

Now for the women who want to be clients: They don't wake up one day like a man does and say, "I am hiring a financial planner today." Instead, in almost every case, they need to hire a financial planner when they are in a crisis: death, divorce, downsizing, etc. Unfortunately, most female clients don't know where to look, who to trust, and so on. And generally, the profession is not full of empathetic people. They care enough to get the assets, but will they take a call on the weekend if a client is crying about their life falling apart? Will they accompany a client who needs to retrieve her car from an impound lot because her boyfriend drove drunk? Will they work with clients to make their lives better, or do they only care about their money?

It's also important to note that women clients have a longer sales cycle and are more complex than men. Most of them don't even trust the stock market; they have to be educated about it. And guess what? They are very open to that.

What if the language was about the "softer side of planning?" Consider the following examples:

- How can you maximize your happiness?
- How can you live your best life?

- How can you have freedom?
- How can money give you choices?
- How can we collaborate? (Not saying, "Don't worry your pretty head about this; I got you.")
- I don't have all the answers, but I want to start a dialogue.

In this male-dominated industry, there is a gross lack of awareness. Many advisors have unconscious bias or are just doing what works for men—who usually make up most of their clients.

But women also have conscious or unconscious bias. I had a female client refer a female friend to me and that prospect told me, "I would never work with a woman; a man can take better care of me." Ouch that hurt!

By 2030, which is only five short years away and counting, women will control two-thirds of the nation's wealth, according to some estimates. This industry must change to meet these needs. That is what this book is all about!

Solution

To address these challenges, a multifaceted approach is necessary:

1. **Redefining Success Metrics:** The industry should broaden its metrics for measuring advisor success beyond traditional financial indicators like AUM and GDC. New metrics could include the number of families served, the depth of client relationships, client satisfaction, and the impact on clients' lives. This shift would better capture the value of female advisors, who often excel in building strong, trust-based relationships with clients.

2. **Promoting Inclusivity and Support:** Creating a supportive environment for women in the industry involves addressing unconscious biases, providing mentorship, and offering flexible career paths that acknowledge the different roles women may play. Initiatives could include networking groups, leadership programs specifically for women, and policies that support work-life balance.

3. **Enhancing Safety and Networking:** Addressing the unique safety and networking challenges women face is crucial. This could involve organizing professional networking events that are inclusive and considerate of women's safety and comfort, such as avoiding late-night events or providing secure transportation options.

4. **Client Education and Relationship Building:** Adapting the language and approach used with female clients to emphasize collaboration, education, and empathy can help build trust and meet their unique needs. Advisors should focus on holistic planning that considers life goals, well-being, and long-term financial security rather than just financial transactions.

5. **Raising Awareness and Advocacy:** Industry leaders and organizations need to actively raise awareness about the underrepresentation of women and the unique challenges they face. This includes advocating for more women in leadership positions and ensuring that female voices are represented in industry discussions and decision-making.

Questions for Financial Advisors to Ask Themselves

1. **Awareness of Gender Representation**
   - How well do I understand the unique financial challenges faced by women, such as the gender pay gap and longer life expectancy?
   - Am I aware of the representation of women among my clients, and do I make a conscious effort to engage and support them?

2. **Addressing Gender-specific Needs**
   - Do my financial planning strategies account for the specific needs and circumstances of female clients, such as career breaks for caregiving or lower lifetime earnings?
   - How can I better educate myself on the financial concerns that disproportionately affect women, such as retirement savings shortfalls or healthcare costs?

3. **Promoting Inclusivity**
   - Am I using inclusive language and communication styles that resonate with female clients?
   - How can I ensure that my practice is welcoming and supportive of women, including providing resources and advice that address their specific financial situations?
4. **Client Engagement and Education**
   - What steps am I taking to empower my female clients to take an active role in their financial planning?
   - Do I offer tailored educational materials and workshops that address topics of particular interest to women, such as financial independence, retirement planning, and investment strategies?
5. **Professional Development**
   - How can I continue to develop my understanding of gender dynamics in financial planning, and what training or resources are available to enhance my skills in this area?

KEY TAKEAWAYS

1. **Severe Underrepresentation of Women Advisors:** The financial advisory industry remains male-dominated, with women accounting for less than 25% of certified advisors. The scarcity of women in rainmaking and leadership roles persists despite millions of dollars invested by institutions like the CFP Board's Center for Financial Planning.

2. **Gendered Metrics for Success:** Traditional success measures like AUM and GDC are male-centric and do not capture the strengths of women advisors, who tend to excel in relationship-building and holistic service rather than transactional sales.

3. **Unique Challenges for Women Advisors:** Women face unique safety and networking challenges in the industry, such as concerns around late-night events, business travel, and male-dominated conferences, which create barriers to full participation and career advancement.

4. **Women's Different Approach to Client Acquisition:** Female advisors often acquire clients through nontraditional means, such as building deep relationships and providing consultative services rather than through aggressive sales tactics. These relationship-based approaches are undervalued by current industry standards.

5. **Female Clients' Different Financial Needs:** Women typically seek financial advisors during crises (e.g. divorce, death, or financial upheaval) and value empathy, collaboration, and long-term relationships over purely transactional advice. Advisors need to tailor their approach to women's unique financial situations and preferences.

6. **Barriers to Women Entering and Staying in the Industry:** Systemic issues such as unconscious bias, lack of mentorship, limited work-life balance options, and lack of representation contribute to women leaving the profession or avoiding it altogether. The industry's culture can often "chew up and spit out" women advisors.

7. **Awareness of Women's Growing Wealth Control:** By 2030, women are expected to control two-thirds of the nation's wealth. Yet, the industry remains unprepared to meet the needs of this emerging client base, with insufficient empathy and understanding in serving female clients.

8. **Rethinking Industry Metrics:** Success in the financial services industry should be measured by new metrics that emphasize the quality of client relationships, the number of lives positively impacted, and overall client satisfaction, rather than focusing solely on AUM and revenue.

9. **Need for Inclusivity and Support:** Addressing the gender disparity requires deliberate inclusivity efforts, mentorship opportunities, flexible career paths, and safety-conscious networking events. Women in leadership roles should be celebrated and supported to foster a more diverse industry.

10. **Empowering Female Clients Through Education:** Financial advisors should adopt a more educational and collaborative approach when working with female clients, focusing on life goals, well-being, and long-term security. Educating women about financial independence and investment options is key to building trust.

Bridgette Grimes, Fearless Girl, Katie Burke, and the Author

CHAPTER FIVE

HISTORY OF WOMEN AND MONEY

We'll never solve the feminization of power until we solve the masculinity of wealth.

–Gloria Steinem

PROBLEM

I was a history major, and I always feel historical context is so important. I bet you will not know half of the story here! Historically, women faced systemic barriers to financial independence and economic participation. These barriers included limited access to education and professional training, legal restrictions on property ownership, exclusion from certain professions and trades, and societal norms that prioritized male financial control. These factors collectively constrained women's ability to earn, save, invest, and manage money, perpetuating economic dependency and gender inequality.

The history of women and money is a complex narrative intertwined with social, economic, and legal changes over centuries. Following is an overview of some key developments.

COVERTURE: THE WORD YOU DON'T KNOW BUT SHOULD

I asked my friend who is an attorney if he knew the word. He says I remember it vaguely from law school but no. My husband and I went to apply for a mortgage. As a candidate for a mortgage, I have a longer work history, I have to make more money; in fact, my husband is semi-retired. I've got a longer credit history and a higher score. But the man always goes first. They listed Steve first, as the "borrower" and me second, as "co-borrower." When I pointed this out, our broker, a woman with long experience in her profession, sympathized, but stated that if she had made *me* the primary borrower, the lawyers would just revert to the traditional categories. This was in 2019. This also happens on tax returns. The study, conducted by researchers at the University of Michigan, using data from the U.S. Treasury Department, found that nearly 90% of married heterosexual couples who filed joint federal income tax returns listed the man's name before the woman's name. I make sure I am first on the tax returns too on principal.

What I had just encountered was a vestige of the legal practice of coverture. This is a term most Americans don't know, but it has been a goal of mine to ensure that all literate, well-educated Americans be as familiar with the idea of *coverture* as they are with other historical terms such as *liberty, democracy,* and *equal rights.*[1]

Coverture was a long-standing legal practice rooted in colonial times, particularly based on English law, though Spanish and French versions existed in the New World. Under coverture, women had no legal identity. At birth, a girl was legally "covered" by her father, and upon marriage, by her husband. The husband and wife were considered one person in law, with the husband's identity prevailing. This practice is why women took their husband's last names, becoming "feme coverts," or "covered women."

Married women could not own property, enter contracts, or work in business, as they legally did not exist. They had no rights to their children, meaning divorce or separation often meant losing them. Women also had no control over their own bodies, as a husband's sexual rights were assumed within marriage, making nonconsensual sex legally permissible. While men could not kill their wives, they were legally allowed to beat them. Coverture's reach extended into nearly every aspect of a woman's life, reinforcing male dominance in both the household and society.

Even though women couldn't legally own property, some men found clever ways to ensure their wealth was passed down to future generations through their daughters, avoiding the hands of their sons-in-law. Commerce also found loopholes–while women couldn't officially sign contracts, many did business anyway. Some operated under a legal exception called "feme sole," allowing them to trade independently, while others managed businesses when their husbands were away. In many cases, wives worked right alongside their husbands, with the community keeping an eye on things.

As for marital rights, though the law granted husbands the upper hand in sexual relations, it's likely that behind closed doors, there was more negotiation than the legal framework would suggest.

Fast forward to 1776, as John Adams and the Continental Congress were laying the groundwork for an independent America. Abigail Adams famously wrote her "Remember the Ladies" letter. Contrary to popular belief, she wasn't asking for women's suffrage or equal rights as we know them today. When she said, "Do not put such unlimited power into the hands of the Husbands. Remember all Men would be tyrants if they could," she was talking about coverture. This was the legal doctrine that stripped women of their financial and legal identities upon marriage, handing all control over to their husbands–property, contracts, earnings, you name it. Abigail's words were a plea to limit this total dominance.

Coverture was a major theme discussed during the suffragist movement, and it was prominently featured in the play, *Suffs on Broadway*, which explores the history of women's fight for equality. In the play Carrie Chapman Catt sang in "Let mother vote":

> *We'll keep our country clean,*
> *We'll tidy up our politics until they are pristine,*
> *We'll wash out any stain,*
> *In society's domain.*
> *So, Mister, won't you please let mother vote?*

The suffragists, including figures like Elizabeth Cady Stanton, recognized coverture as one of the most entrenched forms of legal subjugation. Abolishing it became a core objective of the women's rights movement. The activists saw that true equality meant not only gaining the right to vote but also dismantling laws that denied women control over their finances and property.

Where did coverture go? It has been chipped away over time, but it has never been fully erased. The shadow of coverture has lingered over women's lives and still does. It's the reason women couldn't serve on juries until the 1960s and why marital rape wasn't considered a crime

The Broadway Play, Suffs NYC

until the 1980s. It's also why women couldn't get a credit card in their own name until 1974 or apply for a business loan without a man until 1988.

Today, women still run into coverture's remnants in real estate deals, financial transactions, tax issues, and countless employment and housing situations. Sometimes these encounters are serious, but often they're just frustrating barriers—another hoop to jump through. Yet, the subtle remains of coverture continue to hold women back in ways many don't even realize.

Laws began allowing women to own and control property, keep their wages, sign contracts, and inherit assets separately from their husbands. But its legacy persists in ways that still impact women today.

Although there was no official end date to the law of coverture, many states enacted laws that gradually deteriorated its tenants by enabling women to own and control property, keep her wages, sign contracts, and inherit property separate from her husband in the late 1800s.

Modern Implications

While coverture is no longer a legal doctrine, its historical impact is still evident in various legal and societal structures. Understanding coverture provides insight into the long struggle for women's legal rights and equality. It highlights the importance of legal reforms in promoting gender equality and protecting individual rights within marriage.[2]

Married Women's Property Acts: Starting with Mississippi in 1839, various states passed laws allowing married women to own and control property. New York's Act of 1848 was particularly influential. The New York Married Women's Property Act of 1848 was a landmark piece of legislation in the United States that fundamentally changed the legal status of women, particularly married women, with respect to property rights. Following are key aspects and impacts of the Act.

Key Provisions of the Act

1. **Property Ownership**
   - **Before the Act:** Under the common law doctrine of coverture, married women had no independent legal existence from their husbands. Any property a woman owned before marriage automatically became her husband's property, and she could not acquire property independently during the marriage.
   - **After the Act:** Married women were allowed to own and control property. They could receive and hold property acquired by inheritance, gift, or purchase, and manage it without their husband's intervention.
2. **Contractual Rights**
   - **Before the Act:** Women could not enter into contracts independently; their husbands had to do so on their behalf.
   - **After the Act:** Married women gained the right to enter into contracts and conduct business independent of their husbands.
3. **Legal Actions**
   - **Before the Act:** Women could not sue or be sued in their own names.
   - **After the Act:** Women were granted the right to initiate lawsuits and be sued independently, which allowed them to defend and assert their property rights in court.

Influences and Impacts

1. **Economic Independence:** The Act provided married women with significant economic independence, allowing them to engage in economic activities, such as buying and selling property, which were previously restricted to men. This laid the groundwork for broader participation of women in the economy.

2. **Legal Precedent:** The New York Act served as a model for similar legislation in other states. Over the following decades, many states enacted their own married women's property acts, gradually expanding women's rights across the country.

3. **Social Change:** By legally recognizing women's property rights, the Act challenged traditional gender roles and contributed to the broader women's rights movement. It was a stepping stone toward greater legal and social reforms, including the push for women's suffrage.

4. **Judicial Interpretations:** The implementation of the Act led to numerous court cases that further defined and expanded the rights of women. Judges had to interpret and apply the new law, often setting precedents that advanced women's legal status.

Historical Context

- **Antecedents:** The early nineteenth century saw growing movements advocating for women's rights, including property rights. Women's groups and reformers argued that economic independence was crucial for women's social and political empowerment.

- **Broader Reform Movements:** The passage of the Act was part of a broader wave of social and legal reforms during the period, including abolitionism and the early stages of the labor movement. These reforms were interconnected and collectively aimed at expanding rights and freedoms.

The New York Married Women's Property Act of 1848 was a pivotal piece of legislation that transformed the legal landscape for women, providing them with property rights and a degree of economic independence previously denied to them. It set a precedent for future reforms and played a significant role in the broader struggle for women's rights in the United States.

For more detailed information on the Act and its historical significance, you can refer to sources such as the Legal Information Institute and
historical overviews on women's rights.

EARLY TWENTIETH CENTURY

- **Suffrage Movement:** The fight for women's voting rights, culminating in 1920 with passage of the 19th Amendment in the United
  States and similar movements in other countries, empowered
  women politically and economically.
- **World Wars:** Women played crucial roles in the workforce during
  both World Wars, taking on jobs traditionally held by men. This
  demonstrated women's capability in various industries and led to a
  reevaluation of their economic roles.
- **Economic Independence:** The 1920s and 1930s saw more women
  pursuing higher education and careers, although societal expectations and legal restrictions still limited many. In 1935, if you
  were a married woman and working for the government, you
  were let go.

Interwar Period

- **Professional Opportunities:** More women pursued higher education and entered professions such as teaching, nursing, and social
  work. Women like Amelia Earhart and Eleanor Roosevelt became
  prominent public figures.
- **Economic Struggles:** Despite progress, the Great Depression
  severely affected employment and economic stability for

women. Women were the first ones to lose their jobs if they were married.

MID-TWENTIETH CENTURY
World War II

- **Rosie the Riveter:** Symbolizing women's contribution to the war effort, millions of women worked in factories, shipyards, and other industries.
- **Post-war Changes:** After the war, many women were encouraged to return to domestic roles, but the economic landscape had changed, setting the stage for future advancements.

MID-TO LATE TWENTIETH CENTURY

- **Second-Wave Feminism:** The 1960s and 1970s brought a renewed focus on gender equality, including economic rights. The movement pushed for equal pay, access to credit, and anti-discrimination laws.
- **Birth Control:** On June 23 1960, the Food and Drug Administration approved the sale of Enovid for use as an oral contraceptive. This gave women the choice to not have children and have a career. More about this later.
- **Equal Pay Act (1963):** This law aimed to abolish wage disparity based on sex, a significant step toward workplace equality.
- **Civil Rights Act (1964):** Title VII prohibits employment discrimination based on sex, providing legal protection for women in the

workplace. In 1964 and 1965 the passage of the 24th Amendment and the voting rights act finally made voting equal for Black women. The Voting Rights Act was the result of over a century of work by Black women, including Fannie Lou Hamer, Ella Baker, and Diane Nash.

- **The Equal Credit Opportunity Act (1974):** This Act made it illegal to discriminate against women seeking credit.
- **1976:** Women could buy their own houses in Ireland.
- **The Pregnancy Discrimination Act of 1978:** Until 1978 a woman could be fired for getting pregnant. This act amended Title VII of the Civil Rights Act of 1964, 42 U.S.C. §§ 2000e et seq., prohibits discrimination on the basis of pregnancy, childbirth, or related medical conditions.

I was speaking at the Association of African American Advisors (aka Quad A) first Women's Conference in Chicago and one of the other speakers said Title IX is what changed the trajectory for women. So, let's go a little deeper into this topic.

Title IX is a federal civil rights law in the United States that was enacted as part of the Education Amendments of 1972. It is best known for its significant impact on women's rights and gender equality in education. Title IX states:

No person in the United States shall, on the basis of sex, be excluded from participation in, be denied the benefits of, or be subjected to discrimination under any education program or activity receiving Federal financial assistance.

Following are the key implications of Title IX for women:

1. **Equal Opportunities in Education**
   - Title IX ensures that women have equal access to educational programs and activities, including admissions to schools and colleges.

- It prohibits sex-based discrimination in any educational institution that receives federal funding.

2. **Athletics**
   - Requires schools and colleges to provide equal opportunities for women in athletics, including equitable funding, facilities, equipment, coaching, and scholarships for female athletes.
   - As a result, there has been a significant increase in female participation in sports at both the high school and collegiate levels.

3. **Sexual Harassment and Assault**
   - Schools are required to address and prevent sexual harassment and assault.
   - Educational institutions must have procedures in place to handle complaints of sexual misconduct and must take immediate and effective steps to address such issues.

4. **Career and Technical Education**
   - Women must have equal access to career and technical education programs, which have traditionally been male dominated.
   - Gender equality is promoted in fields like science, technology, engineering, and mathematics (STEM).

5. **Pregnancy and Parenting**
   - Title IX protects the rights of pregnant and parenting students, ensuring they have equal access to education and extracurricular activities.
   - Schools must provide reasonable accommodations to ensure pregnant students can continue their education.

6. **Employment**
   - Title IX prohibits discrimination based on sex in employment within educational institutions.
   - This covers hiring, promotions, pay, and working conditions for female faculty and staff.

Title IX has been instrumental in advancing gender equality in education and has provided women with greater opportunities and protections in various aspects of their academic and athletic lives.

LATE TWENTIETH CENTURY

Second-Wave Feminism

Increasing numbers of women attended college and entered professional fields. By the late twentieth century, women were a significant presence in law, medicine, and business.

Financial Independence

The financial services industry was led by (usually White) men. So, eight women came together to turn everything around by opening their own Women's Bank. Carol Green, Judi Wagner, LaRae Orullian, Gail Schoettler, Wendy Davis, Joy Burns, Beverly Martinez, and Edna Mosely founded the bank's board by each pitching in $1,000. On July 14, 1978, the Women's Bank opened for business. People stood in line down the street in downtown Denver to deposit their money. The first day's deposits exceeded $1 million.

Workplace Policies

- Maternity leave policies, antidiscrimination laws, and affirmative action programs improved women's economic opportunities.
- The Women's Business Ownership Act (WBOA) of 1988 prohibited state laws that required women to secure a male relative as their

cosigner on business loans. The definition of "male relative" could range from a woman's husband to her own child. During the committee hearings, one woman testified that she needed her 17-year-old son as a co-signer but was otherwise not granted a loan based on gender alone. Before 1988, a woman could not get a business loan on her own–a surprise to most women today.

- According to the Small Business Administration (SBA), the WBOA spurred exponential women's entrepreneurial ownership and is the fastest entrepreneurship growth segment in the United States.[3] The Act also established Women's Business Centers to provide mentorship and technical assistance dedicated to women. There is at least one such center in every state, with 60% in rural locations. Between 2007 and 2018, the number of women entrepreneurs increased by 58%. For Black women-owned businesses, the growth rate is 164%.

LATE TWENTIETH TO EARLY TWENTY-FIRST CENTURY

Gender Pay Gap

- **Progress and Challenges:** The gender pay gap began to narrow, but disparities remained. Initiatives like pay transparency and advocacy for equal pay continued. More on this later in the chapter.
- **Equal Pay Day:** This is a symbolic day dedicated to raising awareness about the gender pay gap. It represents the additional time women must work to earn what men earned in the previous year. The date varies each year and is different in various countries, reflecting the specific national gender wage gaps. In 2024 it was March 6.

- **Leadership and Entrepreneurship:** Women increasingly started their own businesses and attained leadership positions in corporations. Programs supporting female entrepreneurs grew in number.

CONTEMPORARY ISSUES

Ongoing Economic Inequality

- **Pay Gap and Leadership:** Efforts continue to close the gender pay gap and increase female representation in leadership roles continue. Organizations and governments are implementing policies to support these goals.
- **Financial Literacy:** Initiatives to improve financial literacy among women aim to empower them to make informed financial decisions and achieve economic independence.

The journey of women and money reflects broader social and cultural shifts, highlighting ongoing challenges and the significant strides made toward gender equality.

EARLY TWENTY-FIRST CENTURY

- **Leadership Roles:** Women increasingly occupied leadership positions in business, politics, and academia. Notable figures include Supreme Court Justice Ruth Bader Ginsburg and business leaders like Sheryl Sandberg.
- **Entrepreneurship:** The rise of female entrepreneurs, supported by initiatives and networks focused on women-owned businesses, marked significant economic progress.

Persistent Challenges

- **Gender Pay Gap:** Despite advances, women continued to earn less than men on average. Efforts to address the pay gap included legislative measures and corporate transparency initiatives.
- **Representation in STEM:** Women remained underrepresented in science, technology, engineering, and mathematics (STEM) fields, prompting initiatives to encourage more women to enter and remain in these fields.

CONTEMPORARY ISSUES

Economic Inequality

- **Pay Equity:** Ongoing efforts to achieve pay equity include advocacy, policy changes, and legal challenges. The Lilly Ledbetter Fair Pay Act of 2009 aimed to address wage discrimination. She was the activist who sued Goodyear for employment discrimination.
- **Work-life Balance:** Policies supporting work-life balance, such as paid family leave and flexible work arrangements, are critical for women's economic participation. When they go home from work, they are still responsible for almost everything in the household.

Financial Literacy and Empowerment

- **Educational Programs:** Initiatives to improve financial literacy among women aim to empower them to manage their finances effectively and make informed economic decisions.

- **Investing and Wealth Management:** Women are increasingly participating in investing and wealth management, though there remains a gap in financial advisory roles, which is what this entire book seeks to address.

Digital Economy

- **Technology and Innovation:** The digital economy offers new opportunities for women entrepreneurs, enabling them to start and scale businesses online.
- **Remote Work:** The shift toward remote work, accelerated by the COVID-19 pandemic, has created new opportunities and challenges for women balancing work and family responsibilities.

Increased Workload and Burnout

- Many women experienced an increase in workload due to the dual responsibilities of professional work and household chores. With schools and daycare centers closed, women often took on the primary role of caring for children and managing remote schooling.
- The blurred boundaries between work and home life led to longer working hours and higher levels of stress and burnout.

Job Losses and Career Interruptions

- Women were disproportionately affected by job losses in sectors heavily impacted by the pandemic, such as hospitality, retail, and health care.

- Some women had to leave the workforce entirely to manage childcare and other family responsibilities, leading to career interruptions and setbacks.

Mental Health Strain

- The increased pressures and lack of support systems contributed to a decline in mental health for many women. Anxiety, depression, and feelings of isolation were common.
- Access to mental health resources was often limited, exacerbating these issues.

Adaptation and Resilience

- Despite these challenges, many women adapted by developing new skills, embracing flexible work arrangements, and finding innovative ways to balance their responsibilities.
- Remote work also provided some women with greater flexibility and control over their schedules, which was beneficial for those who could manage the dual demands.

Workplace Policies and Support

- The pandemic prompted many organizations to reevaluate their policies and support systems for remote workers. Companies began to offer more flexible work arrangements, mental health support, and resources for balancing work and family life.
- There was a growing recognition of the need for inclusive policies that address the unique challenges faced by women.

Long-term Implications

- The shift to remote work is likely to have long-term implications for gender equality in the workplace. There is potential for both positive changes, such as more flexible work options, and negative consequences, like reinforcing traditional gender roles.

Political Influence

- **Historic Elections:** Whether you are a Democrat or a Republican, the election of Kamala Harris as vice president in 2020 marked a significant milestone for women in political leadership.
- **Policy Advocacy:** Women's advocacy groups continue to influence economic policy, focusing on issues like childcare, health care, and workplace equality.

Future Outlook

- **Sustainable Progress:** Achieving sustained progress in women's economic empowerment requires continued legal reforms, social advocacy, and policy innovations.
- **Global Influence:** The United States continues to influence global trends in women's economic rights, with American women playing key roles in international organizations and initiatives.

Ongoing Economic Inequality

Pay Gap and Leadership: Efforts to close the gender pay gap and increase female representation in leadership roles continue. Organizations and governments are implementing policies to support these goals.

INTERNATIONAL GENDER PAY GAP

Several countries have implemented measures to address and reduce the gender pay gap, often through comprehensive legislation and policy initiatives aimed at promoting wage equality and transparency. Many, including the following, are doing better than the United States.[4, 5]

1. **Iceland:** Iceland has been a leader in gender pay equality, being the first country to make it illegal to pay men more than women for the same work. Companies and government agencies with more than 25 employees must obtain government certification of their equal pay policies or face fines. This law, implemented in 2018, is part of Iceland's broader effort to eliminate the gender pay gap by 2022.

2. **Luxembourg:** Luxembourg has achieved the lowest gender pay gap among Organization for Economic Cooperation and Development (OECD) countries at 0.4%. This success is attributed to stringent enforcement of equal pay laws and significant penalties for non-compliance. Firms that do not adhere to equal pay standards face fines ranging from €251 to €25,000.

3. **Belgium:** Belgium has also taken significant steps to address the gender pay gap. Since 2012, Belgian companies with more than 50 employees are required to submit biennial reports on their wage structure. This transparency is aimed at identifying and rectifying gender-based pay disparities.

4. **Spain:** Spain requires companies to conduct regular gender audits and report their findings. This has led to notable progress, with Spain seeing a significant reduction in its gender pay gap over recent years.

5. **Denmark:** Denmark mandates that companies with more than 10 employees report on gender pay disparities. Failure to comply can

result in fines, incentivizing businesses to proactively address wage inequalities.

6. **England: Mandatory Gender Pay Gap Reporting:** Since 2017, companies with more than 250 employees are required to report their gender pay gaps annually. This transparency aims to "name and shame" organizations with significant disparities, encouraging them to take corrective actions to avoid reputational damage.[6]

7. **Other European Countries:** Several other European nations, including Austria, Finland, and Portugal, have similar requirements for pay data reporting and gender audits, promoting transparency and accountability in wage practices.

These measures reflect a growing trend among developed countries to address the gender pay gap through legislative action and policy enforcement. Each country's approach varies, but common strategies include requiring pay data reporting, enforcing equal pay laws, and protecting workers who discuss their wages from employer retaliation.

The history of women and money in the United States and the world is a dynamic story of struggle, resilience, and progress, reflecting broader social and economic changes. The journey toward full economic equality continues, driven by legal reforms, social movements, and the persistent efforts of women advocating for their rights.

Solution

The gradual removal of legal and societal barriers has significantly improved women's financial opportunities. Key reforms include the following:

1. **Educational Access:** Increased opportunities for women to pursue higher education and vocational training have expanded their career options and earning potential.

2. **Property Rights:** Laws allowing women to own and control property independently have enabled them to build wealth and financial security.

3. **Employment and Professional Opportunities:** Antidiscrimination laws and changing social attitudes have opened up a wider range of careers and professions to women, enhancing their economic participation.

4. **Financial Literacy and Inclusion:** Initiatives to promote financial literacy and inclusion have empowered women to make informed financial decisions and access credit, investment, and banking services.

Questions for Financial Advisors to Ask Themselves

1. **Understanding Historical Context**
   - How familiar am I with the history of women's rights and financial independence? How does this knowledge impact my approach to advising female clients?
   - Am I aware of how historical legal and societal restrictions on women's financial rights have shaped current attitudes and behaviors toward money?

2. **Recognizing Persistent Inequities**
   - How do historical inequities, such as unequal pay and restricted access to financial services, continue to affect women's financial opportunities today?
   - In what ways can I address or compensate for these historical inequities in my financial advice and planning services?

3. **Cultural Sensitivity and Education**
   - How can I ensure that my financial planning practice is culturally sensitive and acknowledges the unique financial experiences of women?
   - What resources or training can I seek out to deepen my understanding of the historical challenges women have faced in achieving financial independence?

4. **Advocating for Women's Financial Empowerment**
   - How can I use my role as a financial advisor to advocate for policies and practices that support women's financial empowerment and equality?
   - What initiatives or partnerships can I engage in to help educate and empower women about their financial rights and opportunities?

Questions for Financial Advisors to Ask Their Clients

1. **Exploring Personal Financial History**
   - How has your personal or family history influenced your views and behaviors regarding money?
   - Did you have any role models growing up who shaped your understanding of financial independence and money management?
2. **Understanding Financial Challenges**
   - Do you feel that societal expectations or norms about gender have influenced your financial decisions or opportunities?
3. **Empowerment and Education**
   - What areas of financial education do you feel you would benefit from learning more about, considering the historical context of women's financial rights?
4. **Planning for the Future**
   - What steps can we take to ensure that your financial plan considers and overcomes any historical or cultural limitations you might face?
5. **Engaging in Financial Advocacy**
   - Are there ways you would like to advocate for greater financial equality and empowerment for women, either personally or through your financial plan?

- How can I support you in understanding and navigating any historical or cultural challenges related to your financial journey?

KEY TAKEAWAYS

1. **Coverture:** A legal doctrine that denied women property and financial rights, lasting into the modern era, its remnants still affect areas like real estate and tax filings today.
2. **Married Women's Property Acts:** These laws, starting in 1839, allowed women to own property, make contracts, and gain financial independence.
3. **Suffrage Movement (1920):** The 19th Amendment granted women the right to vote, marking political and economic progress.
4. **World Wars:** Women's participation in the workforce reshaped views on gender roles and economic rights.
5. **Second-Wave Feminism:** Laws like the Equal Pay Act (1963) and Equal Credit Opportunity Act (1974) advanced women's rights in the workplace and finance.
6. **Title IX:** This Act ensured gender equality in education and athletics and addressed sexual harassment.
7. **Lingering Bias:** Despite progress, traces of coverture and gender inequality persist, requiring continued reform efforts.

NOTES

1. Allgor, C. (2012). *Coverture: The word you probably don't know but should.* National Women's History Museum. Available at: https://www.womenshistory.org/articles/coverture-word-you-probably-dont-know-should.

2. For further reading, see *The National Archives on Coverture, Legal Dictionary on Coverture,* and *Britannica's* overview of Coverture.

3. US Small Business Administration. (2022). *The Ascent digital platform expands: SBA introduces course in government contracting to online digital learning platform available* [press release]. Available at: https://www.sba.gov/article/2022/feb/07/ascent-digital-platform-expands-sba-introduces-course-government-contracting-online-digital-learning.

4. Holmes, K. and Corley, D. (2017). *International approaches to closing the gender wage gap* (online). CAP 20. Available at: https://www.americanprogress.org/article/international-approaches-closing-gender-wage-gap/.

5. Wending, J. (2024). *The smallest gender wage gaps in OECD countries* (online). Visual Capitalist. Available at: https://www.visualcapitalist.com/the-smallest-gender-wage-gaps-in-oecd-countries/.

6. Murray, J. (2024). *Gender pay gap explained 2024* (online). Save the Student. Available at: https://www.savethestudent.org/student-jobs/uk-gender-pay-gap-guide.html.

CHAPTER SIX

HISTORY OF FEMALE BREADWINNERS

When you invest in women, you invest in a powerful source of global development. Women and girls are not just the beneficiaries of this progress; they are also the key to driving it.
                                                            –Melinda Gates

PROBLEM

Historically, societal norms and legal barriers have limited women's roles to domestic spheres, significantly restricting their participation as primary earners. Women who became breadwinners often faced cultural biases, financial inequalities, and structural obstacles, such as gender pay gaps and limited access to career advancement opportunities. These challenges not only constrained women's economic independence but also perpetuated broader economic disparities.

According to the Pew Research Center, women's economic role in US household earnings has increased significantly over the last 50 years (Figure 6.1). The share of households where men are the primary earners fell 30% during that period. The line chart shows the breakdown of heterosexual marriage, US households by primary earner (men, women, and shared) from 1972 through 2022.[1]

Embracing the Evolution of Female Breadwinners: Implications for Financial Advisors

I had the privilege of hosting a panel with Kimberly Foss from Mercer and Lisa Brown from Corient. We delved into the profound transformation of female breadwinners over time, influenced by changing societal norms, legal shifts, and the empowerment of feminist movements. From overcoming legal barriers in the 1930s to challenging entrenched gender roles in subsequent decades, female primary earners have navigated diverse challenges and opportunities.

I delved into the historical context, cultural shifts, and modern considerations surrounding female breadwinners, highlighting the impact on financial advisors working with these clients. We

Kimberly Foss, Lisa Brown, Cary Carbonaro at Invest In Women 2024.

also acknowledged the significant contributions of figures like Claudia Goldin to the understanding of women's economic contributions.

First, I broke down the female breadwinners throughout history.

Figure 6.1   Gabriel Cortes/CNBC.

Wives are gaining economic influence while carrying a heavier burden at home

% of opposite-sex marriages with each type of earnings arrangement

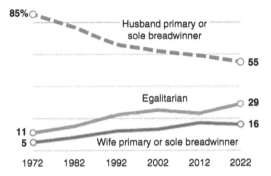

*In **egalitarian marriages**, average number of hours spent on ___ each week*

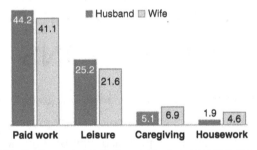

Note: Earnings analysis limited to opposite-sex marriages including spouses ages 25 to 64. In an egalitarian marriage, each spouse earns 40%–60% of the couple's joint earnings. A primary breadwinner earns more than 60% of the couple's joint earnings. A sole breadwinner earns 100% of the couple's earnings.
Source: Pew Research Center analysis of Current Population Survey Annual Social and Economic Supplement (ASEC) and American Time Use Survey, 2016–2021 merged (IPUMS).
"In a Growing Share of U.S. Marriages, Husbands and Wives Earn About the Same"

PEW RESEARCH CENTER

Source: Pew Research Center, Analysis published April 2023

1930S/1940S: LEGAL CONSTRAINTS AND GENDER BIAS

Women encountered significant legal constraints and gender bias in the workforce. Section 214 of the Economy Act of 1932 stated that female teachers would be fired if they married, reflecting societal norms that prioritized women's domestic roles over professional pursuits. Rosie the Riveter took her place in history working in male-dominated roles during World War II. As soon as the men returned, women lost their jobs.

1950S: REINFORCING TRADITIONAL GENDER ROLES AND DOMESTIC EXPECTATIONS

The 1950s reinforced traditional gender roles (Figure 6.2), with women often depicted as homemakers and caregivers in popular culture. Advice columns and media of the time provided tips on how women should prioritize their husbands' needs and manage household responsibilities, perpetuating entrenched gender norms. The outdated belief that women should avoid working due to their delicate biology was historically framed as a protective measure rather than a discriminatory one. After World War II, women were primarily viewed as necessary in their roles as mothers, wives, and consumers, reinforcing traditional gender roles rather than promoting gender equality in the workforce.

Figure 6.2

Tips to look after your husband

(Extract from 1950 Home Economics Book)

Have dinner ready
Plan ahead, even the night before, to have a delicious meal on time. This is a way of letting him know that you have been thinking about him and are concerned about his needs. Most men are hungry when they come home and the prospects of a good meal are part of the warm welcome needed.

Prepare yourself
Take 15 minutes to rest so you will be refreshed when he arrives. Touch up your make-up, put a ribbon in your hair and be fresh looking. He has just been with a lot of work weary people. Be a little gay and a little more interesting. His boring day may need a lift.

Clear away the clutter
Make one last trip through the main part of the house just before your husband arrives, gathering up school books, toys, paper etc. Then run a dust cloth over the tables. Your husband will feel he has reached a haven of rest and order, and it will give you a lift too.

Prepare the children
Take a few minutes to wash the children's hands and faces (if they are small), comb their hair, and if necessary, change their clothes. They are little treasures and he would like to see them playing the part.

Minimise all noise
At the time of his arrival, eliminate all noise of washer, drier dishwasher or vacuum. Try to encourage the children to be quiet. Be happy to see him. Greet him with a warm smile and be glad to see him.

Some don'ts
Don't greet him with problems or complaints. Don't complain if he's late for dinner. Count this as minor compared with what he might have gone through that day.

Make him comfortable
Have him lean back in a comfortable chair or suggest he lie down in the bedroom. Have a cool or warm drink ready for him. Arrange his pillow and offer to take off his shoes. Speak in a low, soft, soothing and pleasant voice. Allow him to relax - unwind.

Listen to him
You may have a dozen things to tell him, but the moment of his arrival is not the time. Let him talk first.

Make the evening his
Never complain if he does not take you out to dinner or to other places of entertainment. Instead, try to understand his world of strain and pressure, his need to come home and relax.

The goal
Try to make your home a place of peace and order where your husband can renew himself in body and spirit.

1960s: Feminist Awakening and Challenging Stereotypes

The 1960s marked a turning point with the rise of second-wave feminism, spurred in part by Betty Friedan's influential book *The Feminine Mystique* in 1963. This period saw a pushback against traditional stereotypes, as women demanded broader opportunities and equal treatment in both professional and personal spheres. This is also when Virginia Slims came out with the campaign, "You've Come a Long Way Baby."

On June 23, 1960 the FDA approved the sale of Enovid for use as an oral contraceptive. This gave women the choice to not have children and have a career.

Muriel Faye Siebert was an American businesswoman who was the first woman to own a seat on the New York Stock Exchange (NYSE) and the first woman to head one of the NYSE's member firms. She joined the 1,365 male members of the exchange on December 28, 1967.

1970s: Strides in Professionalism and Financial Independence

The 1970s witnessed significant strides in women's professional advancements, including the graduation of the first class of certified financial planners (CFPs) in 1973. The introduction of the first

woman's credit card in 1974 symbolized increasing financial autonomy and independence for women.

In 1977, the second woman bought a seat on the NYSE.

1980s: Cultural Shifts and Empowerment Messages

The 1980s saw cultural shifts toward empowering women, with messages challenging traditional gender roles. Iconic commercials for Enjoli perfume included the lyrics, "I can bring home the bacon, fry it up in a pan, and never let you forget you're a man" highlighted women's capabilities as breadwinners while advocating for gender equality.

The comedy-drama movie *Working Girl* premieres in 1988. It stars Melanie Griffith as Tess McGill, a secretary from Staten Island who aspires to climb the corporate ladder in Manhattan. When her boss, played by Sigourney Weaver, is out of town, Tess seizes an opportunity to pitch her ideas by posing as an executive. The film highlights her journey of overcoming sexism and classism in the business world, ultimately proving her competence and achieving professional success.

Working Girl significantly impacted the portrayal of female breadwinners in popular culture by showcasing a woman breaking through corporate barriers. It challenged traditional gender roles and inspired many by demonstrating that women could be ambitious, intelligent, and successful in the business world. Tess McGill's character embodied resilience and ingenuity, encouraging women to pursue their career goals and asserting the importance of recognizing women's contributions in the workforce. The film's success and critical acclaim helped to bring conversations about gender equality and women's empowerment into the mainstream.

1990s: Third Wave of Feminism

As feminist movements evolved in the 1990s, diversity and representation became key themes. It was during this period that the rise of the "smart women" like Hilary Clinton and first female chair of CFP Board, Donna Barwick (1996–97) occurred. The CFP Board has had eight female chairs since.

Today: Diversity, Representation, and Financial Empowerment

As feminist movements evolved, diversity and representation continue to be key themes. Today, female breadwinners are represented by influential figures like Taylor Swift and Beyoncé, showcasing diverse narratives of financial empowerment and success. Kimberly Foss highlighted this, stating, "Lightning-rod figures like Taylor Swift and Beyoncé have popularized the notion of women who are taking charge, both financially and politically." In 2023, we also had the *Barbie* movie breaking records for Margo Robbie and Greta Gerwig. The movie made over $1 billion, and Greta became the first solo female director to reach this milestone.

Claudia Goldin's groundbreaking work in gender economics, culminating in her Nobel Prize win in 2023, has had a profound impact on understanding the economic contributions of women. Her research sheds light on the gender wage gap, occupational segregation, and the economic implications of gender inequality. Additionally, financial advisors play a crucial role in supporting and empowering female breadwinners to achieve their financial goals.

"Our" presentation at Invest In Women, the first question asked of all three of us is, "Are you the breadwinner of the home?" All three of us are! Lisa's husband is a stay-at-home dad. She said he doesn't fit with the stay-at-home moms or the dads. He said the men look down on him, and she said, "It sucks." I said, "Strong women scare weak men."

In 2023, an older male economist in his 80s told me, "We loved working with women in Japan and the USA. They would always work for less than the men and work harder. They took whatever job we gave them; they never negotiated and were just happy to have the job. It was good for the economy." He said this to me as a matter of fact. I was horrified and just walked away. In contrast, however, is the book, *Women Money Power* by Josie Cox, she wrote, "A man is five times as likely to not hire a women who negotiates over salary and 100% more likely to hire a man who does."

Our Invest in Women panel discussed many questions for financial advisors when dealing with the strong trend of women becoming breadwinners, which is currently at 40% and climbing.

Lisa Brown, from Corient, shared her insight highlighting the importance of mutual respect within financial advisory relationships. She emphasized, "It's important for advisors to always treat each spouse with the same amount of respect, regardless of who is the breadwinner or who is the one managing the household finances."

Kimberly Foss, representing Mercer, added valuable perspectives regarding the evolving trends and challenges faced by female breadwinners. She noted, "The trend of female breadwinners isn't going away. Advisors should focus on empowering women by lifting them up and creating opportunities for growth."

At the end, during questions, one young millennial said, "I think we have come a long way, and I am encouraged that more women are breadwinners and that the numbers are increasing." I said, "I can't wait for female breadwinners to become the majority!"

I always figured my current position was a great place to be in because I control my own destiny, but now you know there are factors at work that make it more difficult for women. I am curious how I would rank if I didn't have hurdles to overcome; in other words, how much money would I make if I were a man in my profession?

This goes back to some key differences when the advisor is working with a woman. The planning and strategy should incorporate these considerations:

- Women have longer life spans, so retirement planning is especially concerning.
- Women make less and retire with less due to the gender wage gap.
- Women are generally more conservative than men.
- In retirement, women spend up to $300K more on health care than men do.
- It is more likely that women will spend more years out of the workforce than their male counterparts, due to decisions around child-rearing and providing care for aging parents.
- Seventy-five percent of caregivers are women, and they typically spend 50% more time in caregiving than their male counterparts do.

I took a time labs quiz online, which pulled wage data provided by IPUMS USA and the University of Minnesota, to tell me how much more I would make if I were a man.[2] I was appalled by the results. It said I would make 90% more if I were a man. Excuse me, what? I honestly believed there was a difference. I am a rainmaker! I bring in my own clients and revenue.

The quiz illustrated the pay gap in the financial service field. Male financial advisors within my age range earn an average of $159,000 compared to the $83,000 that females within the same age range. Of course these are the averages, but I still could not believe it. I believe this is one of the reasons it is more difficult to be a female advisor.

COMPANIES WORKING AGAINST THE GENDER WAGE GAP

Several companies have taken proactive measures to address and eliminate the gender pay gap within their organizations. These measures typically include conducting regular pay audits, implementing transparent salary policies, and banning the practice of asking for salary histories from job candidates. Here are a few notable examples:

1. **Salesforce:** Salesforce has committed to equal pay for equal work by conducting annual salary reviews to identify and address any pay discrepancies among employees based on gender or race. This practice has led to multiple adjustments in employee salaries to ensure fairness across the board.

2. **Microsoft:** Microsoft performs regular pay equity analyses and has publicly committed to pay parity, ensuring that employees in the same roles are paid equally regardless of gender or race. The company also provides data on their pay equity initiatives and results, maintaining a high level of transparency.

3. **Accenture:** Accenture has pledged to achieve a gender-balanced workforce by 2025 and conducts comprehensive pay audits. The company publishes its gender pay gap data and has made strides in increasing female representation in leadership positions.

4. **Google:** Google conducts annual pay equity analyses and has implemented policies to ensure that salaries are set based on job responsibilities rather than personal negotiations, which can disadvantage women. This helps to standardize pay across the company.

5. **Reddit:** Reddit has banned salary negotiations altogether to eliminate the disparities that arise from differing negotiation styles between men and women. Instead, they offer transparent pay scales based on the role and experience.

6. **PricewaterhouseCoopers (PwC):** PwC has committed to closing the gender pay gap by providing support networks for women, offering training programs to help women advance to senior roles, and promoting parental leave policies that are equitable for all employees.[3,4]

These companies illustrate that significant strides can be made toward closing the gender pay gap through committed policies, transparency, and regular audits. The actions taken by these organizations serve as models for other companies aiming to achieve pay equity.

TOO AGGRESSIVE BACKLASH

Kara Loewentheil is a graduate of Yale College and Harvard Law School and the founder of the School of New Feminist Thought. She wrote the book *Take Back Your Brain*. She says the socialization women receive around money produced a set of money beliefs that hold women back subconsciously. Spotlighting these "money lies," as she calls them, helps us see how they don't serve women. For example, she writes, "There is no way to win so you may as well not try." This is a lie, but women asking for money or negotiating are often seen as too aggressive. And then they are not well liked in the workplace. Women are 25% less likely than men to ask for a specific amount when negotiating a pay raise partly because women tend to believe if they just work hard, their work will be rewarded without need for negotiation. This is completely in line with the good girl socialization we receive. Many women also think that we should be grateful for being hired or employed and any attempt to negotiate a higher salary, better title, or benefits would make us appear greedy and ungrateful.

I always talk about this in my presentations of "Women, the Workplace, and Money." How do you negotiate for a raise? How do you know your worth? Use sites like Glassdoor and salary.com. Summarize a list of your accomplishments. Here is the difficult part, according to a *Harvard Business Review* article, because as a woman, it is more difficult to negotiate for yourself. You are looked at negatively. A way around this is to get a sponsor or rabbi to do it for you. It can be your boss, colleague, or peer. They can be male or female. They call this the social cost of negotiation for women.[5]

I've been told my entire life that I'm aggressive, but I always saw it as a badge of honor. I also always believed that you have to manage your own career and that you are in control of your own destiny. I am also a pretty big risk taker. I have jumped off a cliff without a net twice in my life, giving up my $500K+ jobs not once but twice so far.

YOU'VE COME A LONG WAY BABY

The *Mary Tyler Moore Show* was an American sitcom that aired on CBS from 1970 to 1977. The show stars Mary Tyler Moore as Mary Richards, a single, independent woman who moves to Minneapolis to start a new life after breaking off an engagement. She lands a job as an associate producer at the fictional WJM-TV news station. The show is notable for its progressive portrayal of a single, career-focused woman at a time when traditional gender roles were being challenged. It combined humor with insightful social commentary, addressing issues such as gender equality, workplace dynamics, and personal growth. It received critical acclaim, winning numerous awards, including 29 Primetime Emmys. It has left a legacy, influencing many subsequent shows and is often cited as one of the greatest TV series of all time. This was a turning point for American women. Here we are 55 years later, and women are set to be majority breadwinners in a few short years. To me, this is progress.

Solution

The evolution of societal attitudes and legal frameworks has been instrumental in supporting the rise of female breadwinners. Key developments include the following:

- **Legal Reforms and Policy Changes:** Laws prohibiting gender discrimination in the workplace, such as the Equal Pay Act and Title VII of the Civil Rights Act, have provided a legal foundation for women to pursue careers and achieve financial independence.

- **Educational and Professional Opportunities:** Increased access to higher education and professional training has enabled more women to enter and excel in a variety of fields. Programs supporting women in STEM, business, and leadership roles have further expanded opportunities.

- **Cultural Shifts and Media Representation:** Positive portrayals of female breadwinners in media and popular culture have helped to challenge traditional gender roles and normalize women's financial leadership. These cultural shifts have been supported by campaigns and movements advocating for gender equality and women's empowerment.

- **Supportive Workplace Policies:** The introduction of family-ly-friendly policies, such as parental leave and flexible work arrangements, has made it easier for women to balance career and family responsibilities. Companies actively working to close the gender pay gap and promote women in leadership also contribute to a more equitable workplace environment.

- **Gender-sensitive Financial Services:** Financial institutions can tailor products and services to meet the unique needs of female breadwinners. This includes offering financial planning, investment advice, and retirement planning specifically designed to address the longer life expectancy, career interruptions, and lower average earnings often experienced by women.

- **Workplace Equality Initiatives:** Companies can implement initiatives to promote gender equality in the workplace, such as unconscious bias training, transparent pay structures, and gender diversity targets. Encouraging a culture of inclusivity and respect ensures that female employees are valued and supported.

- **Educational Campaigns and Media Representation:** Ongoing public education campaigns and positive media representation can help shift societal attitudes toward female breadwinners. Highlighting successful women in diverse roles and industries can inspire others and challenge stereotypes.

- **Research and Data Collection:** Continued research on gender disparities in income, career progression, and financial security can help identify gaps and inform policy and business strategies. Data-driven approaches can lead to targeted interventions that support female breadwinners.

- **Empowering Male Allies:** Engaging men as allies in promoting gender equality can be transformative. Encouraging men to take on caregiving roles, supporting women in leadership, and advocating for equal opportunities creates a more balanced and supportive environment.

Questions for Financial Advisors to Ask Themselves

1. **Understanding the Shift in Roles**
   - How well do I understand the historical and societal changes that have led to an increase in female breadwinners?
   - What knowledge gaps do I have about the unique financial challenges female breadwinners face?

2. **Addressing Bias and Assumptions**
   - Do I hold any unconscious biases or assumptions about gender roles in income earning and financial decision-making?
   - How can I ensure that I do not perpetuate stereotypes about female breadwinners in my practice?

3. **Tailoring Financial Advice**
   - How can I adapt my financial planning approach to better meet the needs of female breadwinners?
   - What strategies can I implement to support female breadwinners in achieving financial security and work-life balance?

4. **Advocacy and Support**
   - In what ways can I advocate for policies or services that support female breadwinners, such as equal pay, childcare support, and flexible work arrangements?
   - How can I better educate myself about the specific financial planning needs of female breadwinners?

Questions for Financial Advisors to Ask Their Clients

1. **Personal Experience and Challenges**
   - Can you share your experience of being a primary earner? How has this role impacted your financial goals and planning?
   - What specific challenges have you encountered as a female breadwinner, and how have you addressed them?

2. **Work-life Balance and Financial Planning**
   - How do you balance your responsibilities as a primary earner with other aspects of your life, such as family and personal interests?
   - Are there areas where you feel you need more support, such as managing stress or planning for future financial security?

3. **Understanding Financial Priorities**
   - What are your top financial priorities as a breadwinner? How do these priorities align with your overall life goals?
   - Do you feel confident in your ability to manage your finances, or are there areas where you would like more guidance?

4. **Navigating Gender Dynamics**
   - Have you faced any challenges related to societal or family expectations about gender roles and income earning?
   - How do these expectations influence your financial decisions and planning?

5. **Future Planning and Aspirations**
   - What long-term financial goals are important to you, and how can we work together to achieve them?
   - How do you envision your financial future, and what steps can we take to ensure that it aligns with your aspirations and values?

6. **Support and Resources**
   - What resources or services do you think would be beneficial in supporting female breadwinners?
   - Are there any specific financial education topics you would like to explore further?

KEY TAKEAWAYS

1. **Historical Obstacles and Cultural Biases:** Women's roles as breadwinners have been constrained by societal norms, legal barriers, and entrenched gender biases, especially from the 1930s through the

mid-twentieth century. Despite these challenges, women like Muriel Faye Siebert and many others paved the way for future generations.

2. **Societal Evolution:** Feminist movements in the 1960s and beyond have reshaped gender dynamics in income earning. The advent of contraceptives, greater educational access, and shifts in media representation played key roles in empowering women to take on the breadwinner role.

3. **Modern Empowerment:** By the 2000s and 2010s, influential figures such as Taylor Swift, Beyoncé, and corporate leaders highlight the narrative of female financial independence, while media (like the *Barbie* movie) and academics like Claudia Goldin further recognize the importance of women's economic contributions.

4. **Financial Advisors' Role:** Financial advisors must adapt to the growing number of female breadwinners, addressing their unique financial needs such as longevity in retirement planning, the gender wage gap, and health care costs. This will change the profession since women will soon be the majority of your clients.

5. **Legal and Workplace Advances:** Legal reforms, such as the Equal Pay Act and Title VII of the Civil Rights Act, alongside family-friendly workplace policies, have gradually improved opportunities for women to be both earners and caregivers.

6. **Challenges Persist:** Despite these advancements, female breadwinners still face pay gaps, underrepresentation in certain industries, and societal expectations about gender roles. Advisors need to account for these factors when offering tailored financial planning.

7. **Actionable Solutions:** Financial services tailored to female breadwinners, workplace equality initiatives, advocacy for better policies, and engaging male allies can further support the rise of women as primary earners.

8. **Questions for Reflection:** Advisors should reflect on their own biases, deepen their understanding of female clients' experiences, and engage in strategies that empower women to achieve financial security and success as breadwinners.

NOTES

1. Fry, R., Aragao, C., Hurst, K., and Parker, K. (2023). *In a growing share of U.S. marriages, husbands and wives earn about the same* (online). Pew Research Center. Available at: https://www.pewresearch.org/social-trends/2023/04/13/in-a-growing-share-of-u-s-marriages-husbands-and-wives-earn-about-the-same/.
2. Showalter, A. (2016). How much would you make if you were a man? *Time Labs*. Available at: https://labs.time.com/story/how-much-would-you-make-if-you-were-a-man/.
3. Coghlan, E. and Hinkley, S. (2018). *State policy strategies for narrowing the gender wage gap*. Institute for Research on Labor and Employment. Available at: https://irle.berkeley.edu/publications/irle-policy-brief/state-policy-strategies-for-narrowing-the-gender-wage-gap/.
4. OECD. (2021). *Pay transparency tools to close the gender wage gap*. Paris: OECD. Available at: https://www.oecd-ilibrary.org/social-issues-migration-health/pay-transparency-tools-to-close-the-gender-wage-gap_eba5b91d-en.
5. Bowles, H.R. (2014). Why women don't negotiate their job offers. *Harvard Business Review*. Available at: https://hbr.org/2014/06/why-women-dont-negotiate-their-job-offers.

CHAPTER SEVEN

UNDERSTANDING THE FEMALE PSYCHE

One is not born, but rather becomes, a woman.
                              –Simone de Beauvoir

PROBLEM

The primary problem addressed in this chapter is the persistent misinterpretation and undervaluation of women's unique perspectives, emotional needs, and cognitive processes by society and industries, particularly in financial services. This issue is compounded by the existence of stereotypes and societal norms that influence how women are perceived and how they perceive themselves, leading to gaps in confidence, representation, and appropriate engagement in various aspects of life, including work, finance, and personal relationships.

Gender is the most powerful determinant of how a person views the world and everything in it. It's more powerful than age, race, or geography. Bridget Brennan, author of *Why She Buys*, says that the color pink is not a strategy. Simply creating a pink version of a male product will not produce results. This is called *pink washing*, and it doesn't work. She insists on social research that underlines why women are different compared to men. Women define achievement differently. They react to emotional scenes and conflict differently. They interact with other members of their own sex differently. These three elements alone mean that most marketing campaigns (built on achievement, conflict, and interaction in typical "male" terms) are done in the wrong language.

ISSUES

1. **Gender Differences and Stereotypes:** While there are structural and functional differences between male and female brains, these do not justify the stereotypes and generalized assumptions often made about women's capabilities and preferences.

2. **Communication and Emotional Needs:** Women and men often have different communication styles and emotional needs, which can lead to misunderstandings and unmet needs in personal and professional relationships.

3. **Imposter Syndrome and Confidence Gap:** Many women experience imposter syndrome and lack confidence, particularly in male-dominated fields, affecting their career progression and financial independence.

4. **Inadequate Industry Approaches:** The financial services industry, among others, often fails to address women's unique needs, focusing instead on generalized or stereotyped approaches, such as pink washing.

Brennan says, "Women are evaluating the salesperson as much as the product." A key driver is ensuring competence and skills by the salesperson. "When women shop, they constantly evaluate how their purchases might impact the people they care about most." This includes family, kids, but also friends and relatives, depending on the status, which means that the sale needs to include multiple stakeholders and in turn drives one of the most important consequences: a positive shopping experience will drive strong word of mouth. *Give her a reason to tell her friends or colleagues about you.*

But women don't want to be sold. Here is a fun story. I was in Costco this weekend, and the people selling in the store started going after a woman with a child to aggressively sell to her. She said, "I am just a housewife, and I have no opinion, and my husband makes all the decisions." I looked back at her and said, "Really? Does that work?" And she said "Yes, like a charm." The salesman said come back with her husband. This is 2024. And my favorite part of this is that she is a school principal, not a stay-at-home woman, and she just uses that tactic to get the aggressive men off her back.

Men Are from Mars, Women Are from Venus, by John Gray and first published in 1992, is a popular book that delves into the inherent differences between men and women and how understanding these differences can improve relationships. The central premise of the book is that men and women are as different as beings from different planets, and that recognizing and respecting these differences can lead to better communication and harmony in relationships. Gray points out some key themes and concepts.

- **Different Communication Styles:** Gray posits that men and women have distinct ways of communicating. Men are more likely to be direct and solution-focused, while women often seek empathy and understanding.
- **Emotional Needs:** According to Gray, men and women have different emotional needs. Men need to feel needed and appreciated, while women need to feel cherished and understood.

- **Stress Management:** The book suggests that men and women cope with stress differently. Men tend to retreat and need space to deal with stress ("go to their cave"), whereas women prefer to talk about their problems to feel supported and understood.
- **Relationship Dynamics:** Gray explores the dynamics of romantic relationships, emphasizing the importance of recognizing and valuing each other's differences rather than trying to change one another.
- **Practical Advice:** The book provides practical advice on how to improve communication and relationship satisfaction by understanding the opposite sex's perspectives and needs.

BRAINS

There is no such thing as a unisex brain. For instance, females tend to have verbal centers on both sides of the brain, while males tend to have verbal centers only in the left hemisphere. Females often have a larger hippocampus (i.e. the "center" of human memory) with a higher density of neural connections in that area. It is why women want to talk more than men. They need to talk and make connections. It makes them better multitaskers than men.

There are differences between male and female brains, but it's important to understand that these differences exist on a spectrum, and there is significant overlap between the sexes. Here are some key points to consider:

- **Structural Differences:** Research has shown that male and female brains can exhibit differences in structure, such as size and connectivity patterns. For example, on average, men tend to have larger overall brain volume, while women often have a higher proportion of gray matter relative to white matter. However, these differences are subtle and do not imply superior or inferior cognitive abilities in either sex.

- **Functional Differences:** Studies have also found differences in brain function between males and females, particularly in regions associated with cognitive tasks such as language processing, spatial-navigation, and emotional regulation. However, these differences are influenced by a complex interplay of biological, environmental, and experiential factors, and individual variation within each gender is substantial.

- **Hormonal Influences:** Hormonal differences between males and females, such as testosterone and estrogen levels, can also affect brain development and function. These hormonal influences contribute to certain sex-specific characteristics and behaviors but do not determine cognitive abilities or personality traits in isolation.

- **Plasticity and Adaptability:** The human brain is highly plastic, meaning it can adapt and change in response to experiences, learning, and environmental factors throughout life. This neuroplasticity enables individuals to acquire new skills, modify behavior, and recover from injury, regardless of gender.

- **Gender Identity and Expression:** It's essential to recognize that brain differences between males and females do not dictate gender identity or expression. Gender identity is a complex interplay of biological, psychological, and social factors, and individuals may identify with a gender that does not align with their biological sex.

- **Cognitive Strategies:** Men and women might employ different cognitive strategies when approaching tasks. For instance, some studies suggest that men tend to use more spatial and object-oriented strategies, while women may rely more on verbal and relational strategies. These differences can influence problem-solving approaches and information processing.

- **Socialization and Cultural Factors:** Societal norms, expectations, and cultural influences also shape how men and women process information. From a young age, boys and girls are often socialized differently, with varying degrees of emphasis placed on certain cognitive skills or behaviors. These societal expectations can influence cognitive development and information-processing styles.

- **Perceptual Differences:** Research suggests that men and women may exhibit differences in perceptual abilities, such as visual-spatial skills and sensitivity to emotional cues. These perceptual differences can impact how individuals interpret and process information from their environment.

While there are some differences between male and female brains, these differences are nuanced and should not be used to make sweeping generalizations about cognitive abilities, behaviors, or personality traits.[1]

FEMALE RESEARCH

A research report published in 2016 refutes three assumptions about how the industry treats female clients.[2] Researchers asked 30 affluent women, aged 35–55, to keep a personal diary of their ups and downs over the course of a week. Trends in those findings were then compared to a national sample of 1,000 women.

SUMMARY OF DEMOGRAPHIC FINDINGS

In the general population, higher income and assets tend to be associated with the following:

- A desire to reduce work and driving time
- A greater interest in more time and energy than in more money
- Seeing money as a way to earn more money instead of achieve life goals

Younger women tend to experience the following:

- Frustration with working and spending (versus investing and saving)
- Time spent in pampering themselves and self-improvement rather than "trying to keep up"
- Need to spend an extra hour in the day doing something romantic with their partner (as opposed to family time, "me" time, or working)

Having higher expectations of oneself and others is a characteristic associated with more education, income, and asset levels.

Finding 1: It's not about saving and investing. It's about working and spending. This is revolutionary! As financial planners/advisors we talk about saving and investing, not working and spending. This is a small change that could make a world of difference with your female clients.

Finding 2: It's not about being a woman. It's about being a person.

Finding 3: It's not about the money. It's about having high standards and expectations for life.

Finding 4: Women sacrifice most of their resources trying to achieve their ideals.

Finding 5: Time is women's scarcest resource, not money.

MYTH 1: WOMEN ARE LOW IN CONFIDENCE

Diary research as well as survey responses indicated that the so-called "confidence gap" between men and women results from women having higher standards than men—not self-esteem issues. Eighty percent of the women surveyed said they feel frustrated when others do not live up to the right standards, while 90% said they sacrifice time, energy, and money to make sure tasks are done properly. More than half of diary "elation" and "frustration" responses resulted from expectations being met or broken.

"When it comes to financial confidence, women are not slower or less sure of themselves; they just want things done right," says the study.

MYTH 2: WOMEN ARE SHORT ON MONEY

What women are really short on is time. "Women are facing a crisis of time that nobody in the industry is talking about or trying to solve," the study states.

Of the 743 frustration responses included in the diary findings, a third had to do with time. Meanwhile, 77% of respondents in the national study said they feel as though they do everything without help, with more than half of respondents saying time is their scarcest resource.

MYTH 3: WOMEN ARE CHARACTERIZED BY THEIR GENDER

"Despite the financial industry's insistence on developing female-specific financial services featuring pink brochures, women do not experience financial life in terms of their sex," the study says.

Only 3% of all financial-related elations and frustrations were reported as "only happens to my gender" in the diary findings, while more than three-quarters of survey respondents said they agree or strongly agree that daily ups and downs are not gender-specific.

More than 70% of women surveyed said they are "most dissatisfied" with the financial services industry over any other and, as a result, are less likely than men to have a financial advisor. The study also indicates that women are likely to change financial advisors if their spouse dies.

This reality exists, says the study, thanks to biased research propagated by faulty research methods: asking questions that confirm false assumptions, treating women as a homogenous group, defining women's financial lives in terms of saving and investing, and viewing women's financial lives as independent from other aspects of life.

The study concludes, "It's clear that for women to start trusting the financial industry, the industry must exhibit the same high standards that women have, create more time for them, and stop focusing on their gender as a starting point for what's important to them."

MORE ON CONFIDENCE

Carol Sankar, an international business consultant, spoke at a Ted-X talk and said, "confidence is the missing link that makes women successful." She calls it the "confidence factor." Is it the way women are raised or society that makes them less confident?

Women are as successful but are less confident than men, according to a report titled "The Status of Undergraduate Women at MIT." Many women suffer from imposter syndrome. Facebook Chief Operations Officer Sheryl Sandberg told us before *Lean In* was published: "There are still days I wake up feeling like a fraud, not sure I should be where I am."

According to Willow, only 20% of women feel confident about their investments.[3] Only 20%. That is very low. This happens with my friends all the time. If they are applying for a job, they will not throw their hat in the ring if they don't have all the qualifications. Let's say they have 8 out of 10. They still will not apply. Men might only have 3 out of 10 and will go for it! It is also an opportunity for us as advisors to shine if we can make them feel confident.

Imposter syndrome is a psychological phenomenon where individuals doubt their accomplishments and have a persistent fear of being exposed as a "fraud." This syndrome is especially prevalent among women, impacting their professional and personal lives. Following are some key points about imposter syndrome for women.

CAUSES OF IMPOSTER SYNDROME IN WOMEN

1. **Gender Stereotypes**
   - Societal expectations and stereotypes about women's roles and abilities can contribute to feelings of inadequacy.
   - Women often internalize societal messages that undervalue their competencies compared to men.
2. **Workplace Dynamics**
   - Women in male-dominated fields may feel like they need to work harder to prove themselves, leading to self-doubt.
   - Lack of representation and role models in leadership positions can exacerbate feelings of not belonging.

3. **Perfectionism**
   - Many women feel pressured to be perfect in both their professional and personal lives. The fear of making mistakes or failing can contribute to imposter syndrome.
   - The expectation to balance multiple roles (career, family, social obligations) can increase stress and self-doubt.

EFFECTS OF IMPOSTER SYNDROME

1. **Career Impact**
   - Women may hesitate to apply for promotions or take on new challenges, fearing they are not qualified.
   - They might undervalue their contributions, leading to lower self-advocacy for raises or recognition.
2. **Mental Health**
   - Imposter syndrome can lead to chronic stress, anxiety, and depression.
   - The constant fear of being exposed as a fraud can take a toll on overall well-being and confidence.
3. **Performance**
   - Paradoxically, women experiencing imposter syndrome often overwork to compensate for their perceived inadequacies, leading to burnout.
   - They might avoid seeking help or mentorship, fearing it will reveal their supposed incompetence.

STRATEGIES TO OVERCOME IMPOSTER SYNDROME

1. **Acknowledge and Normalize**
   - Recognizing that imposter syndrome is a common experience can reduce feelings of isolation.
   - Discussing these feelings with peers or mentors can provide perspective and support.

2. **Cognitive Restructuring**
   - Reframing negative thoughts and focusing on achievements and strengths can help counteract self-doubt.
   - Keeping a journal of accomplishments can serve as a tangible reminder of capabilities and successes.

3. **Seek Support**
   - Mentorship and peer support networks can provide guidance and encouragement.
   - Professional counseling or coaching can offer strategies to manage and reduce imposter feelings.

4. **Set Realistic Expectations**
   - Understanding that perfection is unattainable and that mistakes are part of learning can reduce pressure.
   - Setting achievable goals and celebrating small successes can build confidence over time.

5. **Advocate for Representation**
   - Promoting diversity and representation in leadership roles can provide role models and inspiration for other women.
   - Supporting initiatives that foster an inclusive workplace culture can help mitigate the conditions that contribute to imposter syndrome.

NOTABLE RESEARCH AND RESOURCES

- **Valerie Young:** An expert on imposter syndrome, Young outlines various types of imposter feelings in her book *The Secret Thoughts of Successful Women.*
- **Research Studies:** Various studies have highlighted the prevalence of imposter syndrome among women in academia, corporate environments, and STEM fields.

For more in-depth insights and strategies, you can explore the following resources:

- American Psychological Association
- *Harvard Business Review*
- *Forbes*

Imposter syndrome is a pervasive issue, but through awareness, support, and proactive strategies, women can combat these feelings and realize their full potential.

Confidence Gap: Despite progress, a confidence gap persists. While 78% of women have taken financial actions in the past six months, only 19% feel confident about their money. Actions that improve confidence include contributing to emergency funds, saving more for retirement, investing, and working with financial professionals.[4]

The way teachers react to boys and girls starts early in school, according to Rock the Street:

- Ninety percent of elementary school teachers are female who have little to no certification in math. They inadvertently transfer their math anxieties to the girls in the classroom, but not the boys.

"Having a highly math-anxious female teacher may push girls to confirm the stereotype that they are not as good as boys at math, which in turn, affects girls' math achievement."

- Adolescents are influenced by their parents' perceptions and beliefs during high school. Students whose parents do not encourage them to take such classes will not encounter the experiences in math and science that help them develop needed levels of self-efficacy to pursue math and science careers. Students identify parents as the strongest influence on career and course decisions, particularly when choosing careers in science or engineering.

Despite this, there is a large push to get women interested in STEM fields. I was lucky because my dad was in banking, so I learned about money very early. To me, money was money; I didn't equate it with math. I didn't love math, but I loved money. I would change the problems to money from regular math problems so I would enjoy them more. I remember when I learned in corporate finance about compounding interest, and it was like getting the keys to the kingdom. Albert Einstein once said, "Compound interest is the eighth wonder of the world. He who understands it, earns it; he who doesn't, pays it." While some people question whether the quote was in fact from Einstein, the power of compound interest is unquestionable.

The Ypulse research group published a report and book titled *The Confidence Code for Girls*. It found that today's girls often experience low levels of confidence. Following are some of the study's most troubling findings:

- Around three in four teen girls worry about failing.
- Between ages 8 and 14, girls' confidence levels drop by 30%.
- Between their tween and teen years, girls' confidence that other people like them falls from 71% to 38%–a 46% drop.
- Between ages 12 and 13, the percentage of girls who say they're not allowed to fail increases by 150%.[5]

ADVICE FOR WOMEN IN THE WORKPLACE

- Confidence is a skill that can be taught! Women must learn this.
- Find an advocate or mentor to lobby or negotiate on your behalf.
- Ask for what you want! You will never get it unless you ask!
- Manage your own career! You career is an asset that you hold the keys to.
- If you have girls, teach them to have confidence and speak up for themselves.
- Start today! Little girls with big dreams become women with vision.

Solution Approach

To address these issues, the chapter suggests several strategies:

1. **Acknowledge and Respect Differences:** Recognize that men and women may have different perspectives and needs. This includes understanding that these differences are not deficits but variations that can enrich personal and professional interactions.

2. **Promote Confidence and Overcome Imposter Syndrome:** Encouraging women to build confidence is crucial. This can be achieved through mentorship, advocacy, and creating supportive networks that validate women's experiences and contributions.

3. **Tailored Industry Approaches:** Industries, particularly financial services, should move away from stereotypical marketing and engagement strategies. Instead, they should offer tailored products and services that genuinely address women's needs, such as time management solutions and financial planning that considers women's unique life experiences.

4. **Educational and Societal Reform:** Reforming educational systems to avoid gender bias, promoting STEM education among girls, and addressing societal norms that contribute to confidence gaps can help bridge the divide in how men and women are prepared for and perceive their roles in society.

5. **Encourage Advocacy and Representation:** Women need to be represented in leadership roles and decision-making processes across industries. This representation can help ensure that women's perspectives are included in shaping policies and practices.

6. **Focus on Experience, Not Gender:** Understand that while gender can influence experiences, it should not define them. Industries should focus on individual needs and preferences rather than relying on generalized gender-based assumptions.

Understanding the female psyche involves recognizing brain differences, societal influences, and the need for gender-sensitive approaches in various fields. Women's brains and how they process information is different from men's. It's not about saving and investing. It's about working and spending. Emphasizing confidence, especially in professional and financial contexts, can empower women to achieve their full potential. A woman's gender lens is always on and it colors how she sees the world.

Questions for Financial Advisors to Ask Themselves

1. **Understanding and Training**
   - How well do I understand the unique financial concerns and perspectives of women?
   - What training or resources can I access to improve my understanding of gender-specific financial needs?
2. **Communication and Engagement**
   - How can I adapt my communication style to better meet the emotional and informational needs of my female clients?

- What strategies can I use to ensure I am actively listening to and addressing the concerns of female clients?

3. **Confidence Building**

   - How can I help my female clients overcome financial insecurities and imposter syndrome?
   - What steps can I take to foster a more inclusive and supportive environment for all clients?

4. **Service Customization**

   - Are my financial products and services tailored to address the specific needs and goals of women?
   - How can I better communicate the value of my services in a way that resonates with women?

5. **Representation and Advocacy**

   - How can I advocate for greater representation of women in financial advisory roles and leadership positions?
   - What role can I play in supporting gender diversity within my organization and the broader industry?

Questions for Financial Advisors to Ask Their Clients

1. **Financial Goals and Priorities**

   - What are your primary financial goals, and how can we align your financial plan to support these objectives?
   - How do you prioritize financial stability, retirement planning, and other long-term goals?

2. **Comfort and Confidence**

   - How confident do you feel about your current financial plan and decisions?
   - Are there specific areas of finance that you find challenging or concerning?

3. **Personal and Family Considerations**
   - How do your family responsibilities and personal values influence your financial decisions?
   - Are there specific financial needs or goals for your family that we should consider in your plan?
4. **Experience with Financial Services**
   - How have your past experiences with financial advisors or institutions influenced your views on financial planning?
   - What do you value most in a financial advisor, and how can I best support you?
5. **Time Management and Accessibility**
   - How can I make our financial planning process more convenient and accessible for you?
   - Do you have preferences for how we communicate and manage your financial planning meetings?

KEY TAKEAWAYS

1. **Gender Differences in Perspective:** Gender significantly shapes how individuals view the world, more than age, race, or geography. Understanding these differences is key to serving women effectively in financial planning and other industries.
2. **Rejection of Stereotypes:** While there are biological differences between male and female brains, these should not be used to justify stereotypes or assumptions about women's abilities and preferences.
3. **Communication and Emotional Needs:** Women often have distinct communication styles, valuing empathy and connection. Financial professionals must tailor their communication to meet these emotional needs rather than using generalized approaches.

4. **Confidence and Imposter Syndrome:** Many women experience imposter syndrome, especially in male-dominated industries. This lack of confidence can hinder career growth, even though women may hold themselves to higher standards than men.

5. **The Problem with Pink Washing:** Superficial attempts to market to women, like simply making products "pink," fail because they do not address the deeper emotional and relational aspects that women prioritize in decision-making.

6. **Women Value Relationships:** Women consider how their decisions impact others and often evaluate the person selling to them as much as the product or service. Building trust and demonstrating care for their values leads to stronger relationships and referrals.

7. **Time Is the Scarcest Resource:** Research shows women prioritize time over money. Financial advisors should focus on strategies that save time and reduce stress rather than assuming money is their primary concern.

8. **Confidence Gap in Finance:** Women often lack confidence in their financial decisions. Advisors can bridge this gap by empowering women through education, support, and helping them feel in control of their financial future.

9. **Individuality over Gender:** Women do not want to be defined solely by their gender. Their financial needs are complex and personalized, requiring advisors to move beyond gendered assumptions to build deeper, more meaningful relationships.

NOTES

1. Shapiro, M. (n.d.). *The difference between men and women: Is it all in the brain?* (online) Southern Regional AHEC. Available at: https://www.southernregional ahec.org/men-women-brain/.

2. United Capital. (2016). *What you're really thinking: Understanding the financial lives of women.* Used with permission.
3. Willow. (n.d.). Trust Willow. Available at: https://www.trustwillow.com/.
4. Fidelity. (2024). *Fidelity Investments® study finds three key money moves that minimize financial stress among women* [press release]. Available at: https://newsroom.fidelity.com/pressreleases/fidelity-investments-study-finds-three-key-money-moves-that-minimize-financial-stress-among-women/s/469eaf82-cc28-4a1c-90f4-1edb7db55755.
5. YPulse. (2018). *The confidence code for girls.* Available at: https://static1.square space.com/static/588b93f6bf629a6bec7a3bd2/t/5ac39193562fa73cd8a07a89/1522766258986/The+Confidence+Code+for+Girls+x+Ypulse.pdf.

CHAPTER EIGHT

UNCONSCIOUS BIAS

*Unconscious bias is the result of a lifetime of experiences and is
the sum of our socialization, our upbringing, and our education.*
                                                        –Sheryl Sandberg

PROBLEM: UNCONSCIOUS BIAS IN FINANCIAL SERVICES

Unconscious bias in financial services refers to the automatic, often unintentional prejudices or stereotypes that influence behaviors, decisions, and interactions within the industry. These biases can affect client interactions, hiring and promotions, investment decisions, and overall workplace culture. The problem manifests through the following ways:

1. **Client Interactions:** Biases can lead to differing levels of service based on gender, race, or age, affecting the quality of advice and service received by clients from diverse backgrounds.

2. **Hiring and Promotions:** Affinity bias and gender bias can result in a lack of diversity in the workforce, affecting the inclusiveness and innovativeness of financial institutions.
3. **Investment Decisions:** Stereotypes can influence how financial products are marketed and to whom, potentially limiting access to diverse investment opportunities.
4. **Client Acquisition and Retention:** Cultural and language biases can alienate potential clients from various backgrounds, affecting a firm's ability to serve a diverse clientele.

Unconscious bias in financial services refers to the automatic and often unintentional prejudices or stereotypes that influence the behavior, decisions, and interactions of financial professionals. These biases can impact various aspects of the financial industry, including hiring practices, client interactions, investment decisions, and the overall culture within financial institutions.

Manifestations of Unconscious Bias in Financial Services

Here's a deeper look at how unconscious bias manifests in financial services and its potential consequences:

1. **Client Interactions**
   - **Gender Bias:** Financial advisors might unconsciously assume that male clients are more knowledgeable than female clients about investments, leading to less detailed explanations or different investment recommendations.
   - **Racial Bias:** Advisors might offer different levels of service or products based on assumptions about a client's race, potentially resulting in less favorable financial advice for minority clients.

- **Age Bias:** Younger clients might be perceived as less serious or knowledgeable about financial planning, while older clients might be stereotyped as resistant to new investment strategies.

2. **Hiring and Promotions**
   - **Affinity Bias:** Hiring managers might favor candidates who share similar backgrounds, interests, or educational experiences, which can lead to a lack of diversity within the firm.
   - **Gender Bias:** Women may be overlooked for leadership roles or high-stakes projects due to stereotypes about their capabilities or commitment.
   - **Confirmation Bias:** Managers might favor employees who fit their preexisting notions of what a successful financial professional looks like, often leading to homogeneous work environments.

3. **Investment Decisions**
   - **Stereotype Threat:** Women or minority fund managers might face additional scrutiny or skepticism, influencing their decision-making and risk-taking behavior.
   - **Bias in Financial Products:** Certain products might be marketed differently based on assumptions about demographic preferences, potentially limiting access to diverse investment opportunities for certain groups.

4. **Client Acquisition and Retention**
   - **Cultural Bias:** Financial institutions might tailor their marketing and services to appeal to a specific demographic, inadvertently alienating potential clients from diverse backgrounds.
   - **Language and Communication:** Communication styles and language used in financial planning sessions might be biased toward certain cultural norms, making it difficult for clients from different backgrounds to fully engage and understand.

Consequences of Unconscious Bias in Financial Services

- **Inequitable Service:** Clients from marginalized groups may receive less comprehensive financial advice or less favorable terms, impacting their financial health and long-term wealth-building.
- **Talent Drain:** A lack of diversity in hiring and promotion can lead to a homogenous workforce, reducing the range of perspectives and ideas within the firm, which can negatively affect innovation and problem-solving.
- **Reputational Damage:** Firms that fail to address unconscious bias risk damaging their reputation among clients and the broader public, potentially leading to a loss of business.
- **Legal and Regulatory Risks:** Discriminatory practices, even if unintentional, can result in legal challenges and regulatory penalties, further harming the firm's standing and financial stability.

Addressing Unconscious Bias in Financial Services

1. **Training and Education**
   - Provide regular training sessions to raise awareness about unconscious bias and its impact.
   - Hold workshops and seminars that focus on recognizing and mitigating bias in decision-making processes.
2. **Diverse Hiring Practices**
   - Implement blind recruitment processes to minimize the influence of personal biases.
   - Ensure diverse representation in hiring panels and decision-making committees.

3. **Standardized Procedures**
   - Develop standardized protocols for client interactions, investment recommendations, and performance evaluations to reduce subjective judgments.
   - Use data-driven approaches to ensure fairness and consistency in service provision and internal evaluations.
4. **Inclusive Culture**
   - Promote a culture of inclusion where diverse perspectives are valued and encouraged.
   - Create affinity groups and mentorship programs to support underrepresented employees and foster a sense of belonging.
5. **Accountability and Monitoring**
   - Establish mechanisms to monitor and evaluate the impact of unconscious bias initiatives.
   - Hold leaders and employees accountable for behaviors and decisions that reflect bias, ensuring continuous improvement.

By recognizing and addressing unconscious bias, financial services firms can foster a more inclusive and equitable environment, benefiting both their clients and their workforce.

Story 1: The Financial Planning Meeting

Setting: A well-established financial planning firm in San Francisco

Characters:

- **Emily:** A successful marketing executive seeking financial advice
- **Robert:** A senior financial planner with 20 years of experience
- **Lisa:** A junior financial planner who is new to the firm
- **Mark:** Emily's husband, who is less involved in their finances

Story: Emily, a high-earning marketing executive, decides to seek professional financial advice to better manage her growing wealth. She schedules a meeting with a reputable financial planning firm. Although Emily is the primary breadwinner in her household and has been managing the family's finances, she wants expert guidance on investments, retirement planning, and tax strategies.

Emily arrives at the firm's office, accompanied by her husband, Mark, who supports her but is not as financially savvy. They are greeted by Lisa, the junior financial planner, who takes them to a conference room where Robert is waiting. He's known for his expertise and has a solid reputation in the industry.

As the meeting begins, Emily outlines her financial goals and provides detailed information about her income, assets, and current investments. Despite Emily being the main client and providing comprehensive information, Robert directs most of his questions and explanations to Mark. He assumes that Mark is the primary decision-maker and the one with a better understanding of finances.

Emily notices this and tries to redirect the conversation back to herself, emphasizing her role and knowledge. However, Robert continues to use phrases like "Does that make sense, Mark?" and "What do you think about this plan, Mark?" Emily's frustration grows as she feels overlooked and undermined.

Lisa, observing the interaction, steps in and starts addressing Emily directly, acknowledging her expertise and providing more technical details about the investment options. Lisa's intervention helps to somewhat balance the conversation, but Robert's unconscious bias remains evident.

After the meeting, Emily expresses her dissatisfaction to Mark, who also noticed the biased treatment. They decide to seek another financial planner who will respect and acknowledge Emily's role and expertise.

Emily later finds a different firm where she meets with a financial planner who listens to her, respects her knowledge, and provides tailored advice that aligns with her goals. This experience contrasts sharply with the previous one, highlighting the impact of unconscious bias in the financial planning process.

Back at the first firm, Lisa brings up the incident with Robert and the management, advocating for training on unconscious bias. She points out that overlooking clients based on gender can not only damage client relationships but also harm the firm's reputation and business.

The firm takes Lisa's feedback seriously and implements mandatory training sessions to address unconscious bias. Robert reflects on his actions and acknowledges the need to change his approach, understanding that successful financial planning requires recognizing and valuing the input of all clients, regardless of gender.

Conclusion: Emily's experience at the financial planning firm illustrates how unconscious bias can affect client interactions and satisfaction. By addressing and mitigating these biases, financial planners can ensure they provide equitable and respectful service to all clients, fostering trust and better financial outcomes.

Story 2: The Investment Pitch

Setting: A mid-sized venture capital firm in New York City

Characters:

- **Laura:** A seasoned entrepreneur with a successful track record
- **John:** A venture capitalist with 15 years of experience
- **Sarah:** A junior analyst at the venture capital firm
- **David:** Another entrepreneur pitching at the same meeting

Story: Laura, a highly successful entrepreneur with two previous startups that she sold for substantial profits, is gearing up for her pitch to Secure Ventures, a well-known venture capital firm. Laura's new startup, EcoFuture, focuses on sustainable technology and has already garnered significant interest from early-stage investors.

Laura arrives at Secure Ventures' office and is greeted by Sarah, the junior analyst who has been impressed with Laura's business acumen and innovation. Sarah escorts Laura to the conference room where John and other partners are waiting. David, another entrepreneur pitching on the same day, and Laura exchange pleasantries. David's startup, while interesting, is still in its early stages without the proven success Laura has demonstrated.

Laura begins her pitch, detailing her comprehensive business plan, market analysis, and projected growth. Despite her clear expertise and the potential of EcoFuture, John and the other partners seem distracted, frequently interrupting Laura with trivial questions and showing signs of disinterest. Laura notices this but maintains her professionalism, answering each question with confidence and clarity.

After her pitch, David takes the floor. He presents his idea with enthusiasm but lacks the detailed planning and proven success that Laura offered. However, John and the partners seem more engaged, asking insightful questions and providing positive feedback. David, who is less experienced than Laura, receives encouraging nods and smiles throughout his presentation.

Later, in a private discussion among the partners, John expresses concern about Laura's pitch, citing her "lack of aggressiveness" and questioning her ability to handle the pressures of scaling a business. Sarah, who has analyzed both Laura and David's proposals, speaks up, highlighting Laura's successful track record and the solid foundation of EcoFuture. She points out the unconscious bias at play, noting that Laura's calm and measured presentation style was being unfairly judged against the more traditionally assertive style exhibited by David.

Despite Sarah's arguments, John and the other partners remain skeptical. They eventually decide to invest in David's startup, citing his "potential for growth" and "dynamic presence" as key factors, while dismissing Laura's pitch as lacking the necessary "drive."

Disheartened but undeterred, Laura continues to seek funding. She eventually partners with another firm that recognizes her talent and the promise of EcoFuture. Her startup thrives, achieving significant milestones and making a substantial impact in the sustainable tech industry.

Months later, Secure Ventures realizes their mistake as Laura's company gains widespread acclaim and secures additional rounds of funding. John reflects on the decision and starts to recognize the unconscious bias that influenced their choice. He initiates a series of internal workshops and training sessions on unconscious bias and decision-making to prevent similar occurrences in the future.

Conclusion: The story of Laura Bennett and her experience at Secure Ventures highlights the subtle but pervasive impact of unconscious bias in financial services. It underscores the importance of recognizing and addressing these biases to ensure fair and equitable treatment of all entrepreneurs, regardless of gender.

Conclusion

This story of Julia highlights how unconscious bias can affect financial planning sessions, even when unintentional. By recognizing and addressing these biases, financial advisors can provide more equitable and respectful service, ensuring all clients feel valued and understood.

Case Study: Unconscious Bias, Female Client, and ESG

Background

Jane, a high-net-worth female client, is interested in environmental, social, and governance (ESG) investments and approaches a financial advisory firm for portfolio management. Despite her clear preferences and the growing popularity of ESG, she encounters several biases during her interactions with the advisory team.

Observations

Jane observes the following patterns:

- **Initial Consultations:** The male financial advisor, Tom, often dismisses her ESG interests, steering conversations toward traditional investment strategies.
- **Risk Perception:** Jane's preference for sustainable investments is perceived as a lack of understanding of "real" financial risks, leading advisors to provide overly conservative recommendations.
- **Communication Style:** Advisors use technical jargon and a condescending tone, undermining Jane's confidence in her financial decisions.

Analysis

- **Unconscious Bias:** The firm's advisors may unconsciously believe that women are less knowledgeable about financial matters and view ESG investing as a niche or secondary concern.
- **Cultural Norms:** There is a prevalent notion that men are more suited to making "serious" financial decisions, affecting how advisors interact with female clients.
- **Service Dynamics:** Advisors' biases lead to a lack of personalized service for female clients, affecting their investment satisfaction and outcomes.

Impact

- **Client Trust:** Jane feels undervalued and dismissed, leading to frustration and a potential loss of trust in the advisory firm.
- **Investment Outcomes:** Jane's portfolio does not align with her values and goals, resulting in dissatisfaction and potential underperformance.

Solutions

1. **Bias Training:** Implement unconscious bias training for advisors to recognize and address their biases, ensuring equal treatment of all clients.
2. **Inclusive Communication:** Train advisors to use clear, respectful, and inclusive communication, avoiding jargon and condescension.
3. **Client-centric Approach:** Develop a client-centric approach that prioritizes understanding and meeting the unique preferences and goals of each client, including their interest in ESG.
4. **Feedback Mechanisms:** Establish feedback mechanisms to regularly gather and address client concerns, ensuring continuous improvement in service delivery.

Outcome

By addressing unconscious biases and fostering an inclusive, client-centric culture, the advisory firm can better serve female clients like Jane. This leads to higher client satisfaction, stronger client-advisor relationships, and improved investment outcomes that align with clients' values and goals.

Implicit Bias Versus Unconscious Bias

When meeting new clients, financial advisors need to take an objective position to fully understand risk tolerance, goals, and more. But bias, and especially implicit bias, can sometimes get in the way of fully knowing your client.

We all have biases, and being aware of those biases can help ensure you are giving appropriate advice to all your clients. These associations can be based on identity markers, such as gender, age, race, and socioeconomic background. They influence the way advisors approach their work with clients

Implicit bias, sometimes called "unconscious bias," comes from associations we have that automatically come to mind about people based on their social group. Implicit bias and unconscious bias are often used interchangeably, but there are nuanced differences between the two concepts.

Implicit Bias

Implicit bias refers to the attitudes or stereotypes that affect our understanding, actions, and decisions in an unconscious manner. These biases are automatic and often do not align with our declared beliefs or conscious attitudes. Implicit biases are pervasive and can be directed toward a range of social groups.

- **Automatic:** They operate without conscious control.
- **Pervasive:** Everyone possesses them.
- **Impact Behavior:** Behaviors and perceptions are influenced unconsciously.

- **Tested by Implicit Association Tests (IATs)**: Tools like IATs measure the strength of associations between concepts (e.g. Black people, gay people) and evaluations (e.g. good, bad) or stereotypes (e.g. athletic, clumsy).[1]

Unconscious Bias

Unconscious bias, also known as implicit social cognition, encompasses the broader range of unconscious attitudes, stereotypes, and associations that affect our understanding, actions, and decisions. While implicit bias is a type of unconscious bias, unconscious bias also includes more than just stereotypes and prejudices–it can involve broader patterns of thinking and perception that are shaped by our experiences and socialization:

- **Broader Concept:** Includes all types of unconscious attitudes and stereotypes
- **Developed Through Socialization:** Formed over time through personal experiences, cultural norms, and social conditioning
- **Manifest in Various Forms:** Can influence everything from hiring decisions to daily interactions

Key Differences

1. **Scope**
   - **Implicit Bias:** Specifically refers to attitudes or stereotypes that influence our understanding and decisions
   - **Unconscious Bias:** A broader category that includes implicit bias but also encompasses other unconscious influences on behavior and thinking

2. **Testing and Measurement**
   - **Implicit Bias:** Often measured through specific tests like the IAT
   - **Unconscious Bias:** Not as easily quantified and includes a wider range of unconscious processes
3. **Focus**
   - **Implicit Bias:** Focuses on specific attitudes and stereotypes
   - **Unconscious Bias:** Encompasses all unconscious influences on thought and behavior, including but not limited to implicit biases

While implicit bias is a subset of unconscious bias focused on specific attitudes and stereotypes, unconscious bias includes all the unconscious influences that shape our thoughts and behaviors. Both types of biases operate without our conscious awareness, impacting our actions and decisions in significant ways.

By recognizing and addressing unconscious bias, financial services firms can foster a more inclusive and equitable environment, benefiting both clients and the workforce. Addressing these biases not only improves client satisfaction and trust but also enhances the overall effectiveness and reputation of financial advisory services. [2,3,4]

Is AI Biased?

Dani Fava, the chief strategy officer at Carson, posted this on LinkedIn. With permission I reproduce it here:

AI is not biased, we are.

Check out these results:

I asked DALLE to generate an image of someone who has executive presence and is likely to be a good financial advisor; who understands investing and taxes; someone who most people would trust to manage

their money. And then I asked the same question again and said, "…
with long hair."

Here are her results.

AI is more likely to generate a man with long hair to match this descrip-
tion than a woman.

AI didn't do this. The data that trained the multimodal models did.
Our data

In other words, AI is simply generating a digital version of our reality.

AI learns the same way children do–by processing experiences it
encounters.

Let's make sure we change our baseline.

Implicit and unconscious bias in financial services against women
manifests in various forms, from biased client interactions to skewed hiring and promotion practices. Financial advisors might unconsciously
assume that male clients are more knowledgeable about investments,

resulting in women receiving less detailed explanations and less favorable financial advice. In hiring, affinity and gender biases can lead to a lack of diversity, with women often overlooked for leadership roles. These biases are pervasive, operating automatically and without conscious control, and can be measured using tools like the IAT. To counter these biases, financial institutions must implement comprehensive training programs, promote inclusive communication, and adopt standardized procedures to ensure equitable treatment for all clients, particularly women.

Solution: Addressing Unconscious Bias

1. **Training and Education:** Regular training on unconscious bias helps raise awareness among employees. Workshops and seminars can focus on recognizing and mitigating these biases in decision-making processes.
2. **Diverse Hiring Practices:** Implementing blind recruitment processes and ensuring diverse representation on hiring panels can help reduce biases in hiring and promotions.
3. **Standardized Procedures:** Developing protocols for client interactions, investment recommendations, and evaluations helps minimize subjective judgments.
4. **Inclusive Culture:** Promoting an inclusive culture where diverse perspectives are valued can enhance the workplace environment. This includes creating affinity groups and mentorship programs for underrepresented employees.
5. **Accountability and Monitoring:** Establishing systems to monitor the effectiveness of initiatives addressing unconscious bias and holding employees accountable ensures ongoing progress.

Case Studies and Real-World Examples

- **Financial Planning Meeting:** A scenario where a female client, despite being the primary decision-maker, receives less attention from a male financial advisor illustrates gender bias in client interactions.
- **Investment Pitch:** A successful female entrepreneur's pitch is undervalued compared to a male counterpart, highlighting how unconscious bias can affect investment decisions.
- **Retirement Planning Session:** A female client's financial expertise is overlooked, demonstrating bias in assumptions about gender roles in financial knowledge.

Questions for Financial Advisors to Ask Themselves

1. **Self-awareness and Reflection**
   - "What preconceived notions do I have about certain groups of people based on gender, age, race, or socioeconomic status that might influence my professional interactions?"
   - "What assumptions do I make/have I made about a client's financial knowledge or capabilities based on their background or appearance?"
2. **Client Interactions and Communication**
   - "Do I tailor my communication style based on stereotypes rather than individual client needs and preferences?"
   - "Have I ever unconsciously favored certain clients over others based on shared characteristics or familiarity?"
3. **Decision-making and Recommendations**
   - "How do I ensure that my financial recommendations are objective and not influenced by biases or assumptions about what is 'best' for certain clients?"

- "Do I offer the same level of information and options to all clients, regardless of their background or perceived financial sophistication?"

4. **Awareness of Bias Triggers**
   - "What situations or characteristics might trigger my unconscious biases, and how can I mitigate their impact on my advice?"
   - "Am I aware of any patterns in my behavior or decision-making that could suggest the presence of implicit bias?"

5. **Continued Education and Improvement**
   - "How can I educate myself further on unconscious biases and their impact on financial advisory practices?"
   - "What steps can I take to create a more inclusive and equitable environment for all clients?"

6. **Client Feedback and Adjustment**
   - "How do I seek and respond to feedback from clients that might reveal biases or areas for improvement in my practice?"
   - "Am I open to changing my approach based on feedback and new insights into my biases?"

7. **Professional and Ethical Standards**
   - "How do I align my practice with ethical standards and best practices that promote fairness and equality in financial advising?"
   - "What resources or support systems (e.g. diversity training, peer discussions) can I leverage to help reduce unconscious biases in my practice?"

KEY TAKEAWAYS

1. **Definition and Impact**
   - Unconscious bias refers to automatic prejudices that can affect client interactions, hiring, and investment decisions.
2. **Manifestations of Bias**
   - **Client Interactions:** Gender and racial biases can lead to unequal treatment and service quality.
   - **Hiring:** Affinity and gender biases contribute to a lack of diversity.
   - **Investments:** Stereotypes influence product marketing, limiting opportunities for diverse clients.
   - **Acquisition and Retention:** Cultural biases can alienate potential clients.
3. **Consequences**
   - **Inequitable Service:** Marginalized clients receive inferior financial advice.
   - **Talent Drain:** Lack of diversity stifles creativity and innovation.
   - **Reputation Damage:** Ignoring bias risks client trust and public backlash.
   - **Legal Risks:** Discriminatory practices can lead to legal challenges.
4. **Addressing Unconscious Bias**
   - **Training:** Hold regular sessions to raise awareness.
   - **Diverse Hiring:** Blind recruitment and diverse panels.
   - **Standardized Procedures:** Protocols for interactions and evaluations should be set in place.
   - **Inclusive Culture:** Such culture includes affinity groups and mentorship.
   - **Accountability:** Mechanisms aid in monitoring bias initiatives.

5. **Real-world Examples**
   - Case studies highlight the impact of unconscious bias on financial advice and client opportunities.
6. **Importance of Recognition**
   - Acknowledging and addressing bias is crucial for equitable client treatment and enhancing advisory effectiveness.

NOTES

1. To take this test, go to https://implicit.harvard.edu/implicit/selectatouchtest.html.
2. Implicit Association Test. (n.d.). Project Implicit. Harvard University. Available at: https://implicit.harvard.cdu/implicit/takeatest.html.
3. Understanding implicit bias. (n.d.). Kirwan Institute for the Study of Race and Ethnicity. Available at: https://kirwaninstitute.osu.edu/book/export/html/33.
4. Macheel, T. (2016). *How to confront the "unconscious bias" foiling women in banking* (online). American Bankers Association. Available at: https://www.americanbanker.com/news/how-to-confront-the-unconscious-bias-foiling-women-in-banking.

CHAPTER NINE

FEAR AND
BAG LADY FEAR

Everything in the universe has a rhythm, everything dances.
Don't let fear hold you back from dancing your own dance.
                                              –Maya Angelou

PROBLEM: "BAG LADY FEAR" AND FINANCIAL INSECURITY

Growing up in New York City, I would often see older women on the streets, pushing shopping carts with all their belongings. Whether driven by financial hardship or mental health issues, the image has become a powerful symbol of the fear many women face.

The "bag lady fear" describes a deep-seated anxiety many women have about ending up destitute and homeless in their old age. This fear is influenced by factors such as financial insecurity, societal norms, and perceptions of aging. Women often face unique challenges, including lower lifetime earnings, career interruptions due to caregiving, and longer life expectancies, which can contribute to a heightened risk of financial instability. This fear can lead to stress, anxiety, and overly cautious financial behaviors, potentially limiting financial growth and security. According to the Allianz Women, Money, and Power® Study, 49% of women have this fear. Some surveys say more than 50% of women who have it.

Following are some key aspects of the bag lady fear:

- **Financial Insecurity:** Financial insecurity is rooted in concerns about financial instability and the ability to maintain a comfortable standard of living in retirement. Women may worry about factors such as lower lifetime earnings, interrupted careers due to caregiving responsibilities, and longer life expectancies, which can contribute to a greater risk of financial insecurity in old age.

- **Social and Cultural Factors:** Social and cultural factors, including gender norms and expectations, can contribute to this fear. Women may feel pressure to prioritize caregiving responsibilities over their careers, leading to gaps in employment, lower retirement savings, and increased vulnerability to financial hardship later in life.

- **Perceptions of Aging:** Perceptions surrounding aging are often tied to societal perceptions of aging and the portrayal of older women as vulnerable and economically disadvantaged. Media representations and cultural narratives about aging can reinforce fears of financial insecurity and homelessness in old age, exacerbating anxiety about the future.

- **Impact on Mental Health:** The bag lady fear can have significant psychological effects, contributing to stress, anxiety, and feelings of powerlessness or inadequacy. These fears may lead individuals to adopt overly cautious financial behaviors, such as hoarding money or avoiding risk-taking, which can negatively impact their financial well-being in the long run.

- **Addressing the Fear:** Overcoming this fear involves taking proactive steps to plan for retirement and build financial resilience. Steps may include setting realistic savings goals, investing wisely, seeking professional financial advice, and prioritizing financial literacy and empowerment. Additionally, challenging societal norms and advocating for policies that support gender equality and economic security can help alleviate the underlying sources of the bag lady fear.

Overall, the bag lady fear highlights the importance of addressing gender disparities in retirement savings and financial planning and promoting greater awareness and empowerment around financial issues, particularly among women and marginalized groups. By addressing these concerns, individuals can work toward achieving greater financial security and peace of mind in retirement.

THE DESIGNER BAG LADY

The bag lady fear is still present for 27% of women who make more than $200K a year. Even 46% of women of influence, who generally are less worried about their retirement savings, can't shake this fear. These data are based on the Allianz Women, Power, and Money Study. I too have this irrational fear.

We are not always aware of our feelings around money or how we react to money decisions. Our responses come from the messages we have internalized over the years as well as our experiences growing up. They are ingrained. For many of us, the biggest influence on our money decisions is fear. It's the fear that we will not have enough of it.

THE POSITIVES OF FEAR

Fear is one of the most common mentalities concerning money–and it isn't necessarily all that bad. I have personally always made money decisions out of a desire to protect myself. In fact, my therapist has said to me that my idea of safety would be if I built a money nest and sat inside of it. I'm not alone in this fear. Many of my female clients think the exact same way that I do. We love to hoard cash. It is more than just a rainy day or emergency fund.

Those who fall into this fear category tend to be careful, cautious people who live within or below their means. For example, I like to save 50% of what I make. Every time someone hears this; they do a double take: "What? Are you crazy?" But fear-minded folks are prepared for the unexpected.

THE NEGATIVES OF FEAR

I can speak personally to the negatives of having a fear-driven relationship with money. Fearful people are very slow to make decisions and might miss opportunities. Case in point, my hesitation cost me in the cutthroat New York City real estate market. My biggest regret is that I never owned property in New York City, and I see now how my mindset played a part in that. You usually have to make a decision the same day, and I never could. I experience anxiety when faced with big commitments and refuse to be rushed on a big money decision. I would rather walk away.

Fear-minded folks often make personal sacrifices to maintain security too. For instance, I gave up many vacations in my 20s because I could not part with the future value of that money. We overemphasize delayed gratification and often prepare for bad results that never materialize.

FEAR AS AN ALLY

All that said, in my case, my instinct for financial self-preservation protected me greatly when I married a man who committed financial infidelity. *Financial infidelity* occurs when couples with combined finances lie to each other about money. For example, one partner may hide the fact that he (or she) is paying against significant debts in a separate account that the other partner is unaware of. Another common example is when one partner makes large discretionary expenditures without discussing the matter with his or her partner.

In my case, it was all of the above. He hid income and assets, including moving assets out of the country. He lied about tax returns, and then kept them under lock and key. He was an attorney and CPA and used his expertise to lie to me, telling me that he was legally required to be listed on all the real estate titles. I was the only one on the mortgage, but I took his lies as truth.

Our divorce exposed the full extent of his financial infidelity. It took me four years and cost me more than six figures to get out of that mess of a marriage. So, when all my worst financial nightmares came true, my fear mindset prepared me for it.

My fear had made me a saver. My extreme emergency fund–that I saved and invested in for years–rescued me. I can confidently say that being afraid of not having financial protection is what wound up helping me through four years of negative cash flow.

Knowing your mindset when it comes to money can expose both the strengths and drawbacks of your emotional ties to it. I can't emphasize the importance of this enough. After all, when you know your feelings toward money, you might be able to start using those feelings to your advantage.

FEAR VERSUS GREED

Generally, women respond more to fear than greed. Generally, men respond more to greed. Let's examine.

The differing responses to fear and greed between women and men can be understood through a combination of psychological, sociological, and evolutionary perspectives.

Evolutionary Psychology

Following are several key factors explaining why women tend to respond more to fear and men more to greed.

- **Risk Aversion in Women:** From an evolutionary standpoint, women have historically been primary caregivers and thus more risk-averse to ensure their own and their offspring's survival. This inherent risk aversion translates into a greater response to fear-related stimuli.
- **Risk-taking in Men:** Men, on the other hand, have been evolutionarily predisposed to take risks to compete for resources and mates. This predisposition makes them more responsive to opportunities (greed) that promise significant rewards.

Socialization and Gender Norms

- **Cultural Conditioning**
  - Societal norms and cultural conditioning often encourage men to be assertive, competitive, and wealth-oriented. Men are often socialized to pursue success aggressively, which aligns with a greed-driven mindset.

- Women are typically socialized to be nurturing and protective, roles that align more closely with caution and risk avoidance. This socialization makes them more sensitive to fear-related messages that threaten security.

Behavioral Finance and Psychology

- **Emotional Responses:** Studies in behavioral finance suggest that women generally have stronger emotional responses to potential losses (fear) than to potential gains (greed). This loss aversion makes them more likely to react to fear-based scenarios.
- **Overconfidence:** Men are often more overconfident in their financial decisions, leading them to pursue high-risk, high-reward opportunities. This confidence can be linked to a greed-driven response, seeking significant gains.

Biological and Neurological Factors

- **Hormonal Differences:** Hormonal differences, such as higher levels of testosterone in men, are associated with increased risk-taking and competitive behavior, which can drive a greed-oriented approach.
- **Neurobiological Responses:** Neurological studies have found that men and women process risk and reward differently in their brains. Men's brains may show greater activation in areas associated with reward processing when faced with opportunities for gain, while women's brains may show heightened activity in areas associated with fear and risk.

PRACTICAL FINANCIAL CONCERNS

- **Security and Stability:** Women often prioritize financial security and stability, driven by a fear of future uncertainty. This focus can make them more conservative in their financial choices, emphasizing protection over high-risk, high-reward scenarios.
- **Wealth Accumulation:** Men may focus more on wealth accumulation and the status and power that comes with it. This drive for accumulation can lead to a greater emphasis on greed and opportunities for significant financial gain.

Market Behavior and Investment Strategies

- **Investment Behavior:** Women tend to be more conservative investors, often prioritizing safer, long-term investments over speculative opportunities. Men are more likely to engage in frequent trading and speculative investments, driven by the potential for large returns.
- **Reaction to Market Fluctuations:** In times of market instability, women are more likely to pull back and reassess their financial positions (fear response), while men may see volatility as an opportunity to capitalize on market movements (greed response).

Fear can be a powerful motivator, influencing behavior in significant ways.

Positive Aspects

1. **Heightened Awareness:** Fear triggers the "fight or flight" response, making individuals more alert and focused, which can enhance performance in high-stakes situations.
2. **Behavioral Change:** Fear can prompt individuals to adopt healthier or safer behaviors, such as quitting smoking due to a fear of illness.
3. **Goal Achievement:** Fear of failure or negative outcomes can drive people to work harder and achieve their goals.

Negative Aspects

1. **Paralysis:** Excessive fear can lead to inaction, preventing individuals from taking necessary steps.
2. **Stress and Anxiety:** Chronic fear can result in high stress levels, affecting mental and physical health.
3. **Negative Motivation:** Fear-based motivation can lead to a negative work environment and decrease overall morale.

Application

- **In Leadership:** Using fear to motivate employees can yield short-term results but often leads to burnout and high turnover. Positive reinforcement is generally more sustainable.
- **Personal Development:** Balancing fear with positive motivators like passion and curiosity can lead to more holistic growth.

The differences in how women and men respond to fear and greed are influenced by a complex interplay of evolutionary, social, psychological, biological, and financial factors. Understanding these differences can help financial advisors tailor their strategies and communication approaches to better meet the unique needs and preferences of their clients.

Understanding the bag lady fear and the differences in how women and men respond to fear and greed is crucial for financial advisors. Women's fear is a powerful motivator but can also lead to inaction. Addressing this fear through empathetic communication and tailored financial planning can help women achieve greater financial security and peace of mind.

By recognizing and addressing these concerns, financial advisors can better support their female clients, helping them navigate their fears and make informed, confident financial decisions.

Solution: Addressing the Bag Lady Fear

1. **Financial Education and Empowerment:** Encouraging financial literacy and providing access to professional financial advice can help women make informed decisions about saving, investing, and retirement planning. Understanding one's financial situation and future needs is crucial in alleviating fears of insecurity.

2. **Proactive Financial Planning:** Setting realistic savings goals, investing wisely, and maintaining a diverse investment portfolio are essential steps. Women should be encouraged to plan for retirement early and regularly review and adjust their financial plans as needed.

3. **Challenging Societal Norms:** Addressing and changing societal and cultural norms that place disproportionate caregiving responsibilities on women is crucial. This includes advocating for policies that support gender equality in the workplace, such as equal pay, parental leave, and flexible working arrangements.

4. **Emotional and Psychological Support:** Understanding the psychological impact of the bag lady fear and providing support through counseling or therapy can help women manage their anxieties and develop healthier attitudes toward money.

5. **Promoting a Balanced Perspective:** While fear can motivate caution and savings, it's important to balance this with opportunities for growth. Encouraging women to take calculated risks and seize financial opportunities can help build wealth and financial security.

Questions for Financial Advisors to Ask Their Clients

1. **Awareness of Fears and Anxieties**
   - Have you ever heard of the term "bag lady fear"? How do you feel about it, and do you identify with this fear?
   - What specific financial concerns or anxieties do you have about your future, particularly in retirement?

2. **Current Financial Situation and Planning**
   - How confident do you feel about your current financial situation and your plans for the future?
   - Do you have a clear understanding of your retirement savings and whether they align with your future goals and needs?

3. **Investment and Savings Behavior**
   - How do you approach savings and investment decisions? Do you consider yourself more cautious or risk-tolerant?
   - Have you ever avoided financial opportunities due to fear or uncertainty? If so, can you share an example?

4. **Influence of Past Experiences and Beliefs**
   - How do your past experiences and upbringing influence your current financial mindset and decisions?
   - Do you think cultural or societal norms have impacted your approach to money and financial planning?

5. **Emotional and Psychological Factors**
   - How do emotions like fear or anxiety affect your financial decision-making process?
   - Have you ever sought advice or counseling to help manage financial stress or anxiety?
6. **Future Planning and Goals**
   - What are your primary financial goals for the next 5–10 years, and how do you plan to achieve them?
   - What steps have you taken to ensure financial security in retirement, and are there any areas where you feel uncertain or need more guidance?
7. **Support and Resources:**
   - Do you feel you have access to the resources and knowledge you need to make informed financial decisions?
   - Would you be interested in educational resources or workshops to help you better understand financial planning and investment strategies?

What Keeps Women Up at Night

- Bag lady fear
- Healthcare costs
- Fear of raising entitled children
- Anxiety about work
- Fear of success (higher we climb, the more we get judged)
- Marianne Williamson said it best: "Our deepest fear is not that we are inadequate. Our deepest fear is that we are powerful beyond measure. It is our light, not our darkness, that most frightens us."

KEY TAKEAWAYS

1. **Prevalence of "Bag Lady Fear":** Many women, even high earners, fear ending up destitute and homeless in their old age. This anxiety stems from financial insecurity, societal pressures, and the perception that women are more vulnerable in retirement due to lower lifetime earnings, career interruptions, and longer life expectancies.

2. **Financial and Cultural Factors:** Women's financial concerns are often compounded by societal expectations, such as caregiving responsibilities, which can lead to employment gaps and less retirement savings. These factors increase the risk of financial instability and reinforce the bag lady fear.

3. **Psychological Impact:** The fear of financial ruin has a significant psychological toll, leading to stress, anxiety, and overly cautious financial behavior. This can cause women to avoid risk-taking and miss out on wealth-building opportunities, ultimately limiting their financial security.

4. **The Designer Bag Lady:** This fear is not limited to women with modest incomes. Even 27% of women earning more than $200K a year and nearly half of "women of influence" still harbor this fear, highlighting its deep psychological roots.

5. **The Role of Fear in Money Decisions:** Fear isn't always negative—it can drive women to be cautious, save more, and live within their means. However, it can also lead to inaction, missed opportunities, and personal sacrifices in the pursuit of security.

6. **Balancing Fear with Opportunity:** Advisors need to help women balance their fear-driven desire for security with the need to take calculated risks. By encouraging a more balanced approach, women

can overcome the paralysis that fear sometimes creates and seize opportunities for financial growth.

7. **Impact of Financial Infidelity:** My personal experience with financial infidelity highlights the importance of financial transparency in relationships. My fear mindset, which drove me to save diligently, ultimately protected me during a financially devastating divorce.

8. **Gendered Differences in Response to Fear and Greed:** Women tend to be more motivated by fear, while men are often driven by greed. This difference is rooted in both evolutionary and social factors, with women prioritizing security and men more likely to pursue risky, high-reward financial opportunities.

9. **Financial Advisors' Role in Addressing Fear:** Advisors can help alleviate the bag lady fear by promoting financial literacy, creating realistic savings and investment plans, and offering emotional support. Helping clients understand their emotional relationship with money is crucial to reducing financial anxiety.

10. **Challenging Societal Norms:** Long-term solutions to bag lady fear involve advocating for policies that support gender equality in the workplace, such as equal pay and caregiving benefits, which can alleviate some of the underlying financial pressures women face.

CHAPTER TEN

BRO CULTURE AND LAWSUITS

Women belong in all places where decisions are being made.
It shouldn't be that women are the exception.

—Ruth Bader Ginsburg

PROBLEM

"Bro culture" in the financial services industry refers to a predominantly male, fraternity-like atmosphere that often excludes women and minorities. This culture can lead to discriminatory practices, a lack of career advancement opportunities for underrepresented groups, and a toxic work environment. Notable characteristics include exclusionary practices, aggressive behavior, sexist attitudes, and a lack of work-life balance. The presence of this culture has led to numerous high-profile lawsuits alleging gender discrimination, sexual harassment, and hostile work environments.

Characteristics of Bro Culture in the Financial Sector

1. **Exclusionary Practices:** Women and minorities may feel excluded from informal networks and social gatherings, which can be critical for career advancement.
2. **Informal Networking:** Business deals and promotions might be discussed and decided during activities like golfing, drinking sessions, or sports events, where women and minorities might not be invited or not feel comfortable participating.
3. **Aggressive Behavior:** A competitive, "winner-takes-all" mindset can prevail, encouraging aggressive sales tactics and risk-taking.
4. **Sexist Attitudes and Behavior:** This can include inappropriate jokes, sexual harassment, and a general lack of respect for female colleagues.
5. **Homogeneity:** Hiring and promotion practices might favor those who fit into the existing culture, perpetuating a cycle where similar types of individuals are continually brought in.
6. **Lack of Work-life Balance:** The culture often values long hours and a relentless work ethic, which can disadvantage those with caregiving responsibilities, who are often women.

Impact on Women and Minorities

- **Career Advancement:** Women and minorities may face barriers to advancement due to exclusion from key networks and opportunities.
- **Retention:** High turnover rates among women and minorities can result from feeling undervalued and marginalized.
- **Workplace Climate:** A toxic workplace culture can lead to lower job satisfaction and mental health issues among employees.

- **Talent Pool:** The financial services industry may struggle to attract a diverse talent pool if it is perceived as unwelcoming to women and minorities.

Examples in the Financial Industry

Several high-profile cases and studies have highlighted the presence and impact of bro culture in financial services:

- **Lawsuits:** There have been numerous lawsuits against major financial institutions alleging gender discrimination, sexual harassment, and hostile work environments.
- **Publicized Incidents:** Stories of inappropriate behavior, such as sexual harassment at company events or demeaning treatment of female employees, have surfaced in media reports.
- **Industry Reports:** Studies and reports by organizations like Catalyst and the Financial Women's Association have documented the challenges women face in the financial industry due to entrenched cultural issues.

Efforts to Address Bro Culture

1. **Diversity and Inclusion Initiatives:** Many firms are implementing programs to promote diversity and inclusion, such as unconscious bias training and diversity hiring targets.
2. **Mentorship and Sponsorship Programs:** Establishing mentorship and sponsorship programs can help women and minorities gain the support and networking opportunities they need to advance.

3. **Policy Changes:** Stronger policies and procedures to address harassment and discrimination can help create a safer and more inclusive work environment.
4. **Cultural Change:** Leadership commitment to changing the workplace culture, including promoting work-life balance and valuing diverse perspectives, is crucial.
5. **Accountability:** Individuals must be held accountable for behavior that undermines a respectful and inclusive workplace through clear consequences for misconduct.

Bro culture in financial services is a significant barrier to creating a diverse, equitable, and inclusive workplace. Addressing this culture requires comprehensive and sustained efforts across all levels of an organization, from leadership commitment to grassroots cultural changes. By fostering a more inclusive environment, financial institutions can benefit from a wider range of perspectives, improve employee satisfaction, and ultimately enhance their business performance.

The term "bro culture" in financial services has been highlighted in several high-profile lawsuits, with one of the most notable being the "Boom-boom Room" lawsuit against Smith Barney in the late 1990s. Here are some detailed examples of such lawsuits:

Case Overview: "Boom-boom Room" lawsuit

- **Year:** 1996
- **Defendant:** Smith Barney (now part of Morgan Stanley)
- **Plaintiffs:** A group of female employees led by Ann Hopkins and others
- **Allegations:** The plaintiffs alleged widespread sexual harassment and discrimination. They claimed that a basement party room at the Garden City, New York branch, known as the "Boom-boom Room," was used for lewd and inappropriate behavior by male

employees. Women alleged that they were subjected to groping, obscene jokes, and other forms of sexual misconduct. I grew up in Long Island so this one was part of my local zeitgeist.

- **Outcome:** The case was settled in 1998. Smith Barney agreed to implement significant changes, including revising their policies on sexual harassment and discrimination, establishing a monitoring and reporting system, and creating a fund to compensate affected women.

Case Overview: Gender discrimination lawsuit

- **Year:** 2007
- **Defendant:** Merrill Lynch
- **Plaintiffs:** A group of female brokers
- **Allegations:** The plaintiffs alleged that Merrill Lynch engaged in discriminatory practices, including unequal pay, lack of promotion opportunities, and a hostile work environment characterized by a "boys' club" culture.
- **Outcome:** Merrill Lynch settled the lawsuit for $46 million in 2010. The settlement included significant changes to its policies to ensure more equitable treatment of female employees.

Case Overview: Gender discrimination lawsuit

- **Year:** 2004
- **Defendant:** Morgan Stanley
- **Plaintiffs:** Allison Schieffelin, along with other female employees
- **Allegations:** The plaintiffs alleged that Morgan Stanley discriminated against women in terms of pay, promotions, and other employment opportunities. The lawsuit highlighted a hostile work environment where women were often excluded from important networking opportunities.

- **Outcome:** Morgan Stanley settled for $54 million. The settlement included agreements to implement workplace policy changes and to monitor the company's compliance with antidiscrimination laws.

Case Overview: Class action gender discrimination lawsuit

- **Year:** 2010
- **Defendant:** Goldman Sachs
- **Plaintiffs:** A class of female employees led by Cristina Chen-Oster and Shanna Orlich
- **Allegations:** The plaintiffs alleged that Goldman Sachs had a pervasive culture of gender discrimination that affected pay, promotions, and evaluations. The case also described a workplace culture where women were subject to demeaning comments and excluded from networking opportunities.
- **Outcome:** The case saw ongoing legal battles, with significant court rulings allowing the class-action status to proceed. In 2023, it was finally settled out of court. The long-running gender discrimination class action lawsuit against Goldman Sachs, filed in 2010 by plaintiffs Cristina Chen-Oster, Shanna Orlich, Allison Gamba, and Mary De Luis, recently reached a significant settlement. On May 8, 2023, Goldman Sachs agreed to pay $215 million to settle the allegations, which claimed that the firm discriminated against women in terms of pay, performance evaluations, and promotions. This wound up being approximately $50,000 per employee or around one month of pay per woman. I don't believe this was justice at all personally. This doesn't feel equitable. I was at Goldman Sachs and discriminated against. I was in this lawsuit, and I was going to give the entire amount to a women's cause for charity when it was settled. I then received an email from one of the attorneys in the case, and he said the employees from United Capital were specifically

excluded from the case. I said I am the only one, and he said I am sorry to be delivering this news. In my entire 30 year career, I have never been treated the way I was treated by Goldman Sachs.

Case Overview: Gender discrimination lawsuit

- **Year:** 2018
- **Defendant:** Wells Fargo
- **Plaintiffs:** A group of female employees led by Stacey Allerton
- **Allegations:** The plaintiffs alleged that Wells Fargo maintained a culture of gender bias, with claims including discriminatory pay practices, lack of promotions for women, and a hostile work environment.
- **Outcome:** The lawsuit was settled in 2020 for $35 million, with Wells Fargo agreeing to make changes in its policies and practices regarding gender discrimination.

Broader Impact and Industry Changes

1. **Policy Reforms:** Many firms have revised their policies on harassment and discrimination, instituted mandatory training programs, and established clearer reporting and monitoring mechanisms.
2. **Cultural Shifts:** The exposure of these issues has led to increased awareness and efforts to change the "bro culture" within financial services. Firms are increasingly promoting diversity and inclusion initiatives.
3. **Regulatory Scrutiny:** Regulatory bodies have heightened their scrutiny of employment practices within the industry, leading to more stringent enforcement of antidiscrimination laws.

4. **Corporate Accountability:** Companies are now more frequently held accountable for fostering inclusive workplaces, with leadership taking active roles in promoting diversity.

The "bro culture" lawsuits in financial services underscore the challenges women face in the industry and have catalyzed significant changes. While progress has been made, ongoing efforts are necessary to ensure a truly inclusive and equitable work environment for all employees. All these large firms have striven toward change. I know my own experience within Goldman Sachs, but others have had a completely different point of view. I believe it is getting better but much slower than I would hope.

Solutions

1. **Diversity and Inclusion Initiatives:** Implement programs that promote diversity and inclusion, including unconscious bias training and diversity hiring targets.
2. **Mentorship and Sponsorship Programs:** Establish these programs to provide support and networking opportunities for women and minorities.
3. **Policy Changes:** Strengthen policies and procedures to address harassment and discrimination.
4. **Cultural Change:** Promote a shift in workplace culture that values work-life balance and diverse perspectives.
5. **Accountability:** Hold individuals accountable for behaviors that undermine a respectful and inclusive workplace.

Questions for Financial Advisors to Ask Themselves

1. **Self-Reflection on Bias:** Do I recognize and address my own biases and how they may affect my interactions with colleagues and clients?

2. **Inclusive Practices:** How do I ensure that my professional practices and networks are inclusive of women and minorities?
3. **Role in Cultural Change:** What actions can I take to support a more inclusive and equitable workplace culture?
4. **Responsibility and Accountability:** How do I hold myself and others accountable for creating a respectful and inclusive environment?
5. **Ongoing Learning:** Am I committed to continuous learning and improvement in areas of diversity and inclusion?

KEY TAKEAWAYS

1. **Bro Culture Defined:** A male-dominated, exclusionary environment in financial services that marginalizes women and minorities, fostering gender discrimination, harassment, and a lack of work-life balance.
2. **Impact on Women and Minorities:** Barriers to career advancement, high turnover, toxic work environments, and a failure to attract diverse talent.
3. **Notable Lawsuits:** High-profile cases like Smith Barney, Merrill Lynch, and Goldman Sachs have exposed the harmful effects of bro culture and led to settlements and policy changes.
4. **Efforts for Change:** Diversity initiatives, mentorship programs, stronger policies, cultural shifts, and holding individuals accountable are essential to creating a more inclusive workplace.
5. **Questions for Advisors:** Reflect on personal biases, inclusive practices, accountability, and commitment to supporting cultural change in the industry.
6. **Ongoing Progress:** While improvements are being made, change is slow, and more effort is needed to create true inclusion in financial services.

CHAPTER ELEVEN

WHY WOMEN LEAVE THEIR ADVISORS

Women leave their financial advisors when they feel sidelined or underestimated. Effective advisors need to listen actively and engage with their clients' financial goals and challenges to build long-term relationships.

—Barbara Stanny

PROBLEM

Seventy percent of clients leave their usually male advisor. Many women leave their financial advisors, often after the death of a spouse or a divorce, feeling sidelined or underestimated. This issue is compounded by a common dynamic where advisors, typically male, interact primarily with male clients, neglecting the engagement and involvement of female clients. This can result in women feeling ignored, dismissed, or patronized, which erodes trust and leads to a high attrition rate among female clients. Some say it is even higher than that number.

I was doing a presentation about Women in Leadership for Citywire, and one man asked a question. He said, "I have a 100-million-dollar client, and the wife doesn't attend any meetings, but we are friends. I am concerned about what will happen when he dies."

Shannon Eusey (the CEO of Beacon Wealth) said, "She will leave you."

He insisted the wife wouldn't leave, but Eusey insisted she would. You could tell he was concerned, but he didn't know how to change it. We, the panel, suggested he discuss estate planning with the client and ask what happens if he passes. Women are more charitably inclined than men, and this could be a good reason to get her engaged. Then I thought of all the things I didn't say, like, "Have your thought about bringing a woman on your team?"

I attended Citywire's conference a few months before and I told the organizers that they don't have one woman on the stage anywhere. They only had "manels" (male panels). They took my feedback and ran with it. They added two female speakers in a one on one with Ian Wenick and our all-female dream team panel with, me, Shannon Eusey, Molly Bernard, Cameron Dawson, and

Citywire Women in Leadership Panel April 2024, Left to Right: Rafia Hasan, Shannon Eusey, Cameron Dawson, Molly Bernard, Cary Carbonaro (author).

Rafia Hasan. We thought everyone (90% male audience) would be looking at their phones the entire time. Boy, were we surprised. Not only was everyone listening, but they were literally sitting at the edge of their seats leaning in!

Here's a fact: Soon after their husbands die, many female clients leave their financial advisors. I am usually on the receiving end of this. The client attrition rates are even higher after a divorce.

This article was published first in Rethinking 65. As high as these numbers are, they're not really that surprising considering that 40% of women surveyed say their advisors often ignore or dismiss what they have to say, and 62% of women say their advisors don't understand their unique investment needs.

Why is this? I can share some insight about what I've seen among my female clients.

Most clients who come to me are at a crossroad in their life. Most have never worked directly with an advisor. Some have worked indirectly with an advisor hired by their ex- or late husbands. My clients often tell me they felt they were never heard or listened to, and that the advisor always used numbers and investment language they did not understand.

I've also heard, "I was patronized if I asked questions" or "He would not make eye contact with me. I was just there." And even, "Sometimes I would pick up a magazine and start reading it right in the middle of the meeting; he wouldn't even notice." I hear these stories *all* the time.

Clients have also told me that they were not that interested in managing their finances, or that they and their spouse simply divided and conquered tasks. Traditionally, the women did the household and children stuff, and the men did the money stuff. Although these roles are changing, these norms are very deeply rooted. But conquering and dividing doesn't work with divorce or widowhood.

Research shows that women are also more likely to feel stress around finances. Stress is another factor. According to a Bankrate survey conducted in 2024, 46% of women said money had a negative impact on their financial health, compared to 38% of men.[1]

But women are intuitive! And, in fact, women are great planners. They plan weddings, vacations, and parties. They just don't usually plan their retirements! A woman can do anything she puts her mind to.

WHAT WOMEN NEED

Women need planning *more*, not less, than men! They typically live longer, earn less, save less, invest more conservatively, and spend more money on healthcare! In fact, 90% of women will be responsible for their finances exclusively at one point in their lives. Women are more complex clients than men, who generally want to know how much they beat the S&P 500. In my entire three-decade career, I have never had a woman ask me about that.

A financial advisor's job is inherently quantitative. But money is deeply personal, and the process of planning most often involves a client's complex relationship with money. Planners who can engage with these emotions can motivate clients, plan more holistically, and improve planning outcomes.

Some people talk about the softer side of financial planning. It is interesting that there is really no definition for this. "Softer" typically means emotional or touchy-feely stuff that women are usually better at. Connecting with clients on a deeper emotional level or making them part of your world can be especially important with female clients.

GETTING STARTED

That said, you shouldn't assume that every female client is emotional and touchy feely. You have to get to know them individually. Every person is different in how they approach money and what they want out of an advisor relationship.

One of my clients was very nervous when I first met her in her early 70s. She thought she didn't have enough money and was afraid of the stock market. Each time we met, I showed her a year-over-year graph of her net worth. It rose most years, except for 2008. She spent less than she made, and her investments were in a 60/40 balanced portfolio. She always asked me, "How much do I have?" I responded by showing her the graphs and telling her she was okay. Every time, she relaxed a little more. Now, after 20 years working together, she says she can sleep and she never worries anymore, at least about money.

You may also want to consider sharing some details of your life and your goals with your female clients to build trust and lead by example. Advice coming from a trusted friend who is also a fiduciary, to me, is above reproach. If you always put your clients' interest first and don't have conflicts of interest, it makes it easy to deliver and implement.

Women are not taught to believe in financial abundance, that they can create wealth by taking calculated risk and making investments. This is why most women will pick a guaranteed salary over unlimited upside with zero salary. They're not taught that women can create social and economic capital though financial literacy and taking responsibility for their own lives. When I was speaking at a high school in a wealthy neighborhood in Connecticut, I asked the girls in the room, "How many of you think you will be responsible for supporting yourselves financially?" About 5–10% of the hands went up. There were boys in the room, and some girls didn't raise their hands because it was a mixed gendered group. But even accounting for that, the numbers were too low. This was in 2018, not 1968. I told them they should all want to be responsible, and that 90% would be responsible at some point in their lives anyway.

Solutions

Here are some more ideas on how to attract and retain female clients.

- **Be authentic.** Women can feel in their gut if the advisor is being straight with them. Be the person you would want your mom to go to.
- **Listen, hear, and see them.** Get to know who they are, what is important to them, and what they're afraid of. Even if they don't know what questions to ask, tell them, "Think about capital gains and taxes in your portfolio. This is where working with me will add value."
- **Follow their timeline.** They are busy doing it all, so it might take them more time to review, process, and even run your proposal or suggestions by other friends and confidants. They take longer to close but are worth it; don't give up. I only give up if I am getting ghosted, meaning they are ignoring my calls, texts, and emails. It hurts me because I care for these people. I don't understand what would make a person never respond again.
- **Never do a hard sale.** I know that 75% to 85% of men in our industry ask for the business repeatedly. But I never wanted to sound like a used car salesperson. I don't even consider myself a salesperson. Instead, I think of myself as a consultant or an attorney giving advice. They can choose to take it (or reject it) because it is in their best interest. If they reject, this is usually indecision rather than a straight-out rejection. It reminds me of Alanis Morissette's lyric, "It's the good advice that you just didn't take."
- **Be empathetic.** Put yourself in the client's shoes and try to feel what they are feeling. I happen to be an empath, so this is very natural for me, and I am not sure if this skill can be taught. When a client is hurting, I hurt, and I want to ease their pain and anxiety. Money is very emotional and tied to so much more than just the money itself. That's why we are also therapists.
- **Teach her, don't tell her.** Like the well-known proverb, "If you give a woman a fish, you feed her for a day. If you teach a woman to fish, you feed her for a lifetime." I am a teacher by trade. Giving

and imparting knowledge feels good and like the right thing to do. I always say I teach money instead of history, but sometimes I teach the history of money.

A diverse team can help strengthen relationships and is becoming an increasing requirement for success, according to the NY Life Women's study. The percentage of women agreeing that it is important that their financial advisory team have at least one woman was 54% in 2023 versus 29% in 2019. Almost double! The percentage of women agreeing that a woman financial advisor would be more attuned to their needs was 48% in 2023, up from 29% in 2019.

Suzanne Siracuse, a consultant and former Investment News CEO, says, "It should be mandated that advisors meet with both spouses." She talked about a story of one of her friends who had never went to one meeting and had no idea what is going on or what she had. She always just trusted her husband, and now she was unexpectedly getting a divorce. I told her I had no idea this even happened. I didn't know the wife would be completely left out of the meetings.

Questions Financial Advisors Should Ask Themselves

1. Am I actively involving both spouses in financial discussions?
2. Do I listen to and validate the concerns and goals of my female clients?
3. How can I better educate and empower my female clients about their financial options?
4. Is my advisory team diverse enough to meet the needs of all clients?
5. Am I assuming that my clients understand the financial jargon I use, or am I trying to communicate clearly?
6. What steps can I take to ensure that my female clients feel heard, respected, and valued in our interactions?
7. How can I build a relationship of trust with my clients, particularly those who may feel marginalized or overlooked?

Women need and should have a financial advocate! If you're unsure of whether your practice is female-friendly, I suggest looking at the questionnaire that Kathleen Burns Kingsbury includes in her book, *How to Give Financial Advice to Women*. See where you are. Most women should be at 100%.

Female-Friendly Practice:[2] Answer each of the following statements as True or False for your practice:

1. My practice is at a minimum equally weighted in terms of female versus male. Clients only include clients you're actively working with either individually or as a member of a couple.
2. Women face a variety of financial hurdles that are different from what men face.
3. When I meet with prospects, I need to know if they are going to sign up for my services within the first two appointments. Otherwise, I'm wasting my time.
4. I offer educational forums and client events specifically for women.
5. When I communicate with my female clients, I find it important to stress my expertise, so that they feel comfortable working with me.
6. All women prefer to work with female advisors. Therefore, I refer most women clients to my female colleagues.
7. When I am advising a couple, I communicate with the partner who speaks up the most.
8. I adjust my communication style to meet the preferred style of my client.
9. When I am advising a couple, I check in with both partners each time I have a question.
10. I offer individual meetings for my female clients who are members of a couple.

11. I communicate with other members of a clients' financial team, such as their accountant, banker, or an estate attorney regularly.

12. If a female client is not talking, she is not learning.

13. During a client annual review, I spent a fair amount of time talking about investment performance relative to the benchmarks, such as the S&P.

14. I find it important to tie investment performance results to real-life events for my female clients.

15. When I develop a financial plan, I make sure the client articulates clearly her family values, life, goals, and wishes for the next generation.

16. I offer intergenerational wealth services as part of my practice.

17. I avoid talking about emotional issues related to money with my clients.

18. I am open to and/or work with family, wealth, consultants, family, therapist, and other consultants to help my female client manage and pass on their wealth.

19. I do not offer financial literacy resources training to my clients as I don't see this is part of my job.

20. The majority of women view wealth the same as men do, i.e. means to power and control.

Answer Key: Give yourself 2 points for every correct answer.

1. True
2. True
3. False
4. True
5. False
6. False

7. False
8. True
9. True
10. True
11. True
12. False
13. False
14. True
15. True
16. True
17. False
18. True
19. False
20. False

Points

36–40 Points: Congratulations you are a female-friendly advisor!
22–34: Nice job but you have a little work to do.
0–20: You have some work to do, but now you know what you don't know!

KEY TAKEAWAYS

1. **High Attrition Rates Among Female Clients:** Seventy percent of clients leave their financial advisors, and many of them are women. Women commonly leave their advisors after significant life events like widowhood or divorce due to feeling sidelined, underestimated, or ignored by their (usually male) advisors.

2. **Lack of Engagement:** A recurring issue is that many male advisors primarily engage with the male spouse, leaving women out of financial conversations. This disengagement creates a disconnect that can erode trust and lead to clients leaving when they become solely responsible for their finances.

3. **Women Want Involvement:** Research shows that 40% of women feel their advisors often ignore their input, while 62% believe their unique financial needs are not understood. Women want to be involved, listened to, and respected in financial planning discussions.

4. **Emotional Connection and Personalized Communication Matter:** Women value empathy, understanding, and deeper connections. Advisors who recognize and address emotional aspects of financial planning can build stronger relationships with female clients. A personalized approach rather than a one-size-fits-all model is essential.

5. **Challenges Women Face:** Women often live longer, earn less, and invest more conservatively than men. They are more likely to face financial stress and have higher healthcare costs. Advisors need to understand and address these complexities to effectively serve their female clients.

6. **Education and Empowerment Are Key:** Advisors must educate and empower their female clients, ensuring they understand financial decisions and are prepared for future challenges. Women are often not taught to take financial risks, and many are uncomfortable with financial jargon or investment conversations.

7. **Diverse Teams Build Trust:** Having women on the advisory team can increase trust and engagement. A diverse team better meets the needs of all clients, with 54% of women saying in 2023 that it's important to have at least one woman on their advisory team, up from 29% in 2019.

8. **Solutions for Retaining Female Clients**
   - Involve both spouses in financial discussions and ensure both partners feel heard.
   - Avoid hard selling; instead, focus on being a trusted consultant.
   - Understand the personal side of financial planning–emotions, goals, and life challenges.
   - Regularly check in with both partners, ensure clear communication, and avoid making assumptions about clients' knowledge.
9. **Advisors Must Evolve:** Financial advisors need to reflect on their practices and make changes to better serve their female clients. These changes include adjusting communication styles, involving both partners equally, and building a relationship based on trust, empathy, and mutual respect.

NOTES

1. Ngo, S.M. (2024). *Most Americans are significantly stressed about money–here's how it varies by demographic* (online). Bankrate. Available at: https://www.bankrate.com/banking/money-and-financial-stress-statistics/#trends.
2. Printed with permission from, *How to Give Financial Advice to Women* by Mcgraw Hill and Kathleen Kingsbury.

CHAPTER TWELVE

IGNORED TO INVESTED: HOW TO ATTRACT AND KEEP WOMEN AS CLIENTS

Ignoring women's financial needs is a lost opportunity. Investing in women's financial health and potential creates a ripple effect that benefits everyone.

–Brené Brown

Women are the sole or primary breadwinner in 16% of marriages today, compared with 5% in 1972, and in nearly a third of marriages, both spouses earn the same income.[1] In addition, by 2030, women are expected to control two-thirds of the nation's wealth.[2]

These female breadwinners and economically empowered women are coming up against a fundamental issue with the financial services industry: It was created by and for men. Women have come a long way since the Equal Credit Opportunity Act of 1974, but before then a bank could deny a credit card to a woman without a male cosigner. This long-ago idea that women couldn't take responsibility for their own financial affairs still haunts us. One survey showed that 40% of women say their advisors often ignore or dismiss what they have to say.[3]

WOMEN ARE DEALING WITH FINANCIAL STRESS

As one of the few female advisors, I've made it my life's work to try and change the industry to make it more female-friendly. The problem is more urgent than ever, with women saying the number-one word for how they feel about finances is "stress."[4] Advisors who are ready to listen and serve these women on their own terms are desperately needed.

In my own practice, I've seen some heartbreaking cases of financial abuse. The story of one client whose husband died has remained with me. She had a young child, and she began dating someone. He was financially abusive toward her and was spending all her money.

She calls me crying one day and says, "Can you come with me?"

I said, "Sure, what do you need?"

She needed to get her $100,000 Mercedes out of the impound lot after her boyfriend was caught driving drunk in it. After that day at the impound yard, I helped her find a therapist. I always wonder what would have happened if I hadn't been there. Women need that personal connection with their advisor.

It's not just the right thing to do; there is an actual business case for tailoring financial services to women's needs and preferences. We need to get this right and not just "pinkwash" it. One study showed that retaining baby boomer women as clients could result in one-third higher revenue potential, and firms that gain and retain younger women as clients could experience nearly four times faster revenue growth.[5]

MY COMMON THREAD

Women make up half the population, but we're only 23% of Certified Financial Planners® (CFP).[6] That's why I've spent a decade as a CFP Board ambassador, and with the CFP Board Center for Financial Planning, working to get more women into the profession. I'm also involved in fundraising, and I'm a legacy donor for that cause. I practice what I preach.

To help on the client side, I've written a book, *The Money Queen's Guide*, inspired by my own experiences with finances during a drawn-out divorce. I said, "If it can happen to me, it can happen to anybody," so I wrote a guide to what women should be doing decade by decade in their 20s, 30s, 40s, 50s, and 60s to be financially independent.

I also serve on the foundation board for SUNY College at Cortland, where I earned my undergraduate degree. I set up a named scholarship for a woman in business there. Again, I'm putting my money where my mouth is.

All of this is related to making the industry more female-friendly, recruiting more women, and empowering women to become financially independent. It's all related. It's the one thread that always runs through what I'm doing, what I'm talking about, and what I believe in.

FINDING THE WAY FORWARD

However, I'm only one person. I would love to see the leaders of wealth management enterprises make strides in changing the industry as well. Here are a few ideas:

- **Stop measuring women with a male-oriented measuring stick.** I've said it before: things like gross dealer concession (GDC) and assets under management (AUM) sound like male measuring sticks. Some practices don't even charge based on AUM anymore, so that should be less important. Why don't we try measuring the contribution to a firm by how many lives an advisor has impacted? How many relationships does an advisor have? How deep are the relationships? That feels more meaningful.
- **Hire an expert in women and wealth to evaluate your firm.** Every firm should be motivated to do this because it's the right thing for the business and in the eyes of the public. There are blind spots you're not aware of. You don't know how female-friendly your practice is. I use a quiz where firms can score themselves to reveal how female-friendly they are. We're finding many opportunities to improve.

What Women Want from Their Financial Advisors

When it comes to the best practices for working with women wealth management clients, what sounds like common sense isn't always common practice in the industry. Lacy Garcia is the Founder & CEO of Willow (trustwillow.com), an award-winning wealthtech platform that helps advisors to acquire, grow, and retain relationships with historically underserved clients who are now becoming the new majority of investors: women and NextGen clients. She asks, "What exactly are women looking for when it comes to their relationship with their advisors?"

1. **A Trusted Relationship:** She wants to feel a personal connection to you. This connection begins by showing her who you are as a person and why you want to help her and by asking open-ended questions that demonstrate your genuine interest.

2. **Alignment:** She wants to know that you care about her values and life goals and that her financial plan and investments are aligned with her values and goals. Creating a collaborative relationship and practicing active listening are key to achieving this.

3. **Expansive Support:** She wants support across all life's journeys, particularly emotional transitions with big financial implications such as divorce, widowhood, entrepreneurship, career transitions, family planning, and fertility or adoption.

4. **User Friendliness:** She wants modern and streamlined technology, digital tools, and communications that make life easier and bite-sized. And she wants you to be able to meet with her virtually and communicate by email or text. She doesn't necessarily have the time to come meet with you in your office given the demands of career and/or family.

5. **Relevance:** She wants inspiring, actionable, and bite-sized recommendations and communications that are relevant to her and her family's daily life and life journeys.

6. **Equity and Eco-mindset:** She wants to know that you care about diversity, equity, inclusion, and sustainability–and many women want to see people on your team and in your network who look like them and share similar life experiences.

When working with women clients, advice must become equal parts financial guidance and human understanding. You must create a collaborative client relationship centered on trust and a personal connection. It's about "her" and her life first, and her finances second.

It requires educating her so she is knowledgeable and able to make better financial and investment decisions, versus throwing jargon and spreadsheets at her and being patronizing, which can exacerbate her fears and stress and make her feel that you don't understand or care about her.

A collaborative and personal approach will lead her to feel more connected to you, more confident about her financial situation, and overall more empowered instead of underserved or alienated and needing a new advisor.

Empowered clients make more loyal and profitable clients who are also apt to make more referrals to their amazing financial advisor. Women clients are more advisor dependent and make on average 11 times more referrals than men to their financial advisor—a point I've made throughout the book.

If you aren't doing the simple task of returning a call or proactively making a follow-up call to the women clients, are you missing a huge, easy opportunity. Call them—it builds rapport, leads to client satisfaction, and may even uncover a new challenge you can help with or new assets that are currently being held elsewhere.

According to the *Financial Times,* "Is Wealth Management Changing for Women," women are very comfortable taking risks with their investments, but at the rate of 11% with a male advisor and 26% with a female advisor. That is more than double. Women need to be able to be comfortable taking risks, and this is an important number.[7]

I don't have all the answers to how we can fix the gender imbalance among advisors and why we're still not fully meeting women's needs. However, I want to start a dialogue on how we can do things differently.

The Destiny of Demographics at FutureProof, September 2024
Blair DuQuesnay, Laura Combs, Author, Ashley Bleckner

Willow offers training in how to work with women as well as a lead matching program. With the Great Wealth Transfer underway, the time for change is now. Every firm can do its part to create a wealth management industry that is not only financially successful but also truly serves the needs of all clients.

Questions Financial Advisors Should Ask Themselves

1. How can I ensure I am engaging with both partners in a relationship equally, especially women?
2. Am I actively listening to my female clients and understanding their unique financial goals and concerns?
3. How can I make my communication and educational efforts more accessible and less intimidating for clients?

4. Is my advisory team diverse, and does it include women who can relate to the experiences of female clients?
5. Am I proactively following up with clients, and am I responsive to their needs and concerns?
6. How can I better support my clients through significant life transitions that impact their financial well-being?
7. What measures can I take to build deeper, more meaningful relationships with my clients, beyond just the financial aspects?

KEY TAKEAWAYS

1. **Huge Financial Opportunity:** Women will control two-thirds of US wealth by 2030, yet their financial needs remain under-addressed by the industry, which was designed for men.
2. **Women Experience Financial Stress:** Financial stress is the top emotion women associate with money. Advisors must listen to and address these concerns on women's terms.
3. **A Personal Connection Is Key:** Women value trust, emotional connection, and alignment with their values and goals in financial advisory relationships.
4. **Financial Abuse Cases:** Women are particularly vulnerable to financial abuse, making it vital for advisors to offer emotional and financial support.
5. **Tailored Services Drive Growth:** Firms that retain women clients can see significantly higher revenue growth, highlighting the business case for customizing services.
6. **Holistic Approach:** Advisors should support women through life's major transitions (e.g. widowhood, divorce) and provide streamlined, accessible, and relevant services.

7. **Empowering Women Through Education:** Educating women, rather than overwhelming them with jargon, empowers them to make informed financial decisions and builds loyalty.

8. **Diverse Teams Matter:** Women want to see diversity, equity, and inclusion in their advisory team, fostering greater comfort and trust.

9. **Engage and Communicate Proactively:** Simple actions, like timely follow-up calls, build rapport and uncover new opportunities with women clients.

10. **Women Are More Referral-Driven:** Women make 11 times more referrals than men do, underscoring the value of strong, meaningful relationships with female clients.

NOTES

1. Fry, R., Aragao, C., Hurst, K., and Parker, K. (2023). *In a growing share of US marriages, husbands and wives earn about the same.* Pew Research Center. Available from: https://www.pewresearch.org/social-trends/2023/04/13/in-a-growing-share-of-u-s-marriages-husbands-and-wives-earn-about-the-same/.

2. Baghai, P., Howard, O., Prakash, L., and Zucker, J. (2020). *Women as the next wave of growth in US wealth management.* McKinsey & Co. Available from: https://www.mckinsey.com/industries/financial-services/our-insights/women-as-the-next-wave-of-growth-in-us-wealth-management.

3. Shook, R.J. (2020). Women feel ignored by advisors, study says. *Forbes.* https://www.forbes.com/sites/rjshook/2020/08/07/woman-feel-ignored-by-advisors-study-says/.

4. Fidelity Investments. (2023). *Women's history month 2023 survey.* https://preview.thenewsmarket.com/Previews/FINP/DocumentAssets/637610_v2.pdf.

5. Baghai, P., Howard, O., Prakash, L., and Zucker, J. (2020). *Women as the next wave of growth in US wealth management.* McKinsey & Co. Available from: https://www.mckinsey.com/industries/financial-services/our-insights/women-as-the-next-wave-of-growth-in-us-wealth-management.

6. CFP Board. (2024). *CFP® professional demographics.* Available at: https://www.cfp.net/knowledge/reports-and-statistics/professional-demographics.

7. Merrill Lynch. (2020). *Seeing the unseen, the role gender plays in wealth management* [online]. Available from: https://mlaem.fs.ml.com/content/dam/ML/Registration/seeing-the-unseen-whitepaper.pdf.

CHAPTER THIRTEEN

WIDOWS AND DIVORCEES ARE NOT THE ONLY FEMALE CLIENTS

Each time a woman stands up for herself, without knowing it possibly, without claiming it, she stands up for all women.
— Maya Angelou

PROBLEM

Financial advisors often focus on traditional client segments such as widows and divorcees, neglecting other critical life events that affect women's financial needs. This limited perspective can result in inadequate support for women navigating diverse and significant life changes, such as career transitions, menopause, and family planning.

Women can use help navigating all or any combination of life events. The first time I wrote this it was to define the segment in my women and wealth job at my current RIA. We used this language as a brochure. Then I used a variation of this and shared it with the industry via Rethinking 65.

Wealth management for women has traditionally focused on widows first, divorcees second, and pretty much nothing else. It is as if all women fall into these two boxes. It may come as a surprise to the wealth management industry that women experience much more than two life events. When I look at women's life events, I come up with seven distinct ones.

Yes, of course, we have the first two: death of a spouse/widowhood and divorce/separation. But advisors should give more thought to all seven of these life events—we'll get to the others shortly—to help their female clients and strengthen their client relationships. Most of these life events are triggers to review financial plans and beneficiaries, and advisors should encourage clients to inform them should these events arise.

Here's a look at the seven events.

1. Death of a Spouse/ Widowhood

As many as 70% of female clients leave their financial advisors soon after their husbands die. I am usually on the receiving end of this.

When women lose their life partner, every decision can seem impossible to make alone. It is a great time to work with an advocate who can help them work on big life and financial decisions while they are dealing with grief. Everyone grieves differently. This is a time for an empathetic financial advisor to shine.

Widows have so many decisions to make: "What do I want the rest of my life to look like without my spouse?" and "Am I staying in the house, and can I afford to?"

If you already have a strong relationship with your widowed client, be sure to be there for her. Whenever a client's spouse dies, I attend the funeral service. One of my clients wanted me to sit next to her; I held her hand the entire time while she cried. I also get many clients right after their spouses dies. Establishing a relationship in the middle of her grief is even more difficult, but the key again is giving them what they need.

2. Divorce/Separation

This is another emotionally charged time in a woman's life. Sometimes this is worse than the death of a spouse. It is a time where they are figuratively burning the house down and starting over. It is scary, but it is another time in their life when you can shepherd them through it, and you can shine.

I get involved early on when their marriage is coming apart, and sometimes it takes years before a divorce is final. I am involved in the mediations and negotiations, and I am a friend and a voice of reason the entire time. For me, the best part is that I can share my personal experiences because I went through a four-year divorce that costs hundreds of thousands of dollars. I always say that since I got through it, you can too—and that it is so beautiful on the other side. I am an open book; I don't hold anything back.

Most of my divorced clients come to me while the divorce proceedings are in process, so I don't know the spouse. One of my client couples has been in the process of divorcing for two years, and I'm still working with both spouses. In such cases, it's critical to communicate with and remain a fiduciary to both spouses.

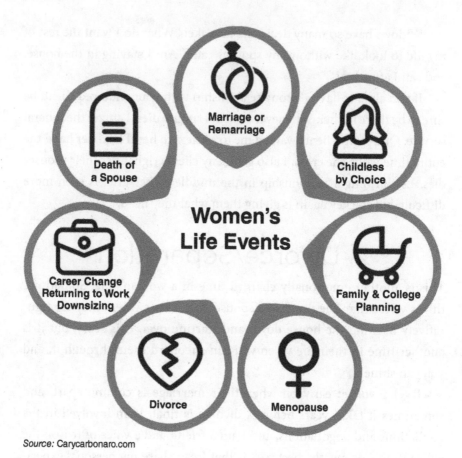

Women's Life Events

- Marriage or Remarriage
- Childless by Choice
- Family & College Planning
- Menopause
- Divorce
- Career Change Returning to Work Downsizing
- Death of a Spouse

Source: Carycarbonaro.com

3. Career Change/Returning to Work

Our careers are important to us. Losing a job not by choice is a life-altering event. I've seen this with my clients over and over. Even when it is their choice, it still is a life change that needs help and guidance to be navigated. I've also worked with clients who want to obtain "returnships" to help them re-enter the workforce after a long gap. You can google which companies offer them.

One of my clients participated in the JPMorgan Chase returnship; my connections helped her land a spot. She was in her 40s at the time and wanted to get back into finance after leaving the workforce to raise her children. The program provided her with lots of training. Returnships can be similar to the management training programs designed for new college graduates—lots of classroom and group learning.

4. Menopause

Menopause is a huge life change when you are in it, and you are in it for the rest of your life. It can have physical, mental, and financial consequences. Menopause is a good time to review retirement plans, healthcare costs, and mental health support with your clients. Every woman's experience is unique. It is a time for reflection.

Menopause is a life stage most financial planners don't address. Menopause is a natural biological process that marks the end of a woman's reproductive years. The average age of menopause is 51, but it can occur anywhere from the late 30s to the early 60s. When a woman hits menopause, she should keep in mind several financial and mental health considerations:

- **Mood swings:** Hormonal changes during menopause can cause mood swings, which can range from mild irritability to severe depression or anxiety.
- **Anxiety and depression:** Menopause can trigger anxiety and depression in some women, which may be related to changes in hormones or the stress of coping with physical symptoms.
- **Brain fog:** Menopause can cause "brain fog," which is a feeling of mental confusion or forgetfulness. This can be frustrating and impact daily life.
- **Insomnia:** Menopause can cause insomnia, which can lead to fatigue, irritability, and difficulty concentrating.

- **Decreased self-esteem:** Menopause can cause physical changes, such as weight gain or loss of muscle tone, which can impact a woman's self-esteem and lead to feelings of depression or anxiety.
- **Sexual function:** Menopause can cause changes in sexual function, which can impact a woman's mental health and relationships.

It's important for women to be mindful of the impact of menopause on their mental health and to seek support if needed. This may include talking to a healthcare provider, a therapist, or a support group. Lifestyle changes, such as exercise, healthy eating, and stress management, can also help support mental health during menopause.

Following are the financial steps an advisor should consider when a client is in menopause:

- **Review and update her retirement plan:** As a woman approaches retirement age, she should review and update her retirement plan. She should consider factors such as her expected retirement age, her retirement savings, and her expected Social Security benefits.
- **Evaluate her healthcare costs:** Menopause can bring about changes in a woman's healthcare needs. She should evaluate her healthcare costs and consider factors such as her health insurance coverage, potential medical expenses, and long-term care needs.
- **Consider her estate planning:** A woman should review and update her estate planning documents to ensure they reflect her current wishes. This includes her will, power of attorney, and healthcare proxy.
- **Reevaluate her budget:** Menopause can also bring about changes in a woman's income and expenses. She should reevaluate her budget and adjust it accordingly to reflect any changes in her financial situation.
- **Focus on her overall financial well-being:** During menopause, it's important for a woman to focus on her overall financial well-being. This includes managing debt, building an emergency fund, and investing for the future.

- **Discuss financial concerns with a financial advisor:** A financial advisor can help a woman navigate the financial challenges of menopause. They can provide guidance on retirement planning, healthcare costs, and estate planning. Make sure you are working with a Certified Financial Planner or a CFP°.

When a woman hits menopause, she should take steps to protect her financial and mental well-being. They may need help! This may include talking to a healthcare provider, a therapist, or a support group. Lifestyle changes, such as exercise, healthy eating, and stress management, can also help support mental health during menopause.

Journalist, menopause advocate, and friend, Tamsen Fadal says, "I want to teach women how to ask questions in all areas of their lives, especially regarding their health and wellness. If they don't feel comfortable with the answers, move on to somebody else and keep going after it. This is your time to thrive, not simply survive." She is the author of a new book coming out in 2024 called *How to Menopause.*

WHAT EXACTLY HAPPENS INSIDE A WOMAN'S BRAIN AFTER MENOPAUSE? A GROUNDBREAKING STUDY HAS THE NEW, EXCITING ANSWERS

We talked about male and female brains earlier in this book. Dr. Lisa Mosconi's groundbreaking 2024 study reveals that menopause significantly impacts the female brain, driven by changes in estrogen levels. Her research provides new insights into women's brain health during and after menopause. This is why it is important to know if your female client is in fact in menopause.

KEY FINDINGS

- **Estrogen Activity in the Brain:** The study shows that estrogen receptors in the female brain increase during perimenopause and postmenopause, indicating a heightened need for estrogen, contrary to previous beliefs that estrogen receptors decline after menopause.
- **Development of a Tracer:** Dr. Mosconi developed a molecule to trace estrogen activity in the brain during PET scans, a first in the field. This enabled detailed imaging of estrogen's impact on the brain.
- **Research Process:** Premenopausal, perimenopausal, and postmenopausal women took an experimental estrogen tracer before undergoing brain imaging.

IMPLICATIONS

- **Brain's Need for Estrogen:** The brain continues to produce estrogen receptors after menopause, showing a strong demand for estrogen, which challenges previous theories.
- **Menopausal Symptoms:** The density of estrogen receptors correlates with menopausal symptoms, suggesting the brain's adaptive mechanism during hormonal changes.
- **Future Research and Applications:** The findings could lead to personalized hormone treatments and a better understanding of Alzheimer's risk in women, with ongoing research to determine the optimal timing for hormone therapy.

Dr. Mosconi's research emphasizes the adaptability and resilience of the female brain, advocating for more informed and supportive approaches to menopause and women's brain health.

Women in this stage of their lives should review and update their retirement plan, evaluate healthcare costs, reevaluate budgets, and focus on overall financial well-being so that they can position themselves for a secure financial future.

Talk to each woman in this stage of life about her expected retirement age, her retirement savings, and her expected Social Security benefits. Evaluate her healthcare costs: menopause can change a woman's healthcare needs because it's often a time when new medical conditions develop. Factors to help her consider are her health insurance coverage, her potential medical expenses, and her long-term care needs.

5. Marriage or Remarriage

Getting married or remarried is a huge life event for clients. They are not only merging their lives, but they are also merging their money. They need a financial planner to make sure they are aligned with their new partner. Do they have the same goals? Is one a saver and one a spender? Have they gotten financially naked? This means being honest and sharing info such as net worth (including *all* assets and liabilities). If either partner has credit card debt or student loans, the other one needs to know this.

Money is one of the top reasons for divorce, so getting on the same page is a great first step in a new marriage. Most couples need an expert to help navigate this. I've had conversations with clients about prenuptial agreements and have recommended attorneys. When a client has significantly more wealth than their spouse-to-be or new spouse, I strongly recommend a prenuptial agreement.

6. Childless by Choice

Yes, this is a thing and an entire category of women. A woman without a child does not need to do any additional financial or estate planning than women with children. She has to decide who her beneficiaries are, and she needs to have a will, a healthcare proxy, and a power of attorney. She can also decide if she needs a trust.

Some people say that women who are childless by choice have to worry about not having a child to take care of them as they age. However, women without children often have more money to pay for top-notch care, often from spending more time in the workforce and not incurring the expense of raising and supporting children, and there are many choices for care. And the reality is, children don't always help their parents.

It is also important not to be judgmental of women who are childless by choice. Many people think a woman who chooses this life hates children and that is often untrue. I identify closely with this group because I am part of it. I never felt less than or not fulfilled because I got so much satisfaction from my career. I was also married to "Mr. Wrong" during my childbearing years. I did an NPR interview on this subject.[1]

And never ask a woman if she regrets her life choices. In the Netflix show, *House of Cards*, Claire Underwood is asked, "Do you ever regret not having kids?"

She replies, "Do you ever regret having them?"

7. Family and College Planning

I've worked with many clients who have said to me that they wanted to plan for having a baby. Some questions to consider: Will they or their spouse stay home, or will they get a nanny? Will they take a sabbatical from work? Will they want to fund college? How much life insurance will they need now that they are responsible for a human life? These are also huge financial decisions that you as their advisor can help them think through.

The cost of raising a child or children can be huge, especially if they attend private school from kindergarten through high school. The cost of nannies and summer camp can also add up. The average cost of summer camp is $178 a day for day camp and $448 a day for sleepaway camp, according to the American Camp Association.[2]

I worked with a couple where the dad stayed home for three years. After crunching the numbers, I told him he had to go back to work after that, but he never did. His working wife grew resentful, and they eventually divorced. To date, I've never worked with a single woman who wanted a child, but this would also require a lot of planning.

What if your child is special needs? Planning for a child with special needs requires a comprehensive and thoughtful approach to ensure their long-term financial security, care, and quality of life. It begins with understanding their unique medical, educational, and personal needs while considering the potential costs over their lifetime. Key components often include establishing a special needs trust to protect eligibility for government benefits like Medicaid and Supplemental Security Income (SSI), creating a letter of intent to outline care preferences, and leveraging financial tools such as life insurance and investment accounts. It's also vital to collaborate with specialized advisors, legal experts, and advocacy groups to navigate complex regulations and ensure the plan evolves with the child's needs. Proactive and tailored planning offers peace of mind and the assurance that the child will be cared for, even when parents or guardians are no longer able to provide direct support.

EMPOWERING WOMEN

In recognizing and addressing the diverse life cycles of women, the wealth management industry can break free from traditional stereotypes. By providing tailored and empathetic financial guidance throughout these distinct phases, financial advisors can empower women to navigate their unique journeys successfully. Embracing the richness of women's financial experiences goes beyond widows and divorcees. We can and should create a more inclusive and supportive wealth management landscape for all women.

Solution

Advisors should broaden their approach to include the seven distinct life cycles impacting women. By proactively addressing these events—widowhood, divorce, career changes, menopause, marriage/remarriage, childlessness, and family planning—advisors can provide more comprehensive, empathetic, and tailored financial guidance. This holistic approach helps in building stronger client relationships and better supporting women through various life stages.

Questions for Financial Advisors to Ask Themselves

1. Are we considering all significant life events that impact our female clients, or are we focusing too narrowly on traditional categories?

2. How can we integrate empathy and tailored advice into our services for clients experiencing major life changes?

3. Do our financial planning strategies address the specific needs associated with menopause, career changes, or remarriage?

4. Are we staying informed about new research and trends that impact women's financial health, such as Dr. Mosconi's study on estrogen and brain health?

5. How can we better support clients who are childless by choice or planning for future family needs?

KEY TAKEAWAYS

- **Beyond Widows and Divorcées:** The wealth management industry often focuses on widows and divorcées, but women experience many significant life events, such as career changes, menopause, marriage, and family planning, that require tailored financial support.
- **Seven Key Life Events:** Financial advisors should consider seven distinct life cycles for women—widowhood, divorce, career transitions, menopause, marriage/remarriage, being childless by choice, and family planning. Each event triggers financial decisions and requires a proactive approach.
- **Empathetic Guidance:** Each life stage can be emotionally charged, such as dealing with grief, divorce, or menopause. Advisors should act as advocates, offering empathy and support during these transitions.
- **Personal Experience Adds Value:** Sharing personal experiences, like navigating a divorce, can help build trust with clients. Real-life advice from advisors who have faced similar situations can empower and comfort clients.
- **Holistic Planning:** Financial planning should address more than just immediate financial needs, including retirement, estate planning, healthcare costs, and overall financial well-being. This comprehensive approach ensures women are well-prepared for any stage of life.
- **Empowering Clients:** By understanding and addressing women's varied life events, financial advisors can create deeper client relationships and better support their clients, moving beyond stereotypes to provide meaningful, lasting advice.

NOTES

1. Segarra, M. (host). (2023). *So you don't want kids. Here's how to respond to unwanted comments*. NPR: Life Kit. Available at: https://www.npr.org/transcripts/1169740774.
2. $448 a day for sleepaway camp.

CHAPTER FOURTEEN

TYPES OF FEMALE CLIENTS, PART II

Women are not a monolith. They have diverse financial needs and goals, and understanding this diversity is key to providing effective financial advice and solutions.

—Melody Hobson

W omen may not be a monolith, but they also are not a niche. As a matter of fact, we are all completely different. The more you understand the differences, the more you can help them.

PROBLEM

Financial advisors often face challenges in effectively serving female clients due to a lack of understanding of women's diverse needs, goals, and financial preferences. They come from varied backgrounds, life stages, and financial situations, which necessitates a more nuanced and personalized approach to financial advising.

Beyond this list there are female clients of mine whose sole reason for hiring me is to get smarter around money. I have clients who are too busy to do this, so they want to delegate and trust me. I have some clients to whom I give my guidance and advice, and they don't take it. I lose sleep over those. There are the ones driven by fear and sometimes can't even make decisions. I find the ones who most need to be invested in stocks are the most afraid, which keeps them from meeting their goals. Most of them just want to be told everything is going to be okay.

I was very liberal with types of clients. They varied in age, demography, life stage, career, marital status, psychographics, and risk tolerance. This is by no means an exhaustive list, just a sample in addition to the previous chapter. I didn't break down niches within professions. For example, some financial advisors work with only attorneys or only doctors. There are also smaller ones like a planner in Vegas who works with sex workers. Depending on where you live you can also specialize and know the firm benefits inside and out. For example, if you live on Long Island you can specialize in Estee Lauder employees. If in Florida you can work with all Publix employees.

Young Professionals

- **Characteristics**
  - Early in their careers, often in their 20s or early 30s
  - Single or in a relationship, possibly with no children
  - Focused on career advancement and personal development
- **Financial Goals**
  - Building an emergency fund
  - Paying off student loans or other debts

- Starting retirement savings (e.g. 401[k] or IRA)
- Saving for major purchases like a car or home
- **Tailored Advice**
  - Create a budget to manage expenses and prioritize savings.
  - Establish an emergency fund with 3–6 months' worth of expenses.
  - Advise on employer-sponsored retirement plans and the benefits of early contributions.
  - Discuss strategies for debt repayment (e.g. snowball versus avalanche method).

Young Families

- **Characteristics**
  - Recently married or with young children
  - Balancing work and family life
  - Increasing household expenses
- **Financial Goals**
  - Saving for children's education (e.g. 529 plans)
  - Buying or upgrading a home
  - Managing household budgets and expenses
  - Starting or increasing retirement savings
- **Tailored Advice**
  - Develop a comprehensive family budget.
  - Educate on the benefits of tax-advantaged education savings accounts.
  - Assist in finding appropriate life and disability insurance coverage.
  - Plan for long-term financial goals, including retirement and college savings.

Established Professionals

- **Characteristics**
  - Mid-career with significant professional experience, often in their 40s or 50s
  - Higher income levels and greater financial complexity
  - Potentially managing dual-income households
- **Financial Goals**
  - Maximizing retirement contributions and investments
  - Diversifying investment portfolios
  - Tax planning and efficient wealth management
  - Planning for children's higher education costs
- **Tailored Advice**
  - Optimize contributions to retirement accounts (401[k], IRA, etc.).
  - Review and adjust investment strategies for growth and risk tolerance.
  - Implement tax-efficient investment and savings strategies.
  - Plan for major expenses, such as college tuition, using tax-advantaged accounts.

Business Owners/Entrepreneurs

- **Characteristics**
  - Owns or manages a business
  - Balancing personal and business finances
  - Focused on business growth and sustainability
- **Financial Goals**
  - Managing business finances and personal financial stability
  - Planning for business succession or exit strategies
  - Diversifying investments outside of the business
  - Ensuring proper insurance and risk management for the business

- **Tailored Advice**
  - Provide guidance on business financial planning and cash flow management.
  - Assist with retirement planning that integrates personal and business goals.
  - Advise on business insurance needs (liability, property, key person insurance).
  - Develop succession or exit strategies, including potential sale or transfer of ownership.

Pre-retirees

- **Characteristics**
  - Nearing retirement age, typically in their late 50s or 60s
  - Focused on securing their financial future and transitioning to retirement
- **Financial Goals**
  - Ensuring sufficient retirement income
  - Protecting and preserving accumulated wealth
  - Planning for healthcare and long-term care costs
  - Reviewing estate planning needs
- **Tailored Advice**
  - Create a detailed retirement income plan, including Social Security and pension options.
  - Review and adjust investment portfolios to reduce risk and increase income potential.
  - Plan for healthcare expenses, including Medicare and long-term care insurance.
  - Update estate planning documents (wills, trusts, powers of attorney).

Retirees

- **Characteristics**
  - Fully retired or in the transition phase
  - Focused on maintaining their standard of living and managing retirement savings
- **Financial Goals**
  - Managing retirement income and withdrawals
  - Preserving wealth and minimizing taxes
  - Planning for potential healthcare and long-term care costs
- **Tailored Advice**
  - Develop a withdrawal strategy to ensure sustainable retirement income.
  - Implement tax-efficient withdrawal plans from retirement accounts.
  - Plan for required minimum distributions (RMDs) from retirement accounts.
  - Assist with long-term care planning and insurance options.

High Net Worth Individuals

- **Characteristics**
  - Significant wealth and complex financial needs
  - Includes executives, investors, and inheritors
- **Financial Goals**
  - Advanced estate planning and philanthropy
  - Sophisticated investment strategies
  - Risk management and tax optimization
- **Tailored Advice**
  - Develop comprehensive estate plans, including trusts and charitable giving strategies.

- Advise on complex investment strategies, including private equity and hedge funds.
- Implement advanced tax planning techniques to minimize tax liability.
- Plan for wealth transfer to future generations.

Caregivers

- **Characteristics**
  - Balancing their finances while caring for aging parents or family members with special needs
  - May experience career interruptions and financial strain
- **Financial Goals**
  - Planning for caregiving expenses
  - Protecting their retirement savings
  - Seeking support and resources for balancing work and caregiving responsibilities
- **Tailored Advice**
  - Develop a budget that includes caregiving expenses.
  - Explore options for financial assistance and benefits for caregivers.
  - Advise on strategies to protect retirement savings and plan for future needs.
  - Provide resources and support for balancing work and caregiving.

Single Women

- **Characteristics**
  - Includes never married, divorced, and widowed women
  - Often focused on maintaining independence

- **Financial Goals**
  - Ensuring long-term financial security
  - Building and managing investments
  - Planning for future healthcare needs
- **Tailored Advice**
  - Create a comprehensive financial plan focused on independence and security.
  - Advise on investment strategies to build and grow wealth.
  - Plan for future healthcare costs, including long-term care insurance.
  - Ensure all legal documents are in place and up to date.

Digital Nomads

- **Characteristics**
  - Women who work remotely and travel frequently
  - Often freelancers, entrepreneurs, or employees with flexible work arrangements
- **Financial Goals**
  - Managing income and expenses across different currencies and tax jurisdictions
  - Building a portable investment and savings plan
  - Ensuring adequate insurance coverage while traveling
- **Tailored Advice**
  - Advise on international banking solutions and currency exchange options.
  - Develop a globally diversified investment portfolio.
  - Provide guidance on tax implications and strategies for multiple countries.
  - Recommend travel insurance and global health insurance plans.

Impact Investors

- **Characteristics**
  - Women who prioritize social and environmental impact in their investment decisions
  - Often involved in philanthropy and social entrepreneurship
- **Financial Goals**
  - Aligning investments with personal values and ethical standards
  - Supporting sustainable and socially responsible businesses
  - Measuring the impact of investments alongside financial returns
- **Tailored Advice**
  - Identify and recommend socially responsible investment (SRI) funds and environmental, social, governance (ESG) strategies.
  - Assist in creating a portfolio that balances impact and financial performance.
  - Provide resources for tracking and reporting the social impact of investments.
  - Facilitate connections with networks of like-minded investors and social enterprises.

Second-act Entrepreneurs

- **Characteristics**
  - Women who start a new business or career later in life, often post-retirement
  - Leveraging years of professional experience and personal passion
- **Financial Goals**
  - Securing funding and managing startup costs
  - Balancing business risk with personal financial security
  - Planning for eventual succession or sale of the business

- **Tailored Advice**
  - Provide guidance on business planning, funding options, and financial projections.
  - Help structure personal and business finances to protect personal assets.
  - Develop a succession plan or exit strategy for the business.
  - Advise on appropriate insurance coverage, including business liability and health insurance.

Tech-savvy Investors

- **Characteristics**
  - Women who are proficient in technology and prefer digital financial solutions
  - Actively engage in online trading, cryptocurrency, and fintech platforms
- **Financial Goals**
  - Maximizing returns through innovative and tech-driven investment opportunities
  - Staying informed about the latest financial technologies and trends
  - Ensuring cybersecurity and data privacy
- **Tailored Advice**
  - Recommend reputable online trading platforms and fintech solutions.
  - Provide education on cryptocurrency investments and blockchain technology.
  - Advise on cybersecurity best practices to protect financial information.
  - Offer insights into emerging technologies and their potential impact on investments.

Social Media Influencers

- **Characteristics**
  - Women who generate income through social media platforms, often through sponsorships, partnerships, and content creation
  - Manage personal brands and online presence
- **Financial Goals**
  - Managing variable income streams and monetizing social media presence
  - Planning for taxes and business expenses
  - Building long-term financial security beyond social media earnings
- **Tailored Advice**
  - Assist with budgeting and managing irregular income.
  - Provide guidance on business expenses, deductions, and tax planning.
  - Develop investment strategies to diversify income sources and build wealth.
  - Advise on protecting intellectual property and brand assets.

Philanthropists and Legacy Builders

- **Characteristics**
  - Women who focus on giving back to their communities and creating lasting legacies
  - Involved in charitable activities and setting up foundations or donor-advised funds

- **Financial Goals**
  - Maximizing charitable impact while maintaining financial stability
  - Planning for estate transfer and legacy preservation
  - Structuring donations for tax efficiency
- **Tailored Advice**
  - Assist in setting up and managing charitable foundations or donor-advised funds.
  - Advise on tax-efficient charitable giving strategies.
  - Develop an estate plan that includes philanthropic goals.
  - Provide resources for evaluating and selecting charitable organizations.

Professional Athletes and Entertainers

- **Characteristics**
  - Women with careers in sports, entertainment, or other high-income professions with a relatively short earning period
  - Facing unique challenges of managing sudden wealth and planning for career transitions
- **Financial Goals**
  - Managing and preserving wealth during peak earning years
  - Planning for a career transition and long-term financial security
  - Protecting against financial risks and volatility
- **Tailored Advice**
  - Provide comprehensive wealth management and investment planning.
  - Develop a plan for transitioning to new careers or business ventures.

- Advise on appropriate insurance coverage, including disability and liability insurance.
- Implement strategies for managing fame-related financial challenges, such as privacy and security concerns.

Social Entrepreneurs

- **Characteristics**
  - Women who run businesses aimed at solving social problems
  - Focused on creating both social impact and financial sustainability
- **Financial Goals**
  - Balancing social mission with business profitability
  - Securing funding from socially conscious investors
  - Measuring and reporting social impact
- **Tailored Advice**
  - Provide guidance on impact investing and obtaining funding from mission-aligned investors.
  - Develop business plans that incorporate social impact metrics.
  - Advise on legal structures that support social entrepreneurship (e.g. B corporations).
  - Assist in building networks and partnerships with like-minded organizations.

Cash Hoarders

- **Characteristics**
  - Women who feel more comfortable having cash than investing in the market
  - Feel there is less risk in cash and can't lose money

- **Financial Goals**
  - Not losing money
  - Low risk tolerance
- **Tailored Advice**
  - They are not going to be able to keep up with inflation.
  - Teach them and show them with taxes and inflation they are losing money in the long term.
  - Get them to keep some in cash and put more away for the long term. Educate them with Callan and Ibbitson charts if they have a 10-year time horizon and they are in a diversified portfolio. They can't lose money, or there has never been a 10-year period in history that has lost money in a balanced portfolio. They need their money to grow to pay for longevity, health care, and so on.

Real Estate Only

- **Characteristics**
  - Women who feel more comfortable just owning real estate because you can touch it then investing in the market
  - Feel there is less risk in real estate and can't lose money
- **Financial Goals**
  - Not losing money
  - Low risk tolerance
- **Tailored Advice**
  - Real Estate is the most expensive asset class to own. Instead of making you money, it costs you money, every month, every year etc. You have insurance, taxes, carrying costs, utilities, and so on.
  - Teach them and show them the true cost. It is a personal use asset, not an investment asset, unless it is going to be a rental long term or short term. Run the numbers with them.

- Depending on where we are in the interest rate cycle and where we are with housing affordability, it may or may not make sense to do this. I have been told, "but if I get a renter to pay my mortgage, I am building up equity over time." This is true, but depending on when you got the house, you may have overpaid. There are high costs to get in and out if you are financing it. You should be financing it if you are taking it as a rental deduction. Things break all the time and unexpected expenses come up. An extreme example: I had a client who transferred $5 million from their portfolio to buy a $5 million house. Nothing changed in their net worth. That portfolio was making them $400,000 a year. Now that house if mortgaged would cost them $400,000 a year for principal, interest, taxes, insurance, maintenance, and so forth. I always say I would rather my asset be working for me than costing me.

These unique client profiles highlight the diverse needs and goals of female clients in financial services. Understanding these nuances enables financial advisors to provide personalized, effective advice and support that aligns with each client's specific life circumstances and aspirations.

Questions Financial Advisors Should Ask Themselves

1. **Understanding Clients**
   - How well do I understand the unique needs and financial goals of my female clients?
   - Do I make assumptions based on gender, or do I treat each client as an individual with distinct needs?
2. **Communication and Education**
   - Am I effectively communicating with my clients, and are they comfortable discussing their financial concerns with me?

- How can I improve my approach to educating clients about financial matters?

3. **Personalization and Inclusivity**
   - Are my services and advice tailored to address the diverse backgrounds and situations of my female clients?
   - How can I ensure that my practice is inclusive and welcoming to all clients, regardless of gender or life stage?

4. **Use of Technology**
   - Am I utilizing technology effectively to meet the needs of my clients?
   - How can I leverage digital tools to enhance the client experience and provide more flexible services?

5. **Investment Strategies**
   - Do the investment options I offer align with the values and risk preferences of my clients?
   - How can I incorporate more socially responsible and impact investing options into my practice?

KEY TAKEAWAYS

1. **Diverse, Not a Niche:** Women have varied financial needs based on their backgrounds, life stages, and goals. Recognizing this diversity is crucial for effective financial advising.
2. **Advisors Must Adapt:** A lack of understanding of women's unique financial challenges often leads to inadequate service. Tailored strategies are essential.
3. **Client Types:** Women fall into diverse categories, such as young professionals, business owners, retirees, high-net-worth individuals, caregivers, and more. Each group has distinct financial goals, from saving and investing to retirement and legacy planning.

4. **Education Matters:** For clients focused on cash or real estate, educating them on long-term growth, inflation, and investment risks helps shift their perspective.

5. **Personalized Solutions:** Tailoring advice to each woman's life stage, risk tolerance, and financial priorities ensures better outcomes and deeper client trust.

CHAPTER FIFTEEN

WOMEN'S HEALTH EQUALS WOMEN'S WEALTH

So many people spend their health to gain wealth, and then have to spend their wealth to regain their health.

—A.J. Reb Materi

PROBLEM

Women face significantly higher healthcare costs over their lifetimes compared to men. This disparity is due to longer life expectancy, reproductive health needs, and a higher incidence of chronic conditions. These increased costs can strain financial resources, especially in retirement, leading to potential financial instability and reduced quality of life.

Lifetime Healthcare Spending: Women typically incur higher lifetime healthcare costs, ranging from $314,000 to $361,000, compared to men, whose costs range from $268,000 to $316,000. This disparity arises from women's longer life expectancy and greater healthcare needs in older age.

Retirement Healthcare Costs: According to the Employee Benefit Research Institute (EBRI), a woman retiring at age 65 in 2023 needs around $157,000 to have a 50% chance of covering her healthcare costs in retirement, while a man needs about $143,000. To have a 90% chance, a woman needs approximately $197,000. Fidelity Investments estimates that a 65-year-old couple retiring in 2022 will need about $315,000 for healthcare and medical expenses throughout retirement. For single retirees, a woman would need about $157,000, while a man would need about $143,000.

INSIGHTS FROM CAROLYN MCCLANAHAN, CFP AND MD

Carolyn McClanahan, a CFP, and medical doctor, offers valuable insights on managing healthcare costs:

1. **Healthcare Personality:** McClanahan emphasizes understanding your healthcare personality. For instance, she shared an anecdote about a 98-year-old patient who hadn't seen a doctor in decades and only came in because she needed help cutting her toenails. This minimalist approach contrasts with those who visit doctors frequently for minor issues. Knowing your healthcare mindset helps in budgeting for healthcare expenses.

2. **Being an Empowered Patient:** McClanahan highlights that we have a "sick care" system rather than a healthcare system. She advises against routine annual bloodwork or full-body scans unless there's a specific concern. Over-testing due to malpractice fears can lead to unnecessary costs. When facing major health issues, it's crucial to work with an insurance advocate and have a support system for advocacy.

3. **Living a Healthy Lifestyle:** McClanahan recommends living healthily by eating right, exercising, and surrounding yourself with supportive relationships. Avoid toxic substances and environments. Women should also have an aging plan that considers where they will live, transportation options if they can no longer drive, and decision-making if they become incapacitated.

THE VILLAGE MOVEMENT

The Village Movement is a grassroots initiative that coordinates critical services for older adults, allowing them to live independently in their own homes while staying socially engaged within their communities. Originating in 1999, the movement now includes more than 300 villages across the nation. It aims to reduce social isolation, expand access to services, and increase seniors' confidence in aging at home.

Josie Cox's book, *Women Money Power: The Rise and Fall of Economic Equality*, explores the relationship between women's economic power and the American healthcare system. Key themes include the following:

1. **Historical Context of Economic Inequality:** Cox traces the evolution of women's financial opportunities and freedoms, highlighting movements and milestones from suffrage to modern feminism.
2. **The Health-wealth Nexus:** The book delves into how women's health impacts their financial stability, discussing how chronic illnesses can derail careers and retirement plans.
3. **Systemic Barriers:** Cox critiques systemic barriers like the gender pay gap, inadequate parental leave, and lack of affordable childcare, showing how this affects both economic status and health.
4. **Case Studies and Personal Stories:** The book includes real-life stories illustrating the economic impact of health issues on women.

5. **Policy Recommendations:** Cox offers recommendations for health-care reforms, equitable pay policies, and support systems for working mothers and caregivers.

THE HEALTH-WEALTH BOND

Women face unique financial and retirement stresses due to the gender pay gap, caregiving responsibilities, and longer lifespans. Chronic illnesses disproportionately affect women, exacerbating financial instability. Financial planning should incorporate potential health issues to ensure a secure future.

Proactive Financial Planning

- Save early and contribute to retirement plans.
- Secure insurance coverage and build emergency funds.
- Create an estate plan and consider long-term care options.
- Advisors should ask clients about their health and incorporate these factors into financial planning.

Addressing the Health-wealth Gap

Efforts to close the women's health gap include enhancing women-centric research, improving data collection, increasing women-specific care, and creating incentives for investment in women's health innovation. Policies supporting women's health at academic institutions and workplaces are also essential.

Biology as Destiny

The idea that "women's biology is their destiny" is a concept rooted in historical and cultural beliefs that women's roles and capabilities are inherently determined by their biological characteristics, particularly their reproductive functions. I first heard of this in a women's studies class in college. As a matter of fact, women's studies was my minor, but my dad told me not to put that on my resume. He said it would make me look like a radical. My dad was very traditional, and I listened to him. This notion has been challenged and critiqued extensively in modern discussions of gender, biology, and sociology. Following are some perspectives on this topic:

1. **Historical Perspective**
   - Historically, women have been seen primarily as mothers and caregivers. Their biological ability to bear children was often used to justify limiting their roles to domestic spheres and excluding them from education, employment, and public life.
   - Prominent thinkers like Aristotle and later some nineteenth-century scientists argued that women's intellectual and physical capabilities were inferior to men's due to biological differences.

2. **Biological Determinism**
   - Biological determinism is the idea that biological factors such as genetics and hormones determine human behavior and societal roles. This view suggests that women's biology predisposes them to certain behaviors and roles, such as nurturing and caregiving.
   - Critics argue that this perspective ignores the significant impact of social, cultural, and environmental factors on human behavior and capabilities.

3. **Modern Scientific Understanding**
   - Contemporary science recognizes that while biological differences between men and women exist, these differences do not rigidly dictate abilities, interests, or roles. The human brain is

highly adaptable, and socialization plays a critical role in shaping behavior and skills.

- Research in neuroscience and psychology shows that both men and women have a wide range of capabilities that can be nurtured through education, experience, and social support.

4. **Feminist Perspectives**[1]
   - Feminists argue that the idea of biology as destiny is a tool used to perpetuate gender inequality. They emphasize that social constructs, rather than biology, are responsible for the roles and expectations imposed on women.
   - Simone de Beauvoir's famous statement, "One is not born, but rather becomes, a woman," underscores the idea that gender roles are socially constructed rather than biologically determined.

5. **Implications for Policy and Society**
   - Accepting the notion that women's biology is their destiny can lead to discriminatory practices and policies that limit women's opportunities and reinforce gender stereotypes.
   - Policies that promote gender equality, such as equal access to education and employment, challenge the idea that biology limits women's potential and demonstrate that women can excel in diverse fields.

6. **Examples of Women Breaking Biological Stereotypes**
   - Many women have excelled in fields traditionally dominated by men, such as STEM, politics, and business. Figures like Marie Curie, Angela Merkel, and Sheryl Sandberg exemplify that women's capabilities extend far beyond their biological roles.

The idea that women's biology is their destiny is increasingly viewed as outdated and reductive, with modern understanding recognizing the complex interplay of biology, socialization, and individual potential.

Advisors must understand the unique health challenges women face and incorporate these into financial planning to help female clients achieve financial stability and well-being. Proactive planning and open communication about health issues are key to addressing the health-wealth connection and ensuring a secure financial future for women.[2]

Questions for Financial Advisors to Ask Clients

1. Have you considered how your healthcare needs might change as you age?
2. What steps have you taken to ensure you have adequate health insurance coverage?
3. Do you have an emergency fund specifically for healthcare expenses?
4. How are you planning to manage long-term care needs?
5. Are there any lifestyle changes you can make to improve your health and potentially reduce future healthcare costs?
6. What is your approach to regular medical check-ups and preventive care?
7. How comfortable are you with the idea of working with a healthcare advocate if necessary?
8. Do you have a clear plan for your living arrangements and care needs in older age?

Questions for Financial Advisors to Ask Themselves

1. How do I stay informed about the latest trends and costs in healthcare, especially those affecting women?
2. Am I incorporating comprehensive healthcare cost estimates into my clients' financial plans?
3. How can I better educate my female clients about the importance of planning for healthcare expenses?
4. What tools and resources can I provide to help my clients manage healthcare costs effectively?

KEY TAKEAWAYS

1. **Higher Healthcare Costs for Women:** Women generally face higher healthcare costs than men, especially in retirement, due to longer life expectancy and reproductive health needs.

2. **Proactive Healthcare Planning:** Advisors should help clients prepare for healthcare expenses by addressing insurance, emergency funds, and long-term care needs early in the financial planning process.

3. **Empowered Patient Approach:** Clients should be educated on avoiding unnecessary medical expenses, being informed patients, and advocating for themselves in healthcare decisions.

4. **Healthy Living and Aging Plans:** Encouraging women to maintain a healthy lifestyle and plan for aging-related needs–like living arrangements and caregiving–can reduce future healthcare expenses.

5. **The Health-wealth Nexus:** Chronic illnesses and healthcare expenses can derail financial stability, making it critical for women to address both health and financial planning together for long-term well-being.

NOTES

1. Feminist Theory: Works by feminist scholars that critique biological determinism and advocate for gender equality.
2. *The Second Sex* by Simone de Beauvoir discusses how women's roles are socially constructed.

CHAPTER SIXTEEN

WOMEN AND PHILANTHROPY

The more I give, the more I receive. Women are using their wealth and influence to make a difference and lead the way in philanthropy.

—Oprah Winfrey

PROBLEM

Despite the increasing influence of women in philanthropy, they face unique challenges, including lack of recognition, visibility, and mentorship opportunities. Additionally, women may not always be engaged in conversations about estate planning and charitable giving, which limits their potential impact.

Women are increasingly prominent and influential in the realm of philanthropy, bringing unique perspectives and approaches to charitable giving. Following are some key aspects of women as philanthropists.

GROWING INFLUENCE IN PHILANTHROPY

- **Wealth Creation:** As women achieve greater financial independence and success in business and careers, their capacity to contribute to philanthropic causes has significantly increased.
- **Inheritance and Control of Wealth:** Women are more likely to control a significant portion of wealth through inheritance. Many are becoming primary decision-makers in family philanthropy.

UNIQUE APPROACHES TO GIVING

- **Collaborative Giving:** Women often prefer collaborative approaches to philanthropy, engaging in collective giving circles and partnerships that amplify impact.
- **Focus on Relationships:** Women philanthropists emphasize building relationships with the organizations and communities they support, fostering a deeper understanding of the issues and needs.
- **Long-term Commitment:** They tend to commit to long-term support rather than one-time donations, aiming for sustainable impact.

AREAS OF FOCUS

- **Health and Education:** Women philanthropists often prioritize issues related to health, education, and the welfare of women and children, addressing systemic inequalities.

- **Social Justice and Equity:** There is a strong inclination toward supporting social justice initiatives, gender equality, and efforts to empower marginalized communities.
- **Community Development:** Women frequently invest in community development projects that promote local empowerment and resilience.

IMPACT AND STRATEGY

- **Hands-on Involvement:** Many women philanthropists are actively involved in the causes they support, participating in the planning and execution of initiatives.
- **Strategic Giving:** They are strategic in their approach, using research and data to inform their giving decisions and maximize the effectiveness of their contributions.
- **Measurable Outcomes:** Women philanthropists often seek measurable outcomes and impact, focusing on transparency and accountability in the organizations they support.

CHALLENGES AND OPPORTUNITIES

- **Recognition and Visibility:** Despite their significant contributions, women philanthropists are sometimes less visible and recognized than their male counterparts. Increasing awareness of their impact is essential.
- **Mentorship and Networks:** Building networks and mentorship opportunities for emerging women philanthropists can help amplify their impact and ensure the continuation of philanthropic efforts across generations.

- **Women Are Interested in Philanthropy:** Bring her into the conversation about estate planning or gifting while she is alive. There are so many great ways to get her excited about "her" charities and how she can impact them.

INSPIRATIONAL EXAMPLES

- **Melinda Gates:** She is co-chair of the Bill & Melinda Gates Foundation, which focuses on global health, education, and women's rights.
- **Oprah Winfrey:** Through the Oprah Winfrey Foundation and Oprah's Angel Network, she has supported education, empowerment, and disaster relief efforts.
- **Laurene Powell Jobs:** She is the founder of the Emerson Collective, which focuses on education, immigration reform, the environment, and social justice.
- **Beyonce:** The award-winning performer founded the BeyGOOD Foundation, and the BeyGOOD initiative supports various causes, including disaster relief, education, and homelessness. BeyGOOD has partnered with several organizations to provide scholarships and financial support to those in need.
- **Taylor Swift:** In 2024, Taylor Swift donated $5 million to Feeding America to help with relief efforts after Hurricanes Helene and Milton. Swift has donated to food banks at all stops on her Eras tour.

FUTURE TRENDS

- **Increased Philanthropic Participation:** The trend of increasing female participation in philanthropy is likely to continue as more women achieve financial success and control significant wealth.

- **Innovative Philanthropy:** Women are at the forefront of innovative philanthropic models, such as impact investing and social enterprises, which blend charitable goals with business principles to create sustainable change.

WOMEN MOVING MILLIONS

Women Moving Millions is a nonprofit organization that believes if women step into their leadership and make big, bold investments, they can accelerate progress to realize gender equality. This organization curates learning opportunities where members can build a peer network and grow within philanthropy and leadership. Women Moving Millions stands as an important and influential force in shaping the landscape of gender lens philanthropy.

Women Moving Millions members surveyed in 2023 reported that they had collectively invested $135 million in grant funding across all women's issues, $61 million of which was allocated to organizations advancing women and girls. It is estimated that the total amount given to women and girls across Women Moving Millions members, including those who did not complete the survey, was approximately $157 million in 2023, with total overall giving estimated to be $252 million.

"Women Moving Millions is a dynamic impact-lead community on a mission to power the movement for gender equality by fostering members, leadership, cultivating collaboration, and igniting bold philanthropy we are transforming the landscape of philanthropy and acting as a powerful catalyst and driving change," said Sara Haacke Byrd, CEO.

CREATING WIN-WINS

As advisors, we are in unique positions to make a difference in the world with our clients and charities. Charitable gifting vehicles are mechanisms that donors can use to make charitable contributions in a tax-efficient manner.

These vehicles offer various benefits, including immediate tax deductions, the ability to support multiple charities, and sometimes the potential for ongoing income. Following are some common charitable gifting vehicles:

1. **Donor-advised Funds (DAFs)**
   - **How They Work:** Donors contribute to a fund managed by a public charity and receive an immediate tax deduction. The funds can be invested and grow tax-free until the donor decides to make grants to qualified charities.
   - **Benefits:** Flexibility in timing and amounts of gifts, potential for growth, and anonymity if desired

2. **Charitable Remainder Trusts (CRTs)**
   - **How They Work:** Donors transfer assets into an irrevocable trust, receive an immediate tax deduction, and retain an income stream for a specified period or for life. After the income period, the remaining assets go to the designated charity.
   - **Benefits:** Provides income to the donor or other beneficiaries, immediate tax deduction, and potential to reduce estate taxes

3. **Charitable Lead Trusts (CLTs)**
   - **How They Work:** Assets are placed in a trust that provides income to a charity for a set term, after which the remaining assets go to the donor's beneficiaries.
   - **Benefits:** Immediate charitable deductions, potential reduction in estate and gift taxes, and a way to pass assets to heirs at a reduced tax cost

4. **Private Foundations**
   - **How They Work:** Donors establish a private, nonprofit organization to manage their charitable activities. They have control over investments and grant-making decisions.
   - **Benefits:** Full control over grant-making, ability to involve family members, and potential for long-term impact

5. **Charitable Gift Annuities**
   - **How They Work:** Donors make a gift to a charity in exchange for a lifetime annuity. The donor receives fixed annual payments for life, and the charity receives the remaining value after the donor's death.
   - **Benefits:** Immediate tax deduction, fixed income stream, and potential reduction of estate taxes

6. **Pooled Income Funds**
   - **How They Work:** Donors contribute to a fund pooled with other donors' contributions, receiving lifetime income based on the fund's earnings. The remaining funds go to the charity after the donor's death.
   - **Benefits:** Immediate tax deduction, potential income growth, and benefit to multiple donors

7. **Qualified Charitable Distributions (QCDs)**
   - **How They Work:** Individuals over 70.5 years old can transfer up to $100,000 directly from their IRAs to a charity without counting the distribution as taxable income.
   - **Benefits:** Reduces taxable income, satisfies required minimum distributions (RMDs), and directly benefits charities

8. **Bargain Sales**
   - **How They Work:** Donors sell property to a charity for less than its fair market value. The difference between the sale price and market value is considered a charitable contribution.
   - **Benefits:** Immediate cash from the sale, partial tax deduction, and removal of the property from the donor's estate

9. **Gifts of Appreciated Assets**
   - **How They Work:** Donors contribute appreciated securities, real estate, or other assets directly to a charity, avoiding capital gains taxes and receiving a tax deduction for the full market value.
   - **Benefits:** Tax deductions based on full market value, avoidance of capital gains tax, and diversification of assets

10. **Bequests**
    - **How They Work:** Donors designate a charity as a beneficiary in their will or trust, transferring assets upon death.
    - **Benefits:** No impact on current income, potential estate tax deductions, and the ability to leave a legacy

Charitable gifting vehicles provide a range of options for donors to support their favorite causes while optimizing tax benefits and financial planning. Each vehicle has unique features and benefits, allowing donors to tailor their charitable giving to align with their personal, financial, and philanthropic goals.

Women as philanthropists bring distinct and impactful approaches to charitable giving. Their focus on collaboration, long-term commitment, strategic planning, and addressing systemic issues positions them as powerful agents of change in the philanthropic sector. Their growing influence and unique perspectives continue to shape the future of philanthropy, driving progress toward a more equitable and just world.

The amount women give to charitable causes has been a subject of study and analysis, revealing significant trends and insights into their philanthropic behavior. Following are some key points about how much women give.

1. **Giving Trends and Statistics**
    - **Higher Propensity to Give:** Research indicates that women are generally more likely than men to give to charity. Studies have shown that single women and married couples donate more frequently and in larger amounts compared to single men.
    - **Generosity Index:** According to various studies, women give a higher percentage of their wealth and income to charitable causes than men do. For instance, single women are more likely to give to charity and typically give more generously relative to their income.

2. **Wealth and Giving**
   - **Wealthy Women:** Among high-net-worth individuals, women are increasingly influential. They often make significant contributions to philanthropy. For example, women who control substantial wealth or who are part of wealthy families are often primary drivers of philanthropic efforts within those families.
   - **High-net-worth Giving:** Wealthy women are major donors to educational, health, and social justice causes. They often make large, transformative gifts that have significant impacts.

3. **Collective Giving**
   - **Giving Circles:** Women are more likely to participate in giving circles, where they pool their resources with others to make a larger impact. This collective giving approach amplifies the total amount given and can result in substantial contributions to various causes. I was the founding president of my giving circle in Florida. It was part of the Southlake Community Foundation. Ours was called the WGA for the Women's Giving Alliance. It costs $1,000 a year per person, and each member gets one vote. We also instituted a legacy membership where women who donated $25,000 never had to pay annually again. This was also my idea and to stretch it out over a few years as a multiyear pledge. Each year we voted on what we called "strategic philanthropy." We wanted to make transformative gifts to nonprofits in the area benefiting women and children. Women are a force for good when we can come together like this. In 2024 we hit our 10-year anniversary.

4. **Studies and Findings**
   - **Women's Philanthropy Institute:** According to research from the Women's Philanthropy Institute at Indiana University, women are more likely to give and give more generously to charitable causes compared to men. The institute's studies indicate that

Women's Giving Alliance 10 year Anniversary party.

households headed by single women are more likely to give than those headed by single men.

- **Comparison Studies:** Studies show that women are more likely to give to a variety of causes and often spread their giving across multiple charities. This diversification in giving often results in a higher total amount donated across different sectors.

5. **Influence of Wealth Transfer**
   - **Intergenerational Wealth Transfer:** As a significant portion of wealth is expected to transfer from the older generation to women (either as widows or through inheritances), the amount women can give is expected to rise substantially. This wealth transfer is poised to amplify women's role in philanthropy.

6. **Specific Examples**
   - **Mega Donations:** Women like MacKenzie Scott have made headlines for their extraordinary philanthropic contributions. Scott has donated billions of dollars to a wide range of causes in a relatively short period.
   - **Community Impact:** Women at all income levels contribute significantly to community-based organizations, often providing crucial support for local initiatives and smaller charities that might otherwise struggle to secure funding. Anita Knotts of the Lotus

Institute, in a TEDx talk called "The Future of Finance Is Female," says, "Women who are economically and financially empowered use their wealth to reinvest back into their communities, which ultimately helps all of society."

Summary

Women give a substantial and growing amount to charitable causes, influenced by their higher propensity to donate, their strategic approach to philanthropy, and the increasing control they have over significant wealth. Studies consistently show that women are generous givers, often prioritizing long-term, relationship-based philanthropy that seeks to address root causes and create sustainable impact. With the expected intergenerational wealth transfer, the role of women in philanthropy is likely to become even more prominent in the coming years. As an advisor leading with philanthropy or teaching and guiding female clients with philanthropic vehicles will be a win-win-win for you, the client, and the charity.

Solution

Financial advisors can play the following pivotal role in addressing these challenges:

1. **Engage Women in Estate Planning and Philanthropy:** Include women in discussions about charitable giving and estate planning to make them aware of various charitable gifting vehicles and strategies.
2. **Promote Recognition and Visibility:** Highlight and celebrate the contributions of women philanthropists to increase their visibility and encourage more women to engage in philanthropy.
3. **Provide Mentorship and Building Networks:** Create and support networks and mentorship programs to help emerging women philanthropists learn from experienced ones and amplify their impact.

4. **Educating on Strategic Giving:** Guide women on how to approach philanthropy strategically, focusing on long-term impact, measurable outcomes, and sustainable change.

Key Questions Financial Advisors Should Ask Their Clients

1. **Philanthropic Goals and Interests**
   - What causes or organizations are you passionate about?
   - What impact would you like your charitable contributions to have?

2. **Giving Preferences**
   - Do you prefer to give individually, or are you interested in collaborative giving circles or partnerships?
   - Are you more inclined toward one-time donations or long-term commitments?

3. **Involvement Level**
   - How involved would you like to be in the initiatives you support (e.g. hands-on involvement versus strategic support)?
   - Do you want to build relationships with the organizations and communities you support?

4. **Financial Considerations**
   - What percentage of your wealth or income are you comfortable allocating to philanthropy?
   - Are you aware of the tax benefits and financial planning advantages associated with various charitable gifting vehicles?

5. **Legacy and Future Planning**
   - How would you like to incorporate philanthropy into your estate planning?
   - Are there specific causes or organizations you want to support through your will or trust?

6. **Challenges and Concerns**
   - What concerns do you have about charitable giving (e.g. impact, recognition, tax implications)?
   - How can I assist you in overcoming any aversions or barriers to philanthropic giving?
7. **Inspirational Examples and Role Models**
   - Are there any philanthropists or charitable organizations you admire and would like to emulate?
   - How do you see your philanthropic efforts influencing your family and community?

KEY TAKEAWAYS

1. **Women's Growing Role:** Women are leading in philanthropy, using their wealth and influence to create lasting social change.
2. **Wealth and Influence:** Increased financial independence and control over wealth enable women to make significant philanthropic contributions.
3. **Unique Giving Styles**
   - **Collaborative:** Women favor collective giving and partnerships.
   - **Relationship-driven:** They prioritize deep connections with the causes they support.
   - **Long-term Focus:** Women commit to sustained, long-term impact.
4. **Key Areas of Focus**
   - **Health, Education, and Social Justice:** Women often focus on issues affecting women, children, and marginalized communities.
5. **Strategic Giving:** Women are hands-on, data-driven, and seek measurable outcomes from their philanthropic efforts.

6. **Challenges**
   - **Visibility:** Women philanthropists often lack recognition.
   - **Mentorship:** Building networks and mentorship opportunities can amplify their impact.
7. **Future Trends:** With wealth transfer, women's role in philanthropy will expand, and they will continue to lead in innovative models like impact investing.
8. **Advisors' Role:** Advisors should engage women in estate planning and philanthropy, educating them on charitable gifting strategies for maximum impact.
9. **Women Moving Millions:** This group exemplifies women's collective power in philanthropy, investing millions to advance gender equality.
10. **Inspirational Leaders:** Figures like Melinda Gates, Oprah Winfrey, and MacKenzie Scott highlight the transformative power of women in philanthropy.

CHAPTER SEVENTEEN

GETTING TO KNOW YOUR CLIENTS WITH BEHAVIORAL FINANCE[1]

The most important thing in communication is hearing what isn't said.

–Daniel Kahneman

PROBLEM

Many clients make financial decisions driven by emotions and subconscious beliefs about money, which can lead to poor financial outcomes. Women face unique financial challenges and societal pressures that further complicate their financial behaviors. Understanding and addressing these emotional and psychological factors is crucial for providing effective financial advice and planning.

How well do you know your clients? What makes them tick? What drives their financial decisions and what narratives shape their relationships with money? What does money mean to them? Sometimes it is hard for us to find out when they don't know these answers themselves.

Understanding each client's financial behaviors can be like unlocking a secret code. Sometimes their current financial decisions are shaped by what they observed in their childhoods, such as mom and dad fighting over money, or when dad got paid it was a fun day because they would have a family outing. Other times, their decisions may be tied to their current mood. For example, some people may use "retail therapy" to feel uplifted–they might buy a new designer pocketbook to feel better even though they already have many of them and don't need another.

The financial services industry is increasingly recognizing that such behaviors are important to understand when tailoring advice. In 2021, for example, the Certified Financial Planner (CFP) Board added the "Psychology of Financial Planning" to its principal knowledge areas. Many more advisors realize today that a client's attitudes, values, and beliefs play a crucial role in saving, spending, and investing decisions.

FINANCIAL THERAPY

As a result, the concept of financial therapy has taken off in the twenty-first century. It focuses on the evaluation and treatment of cognitive, emotional, behavioral, and economic aspects of financial health.[2]

Financial behavior tends to be more emotional than rational for most people. Consequently, many advisors and other professionals focused on personal financial planning also counsel clients on managing their emotions and avoiding interpersonal conflicts when presented with financial choices.

Admitting You Have a Problem

As women, we truly experience a unique set of circumstances in our financial lives. We are often spoon-fed the notion that we should rely on our partners for financial support while simultaneously being told how important it is to have the most expensive makeup, clothes, purses, car, and house. We are constantly sold an ideal way of life–one that is consumer driven and completely reliant on our ability to spend. The result is we are blinded by what we see around us. We make bad financial decisions for no other reason than we feel it is the socially acceptable thing to do. The fallout can be great. And the worst part is we did it to ourselves.

The idea of financial therapy isn't just a buzz term. These days, it's on the top of my list of client services. It's offered at one time or another to nearly everyone who walks through my office doors…or who asks me out for lunch, or sits next to me on a plane, and so forth.

The reason is simple: as a society, we just haven't been taught to talk about money, or to separate emotional decisions from prudent decisions. That means a huge part of my job is constantly trying to get my clients to make better financial decisions during emotional times.

Usually, that means taking the heart out of the equation. Easier said than done, right?

For example, a successful woman might want to buy her dream home nestled on the water. She thinks she can afford it. She has enough money to buy the house, but that would be it. Her retirement fund would be gone, and living in that house may quickly become uncomfortable, if not impossible. All too many people find themselves in this situation, unable to see past the SOLD sign in front of that beachfront home. The self-gratification quickly wears off and is replaced with self-humiliation when she realizes she is living in a house she cannot afford.

Emotions impact all of us. It is our human nature and simply impossible to separate our emotions from our behaviors. But we can work to ensure our decisions are not driven by our emotions. When it comes to money, making emotional decisions is a trend that binds us all together.

Emotions don't discriminate based on the size of your net worth. If there's one thing I've learned, and that I pass on to nearly everyone I meet, it's the simple truth that no one has ever made a poor financial decision without emotions being part of the mix. They may have played a small role, or even a larger one, but regardless, they are always involved. Whether it's anger, happiness, greed, fear, or any combination of these, it's our feelings that derail us and position us for a great demise.

Emotional Decisions

Emotional decisions–whether based on happiness, fear, or another feeling–occur at every stage of life. Even as we become more connected and in control of our emotions, we will never be fully capable of removing them from the equation. So, what can you do to minimize the role emotions play in your financial decisions? There is no one right answer. It will always change. The answer when you're in college is different from the answer when you enter the real world and begin your career, or when you're getting married, or if you're getting divorced. Further, emotional decisions are sometimes even more clouded by a lack of information. Enormous emotions combined with bad information are almost certainly a disaster waiting to happen.

Later in life, after careers have been forged and investments made, emotional decisions persist. Knowing you're on the right track and having someone guide you can make all the difference. The lessons presented in the forthcoming pages will help you make the right decisions related to money in all the stages and transitions of your life. Education, experience, and therapy have helped me be a rock for my clients. I remain a big proponent of counseling for all kinds of life's struggles, and financial therapy has become part of my own personal brand, as I saw how reconciling my emotions with my reality made for a better, stronger money mind.

In fact, counseling helps to squash those "bag lady fears". Working with an unbiased, impartial, and well-trained financial advisor can offer honest feedback for you to consider. I am not your typical woman worried about ending up penniless. I am an educated, successful, self-sufficient woman of means who enjoys the finer things in life. The key is not to turn into a robot; emotions can help you make decisions. The important gift I would like to give to you is the valuable tips and tools you can use to create a separation between your emotions and your financial decisions. Emotions will always be a factor, but they should never be the driving force. I was often the victim of my emotions. I married the wrong man and allowed him to take advantage of me, and my hard work, every day of our marriage. But eventually, I took the emotions out of it, and recognized that if it were not for my emotions, I could have dodged this one. But the lessons I learned and the experience I had only further positioned me to ensure my clients do not make the same gigantic missteps.

FOUR MONEY BELIEFS

Financial therapists have identified four categories of money beliefs, often formed during childhood: money worship, money status, money vigilance, and money avoidance.[3]

Four Money Beliefs

- **Money Worship:** Belief that money brings happiness
- **Money Status:** Equating self-worth with net worth
- **Money Vigilance:** Controlling spending and living frugally
- **Money Avoidance:** Rejecting the concept of money due to emotional distress

Money worship is the belief that money and purchasing power determine happiness. The money status group encompasses people who equate self-worth with net worth. They sacrifice self-actualization and happiness to consumerism. Their more conservative money vigilance counterparts are at the opposite extreme. They vigilantly control their spending, live frugally, and avoid even those expenses that could make life more pleasant. Money avoidance is associated with heightened emotional distress followed by conflict and a rejection of the very idea of money altogether.[4]

UNDERSTANDING THE WHY

As a woman and wealth expert, I've observed how it is especially important for women to understand why they do what they do. Delving into behavioral finance makes the financial planning process more female-friendly.

For example, one of my female clients believes she is provided money because she deserves it. She spends often and buys the best. Through our discussions, I learned her grandmother told her she was very special and would want for nothing.

When her grandmother passed away, my client was used to spending and always looking her best. She didn't care about the debt piling up because she thought someone else would take care of it. She was passed over for her dream job because they ran a credit check and found she had high debt to income.

A behavioral finance tool showed that she is spontaneous and that money encourages her to enjoy and live in the moment. A reasonable budget would not necessarily stop her behaviors. With this understanding, my client let me counsel her and agreed to work with a financial therapist. A good practice for my client was making savings and investing automatic.

A FEW CHOICES

Today, many behavioral finance tools can help advisors help clients address such issues. These tools provide invaluable insights into the subconscious motivations behind financial choices. Behavioral finance tools not only helped me learn more about my clients, but they've also helped me learn more about myself.

When I was an advisor at United Capital, we used its Money Mind quiz with our clients. This simple seven-question test helped our clients (and us) understand what was driving their financial decisions: fear, happiness, commitment, or a combination. It was a simple way to explore why someone does what they do around money. I found MoneyMind helpful in learning about clients.

Another similar tool is Money Habitudes (https://www.moneyhabi tudes.com), initially released in 2003 and one of the first behavioral finance tools. It offers a game-like assessment–played either via physical cards or online–to help people understand and talk about their finances in a fun, constructive way. Money Habitudes also allows people to pinpoint underlying financial habits, attitudes, and motivations to make real behavior changes. It helps financial professionals bring emotions and personal stories into the conversation in an approachable way.

Money Habitudes also helped me learn a lot of things about myself. I am an 8 out of 9 on planning, which means I act intentionally. I am 5/9 on safety and security. Not surprisingly, I scored 0 on being carefree about money.

Another potentially useful tool is Knomee (https://knomee.com). I haven't used it with clients yet, but I have tried it myself. It helps users confidently create unique financial profiles and securely connect with financial service providers. I presented with Marla Sofer, the founder of Knomee, at Shift, Human First Guidance in March 2024 in Orlando.

The name of our presentation was *Knowing You, Knowing Me.* At our presentation I asked how many advisors talk to their women clients about menopause.

Laughter erupted from the crowd. But I was deadly serious.

I said, "So, only 32% do; interesting. Okay. Everybody knows that financial planning for women is divorced women and widowed women. Guess what? There's a lot more than that. Menopause is a super important chapter in women's lives that can make or break them. I've had clients quit their jobs. I've had clients divorce their husbands. I have clients fight with their kids who never speak with them again because of what happened during menopause. It is a major life event that is going to be with women for the rest of their lives."

I warned the advisors that to succeed they had best know their women clients as a whole person, including their major life changes such as menopause.

WHY THIS MATTERS TO YOU

Women still make only 82 cents for every dollar earned by men. But, Sofer added, more women are graduating from college, the number of women living without a male partner has tripled in 50 years, and so more women are demanding financial independence. And they have money to spend. Sofer said:

Women are going to control 75% of discretionary spending by 2028. Why does this matter to you? Well, right now, there are 65.5 million women in the United States between the ages of 20 and 49. An Oliver Wyman study says that in that group, women alone represent a $700 billion revenue opportunity for financial services.

With all that potential, Sofer said, the financial services industry is getting it wrong about the reality of women's financial lives. Thirty percent of women in the United States today have no retirement savings by the age of 55. But 45% of women are the household breadwinner, with male breadwinners now 55%, down from the 85% it was 50 years ago.

NOT JUST FOR WOMEN

Sofer previously worked at Microsoft, JP Morgan, and BlackRock, among others. "All of that experience really exposed me to the fact that our industry is really, really good at pushing products at people but we're not that good at knowing our customers," she said. "Radical candor, transparency and reciprocity work wonders in getting to know the whole client, but talking to clients about emotions might be out of many advisors" comfort zone. Even if it's out of your comfort zone, your clients want money to help them feel confident and feel freedom," Sofer said.

I have a simple rule about bonding with a client. I share information about her own portfolio, net worth, and tax returns. She calls this her "I'll show you mine if you show me yours" approach.

I have no trust issues; I am on the super-deep level with my clients. Obviously, a lot of people are going to be like, "There's no way I'm ever doing that." But I don't have a problem with it, and it has served me my whole career.

A REAL DIFFERENTIATOR

In an informal survey taken by Sofer at the event, advisors said money primarily means freedom to them, followed by fulfillment, safety, joy, peace, sharing, helping others, and stewardship.

We suggested advisors guide their clients to align their values with their investing, and to acknowledge when money is a source of joy for them, such as spending on a memorable vacation or a meaningful gift.

"When you guide them to align with their values, the more they are going to feel what you're doing for them is valuable. When you're not getting into that vulnerable spot of talking about values, you're subjecting your practice to falling into the trap of generic, undifferentiated advice and you're not going to that personalization that they're looking for," Sofer said.

DATAPOINTS

I also suggest checking out DataPoints. It gives financial advisors multiple tools to uncover their clients' money-related attitudes, beliefs, and values.[5] The company was founded by Sarah Stanley Fallaw, daughter of Thomas J. Stanley, author of *The Millionaire Next Door*. She coauthored *The Next Millionaire Next Door* with her father. Many of her tools are based on their work.

I got my best female clients from the following sources:

- Teaching investments at a local community college
- Referrals from a divorce attorney, CPA, mediator, and life coach
- My online videos
- Social media: #female advocate
- Referrals from my other female clients
- Because women are so social and relational, they will be your best referrers.

Advice will become equal parts financial guidance and human understanding, creating a collaborative client relationship centered on empathy, education, and empowerment. If this is the future, behavioral finance is the way forward.

Solution

Incorporate behavioral finance and financial therapy into financial advising to better understand clients' emotions, attitudes, and beliefs about money. Use behavioral finance tools and techniques to uncover the motivations behind clients' financial decisions and to help them separate emotions from financial choices. Provide education, empathy, and personalized guidance to empower clients to make better financial decisions.

Questions to Ask Clients

1. **Understanding Financial Behaviors**
   - What early experiences with money can you recall from your childhood?
   - How do you feel when you think about your financial situation right now?
   - Have you ever made a financial decision based on your mood or emotions? Can you describe it?

2. **Exploring Money Beliefs**
   - What does money mean to you? Is it security, freedom, happiness, or something else?
   - Do you believe that having more money would make you happier? Why or why not?
   - How do you view your self-worth in relation to your net worth?

3. **Identifying Financial Goals and Concerns**
   - What are your short-term and long-term financial goals?
   - Are there any financial decisions you regret? What were the emotions involved in making those decisions?
   - What financial concerns keep you up at night?

4. **Addressing Emotional Spending**
   - Do you ever use shopping or spending to cope with stress or other emotions?

- How do you feel after making a significant purchase?
- Have you noticed any patterns in your spending habits that you think might be driven by emotions?

5. **Evaluating Financial Planning Tools**
   - Have you ever taken any financial behavior assessments or quizzes? What insights did you gain from them?
   - Would you be interested in trying a tool like MoneyMind or Money Habitudes to better understand your financial habits?

6. **Discussing Major Life Events**
   - Have you experienced any major life changes recently (e.g. marriage, divorce, menopause) that have impacted your financial situation?
   - How do you feel about your financial future as you approach or navigate through these life changes?
   - Are there any upcoming events or transitions that you are concerned about financially?

7. **Building a Collaborative Relationship**
   - How comfortable do you feel discussing your emotions and personal stories related to money with me?
   - What kind of support do you need from me to feel confident in your financial decisions?
   - How can we work together to align your financial plan with your personal values and goals?

KEY TAKEAWAYS

1. **Emotions Drive Financial Decisions:** Many financial decisions are driven by emotions and subconscious beliefs, which can lead to poor financial outcomes. Understanding these factors is critical for effective financial advising.

2. **Behavioral Finance Tools:** Tools like MoneyMind, Money Habitudes, and Knomee help uncover clients' financial habits, attitudes, and motivations. These tools enhance advisor-client relationships by personalizing advice.

3. **Financial Therapy:** Financial therapy addresses the emotional and psychological aspects of financial health. It is a growing trend in financial advising, helping clients make better decisions by separating emotions from their financial choices.

4. **Money Beliefs:** Clients often fall into one of four money belief categories: money worship, money status, money vigilance, and money avoidance. Understanding these beliefs helps advisors offer more tailored advice.

5. **Women and Behavioral Finance:** Women face unique financial challenges and societal pressures, making it essential for advisors to incorporate behavioral finance to better serve female clients. Discussing major life events like menopause can deepen relationships and provide better financial guidance.

6. **Personalization Is Key:** Advisors should guide clients to align their financial decisions with their values, helping them feel more confident and empowered. Building a collaborative, empathetic relationship is crucial for long-term success.

7. **Client Engagement:** Asking questions about financial behaviors, emotions, and life experiences builds trust and opens deeper conversations about money, leading to better financial planning outcomes.

NOTES

1. Much of this chapter was take from an article originally published for Rethinking 65; it is used with permission.
2. Archuleta, K.L. (ed.) (2014). *Journal of Financial Therapy*, 5(2). Available at: https://fta.memberclicks.net/assets/docs/Journal/journal%20of%20financial%20therapy%20vol%205%20iss%202.pdf.

3. Archuleta, K.L. (ed.) (2014). *Journal of Financial Therapy*, 5(2). Available at: https://fta.memberclicks.net/assets/docs/Journal/journal%20of%20financial%20therapy%20vol%205%20iss%202.pdf.
4. Novak, J.R. and Johnson, R.R. (2017). Associations between financial avoidance, emotional distress, and relationship conflict frequency in emerging adults in college. *Journal of Financial Therapy*, 8(2). Available at: https://newprairie press.org/jft/vol8/iss2/5/.
5. DataPoints. (n.d.). About DataPoints. Available at: https://datapoints.com.

CHAPTER EIGHTEEN

EFFECTIVE COMMUNICATION WITH FEMALE CLIENTS

Empathy is the key to successful communication. Understanding and addressing the unique financial concerns of female clients requires a thoughtful and empathetic approach.

–Jane Fonda

PROBLEM

Financial advisors often struggle to effectively communicate with female clients, leading to a lack of trust, engagement, and satisfaction. Women typically have different financial priorities and decision-making processes than men, and traditional advising approaches may fail to address these differences adequately.

Understanding and effectively communicating with women in financial planning requires recognizing their unique perspectives and preferences. Women often approach financial decisions differently than men do, necessitating tailored communication strategies to enhance the advisor-client relationship.

INSIDE-OUT VERSUS OUTSIDE-IN APPROACHES

Approaches to Financial Decisions

- **Men:** Typically evaluate financial decisions from the inside out, starting with their own goals and needs before considering the impact on others.
- **Women:** Often assess decisions from the outside in, beginning with the big picture and community impact, and then aligning choices with personal goals.

Establishing Long-term Financial Needs

1. **Clarify Goals:** Understand the woman's long-term financial objectives and the broader impact of these goals.
2. **Evaluate Strategies:** Discuss specific investment strategies that align with her objectives once her goals are clear.

Focusing on Values and Processes

Do the following when discussing investment performance:

- Emphasize values and the decision-making process rather than delving into overly complex analysis.
- Explain the beliefs and criteria guiding investment choices.
- Use clear, descriptive language to discuss risk-return trade-offs.

Example: ESG Investments

Women often prefer investments that reflect their values, such as environmental, social, and governance (ESG) investments:

- Describe a mutual fund with a patient, value-oriented investment philosophy.
- Highlight its steady, long-term growth and alignment with her financial goals.
- Discuss associated fees, expenses, and overall cost-effectiveness.

ESG AND WOMEN

Women tend to be more interested in Environmental, Social, and Governance (ESG) investing compared to men. Several studies and surveys have shown this trend, highlighting various reasons for this inclination:

1. **Values and Impact**
   - Women often prioritize values-based investing, focusing on the social and environmental impact of their investments. They are more likely to consider the broader implications of their financial decisions on society and the environment.
2. **Risk Awareness and Long-term Thinking**
   - Research suggests that women generally have a lower risk tolerance and a preference for long-term, sustainable growth. ESG investing aligns well with these preferences, as it emphasizes sustainability and ethical practices, which can contribute to more stable long-term returns.
3. **Wealth Transfer and Influence**
   - With the increasing wealth transfer to women, especially as they outlive men, their influence on investment strategies is growing.

Women are using this influence to advocate for responsible and sustainable investment practices.

4. **Corporate Responsibility**
    - Women are often more concerned with corporate governance and ethical business practices. They value transparency, accountability, and social responsibility, which are key components of ESG criteria.

5. **Research and Education**
    - Educational initiatives and research have also highlighted that women are more likely to be engaged with ESG topics. This awareness leads to a greater inclination toward integrating ESG factors into their investment decisions.

WHAT IS YOUR WHY?

Women don't care how much you know until they know how much you care! Share your story and your "why" with them. Why do you do what you do for a living? What makes you tick? As an example, here is my why:

Hi, I'm Cary.

I grew up with my dad who was a senior vice president for JP Morgan Chase. I was his oldest, and we bonded over money rather than sports. We went to foreclosure auctions and Straight Talk with the Dolans, and he took me to work before there was a "take your daughter to work day." Money and financial literacy were in my blood. I thought everyone knew what I knew. When I went to college, I founded a national sorority for women to feel safe. I would also teach everyone how to do budgets. When I graduated college, I went right into banking and working with clients for JP Morgan Chase in the management training program and the executive management training program after I received my MBA. I held various roles at Citibank and Lord Abbett

Mutual Funds before I started my own financial planning firm. I also received my CFP designation. This is Certified Financial Planner, the gold standard in my industry. After starting my own firm, I merged with a larger one, United Capital. I had many ups and downs along the way. I got divorced, remarried, United Capital was sold to Goldman, and it took me years to get out. I wrote a book for women to help them *Build Wealth and Banish Fear*. I started speaking all over the world and doing hundreds of media segments on women and money. I became a CFP Board Ambassador and won a bunch of awards within my industry. I also founded Women's Leadership at United Capital. The "ONE THING" theme throughout my life was to always help women feel safe, secure, and heard. I want women to feel like a victor, not a victim. My profession fails and is least sympathetic to women and can gain the most if it can change its approach. This is my life's work to make the industry female-friendly.

Figure 18.1   Key ways to retain clients.

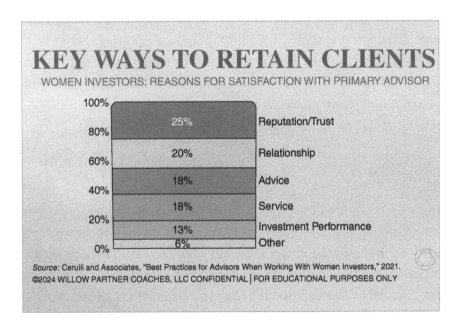

KEY WAYS TO RETAIN CLIENTS
WOMEN INVESTORS: REASONS FOR SATISFACTION WITH PRIMARY ADVISOR

- 25% Reputation/Trust
- 20% Relationship
- 18% Advice
- 18% Service
- 13% Investment Performance
- 6% Other

Source: Cerulli and Associates, "Best Practices for Advisors When Working With Women Investors," 2021.
©2024 WILLOW PARTNER COACHES, LLC CONFIDENTIAL | FOR EDUCATIONAL PURPOSES ONLY

Tell your story! Women want to hear it. Women's satisfaction with their advisors is 25% reputation/trust and 20% relationship followed by 18% advice, 18% service, 13% investment performance, and 6% other (Figure 18.1).

COMMUNICATING EFFECTIVELY WITH WOMEN CLIENTS: WILLOW'S THREE E'S MODEL

Communicating effectively with women clients starts with meeting them where they are–no blame, no shame. Focusing on the client and who they are rather than their assets, their gender/ethnicity/employment status/ marital status/etc. is key.

Willow has a three E's framework for communicating with women clients and it has helped advisors attract and retain clients: Empathy, Education, and Empowerment.

Empathy

Empathy is all about employing active listening. Recent research from Nuveen shows that only 54% of heirs retain the services of their parents' advisor if they meet the advisor as a young adult or older.[1] If the introduction happens when the inheritor is a child or teen, the likelihood of maintaining the relationship rises to 80%. We'll talk more about education later, but giving kids an age-appropriate book about investing is a great place to start.

Following are ways to show empathy:

- Invite everyone to be part of the conversation. Women want to know their children will be taken care of, not only financially but also emotionally. By including her children in the conversation, you are establishing a relationship with them and will act in their best interests now and in the future.
- Reach out to women directly both in a meeting with their spouse and separately. Get to know her!
- Embrace collaborative language and employ active listening. That means focusing on the following:
  - Observe nonverbal cues (eye contact, facial expressions, body language): Do they look uncomfortable talking about money? Do they seem bored?
  - Use inclusive language to validate each spouse's perspective and contributions to the client relationship.
  - Ask open ended questions: What's on your mind? What do you need to know before you leave this meeting comfortable?
- Meet them where they are: They may not be as familiar with some of the investments. Take the time to explain it all and the why behind those are part of the portfolio/strategy.
- Integrating coaching into your practice is key.

Coaching is a management style that differs widely from the command-and-control strategy. It offers a give-and-take, more collaborative style of work than the traditional advisor-advisee relationship. Coaching comes from a place of humility and respect. It enables lasting behavior change through the use of carefully constructed questions that will help clients think deeper, or differently, about their finances. For example, if you have established a relationship anchored in trust, simply asking the client "What's on your mind as we talk about your finances?" can lead to a conversation about how they *really* feel. See Figure 18.2.

Figure 18.2   Show empathy by asking coaching questions.

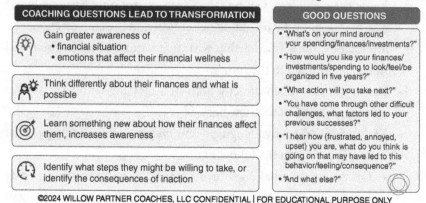

SHOW EMPATHY BY ASKING COACHING QUESTIONS

COACHING QUESTIONS LEAD TO TRANSFORMATION	GOOD QUESTIONS
Gain greater awareness of • financial situation • emotions that affect their financial wellness	• "What's on your mind around your spending/finances/investments?"
Think differently about their finances and what is possible	• "How would you like your finances/ investments/spending to look/feel/be organized in five years?"
Learn something new about how their finances affect them, increases awareness	• "What action will you take next?" • "You have come through other difficult challenges, what factors led to your previous successes?"
Identify what steps they might be willing to take, or identify the consequences of inaction	• "I hear how (frustrated, annoyed, upset) you are, what do you think is going on that may have led to this behavior/feeling/consequence?" • "And what else?"

©2024 WILLOW PARTNER COACHES, LLC CONFIDENTIAL | FOR EDUCATIONAL PURPOSE ONLY

Education

Be honest and transparent, including about fees. While many women are confident investors, others feel overwhelmed or intimidated by the wealth management industry, one which historically has failed to cater to women consumers. Therefore, if an advisor dives right into very specific and convoluted topics to show their expertise, it becomes very off-putting and will likely alienate those you are trying to impress. To avoid this, make no assumptions, ask questions along the way, and read body language.

It's important to think about education not only in the traditional sense of a classroom or a seminar but also in your everyday interactions with clients, their spouses, and their heirs. Education is a great way to build rapport and deliver on the promise of meeting clients where they are. Consider the following topics:

- **Portfolio and Portfolio Management:** This can be as simple as explaining fees, discussing the importance of having beneficiaries listed, and sharing insights as to why you should use one account type over another.

- **Terminology and Jargon:** This helps to demystify some of the investment terms, especially to those who are newer to investing or the responsibility of investing.
- **Wealth Management:** This isn't just for the super wealthy. The basics of estate planning apply to all.
- **Life Stage Considerations:** The typical life stages–starting out, getting married, starting a family, and planning for retirement–need to be considered, but you also have the women-specific considerations around those stages, such as fertility, caring for aging parents, and the potential impact of time away from work to care of aging parents, etc.

We recommend incorporating many ways to educate in your practice. This varies based on the topic but also the person/people you are trying to help. Some people don't want to come to an in-person event, or they may not even want to talk to you about it, so for them a book or some info sheets could be best. Other ideas include the following:

- Hosting regular webinars for your clients and prospects is a great thing to do. We talked about this earlier in your communication strategy as well.
- Doing some "noninvestment" events may get a different part of our client and prospect audience to attend. Bring in a speaker of interest and host a lunch at a local restaurant. These things can be cost effective and still have big impact.
- Hold networking events. Make your clients feel like they are part of a community.
- Consider hosting targeted events for certain subgroups of your base. Maybe it's women or next gen. You cater the agenda to their needs.

EMPOWERMENT

Act has your client's quarterback. Empowerment is a very strong word and means different things to different people. Willow recently asked a group of advisors what empowerment means to them, and following were some of the responses:

- Confidence and the freedom to act
- Being informed and confident to make decisions
- Encourage, inspire, motivate

As an advisor, if you can make your clients feel these things, you are winning and will be successful.

Educational Approach

Women value advisors who educate and build confidence. Do the following to foster engagement:

1. **Define Key Concepts:** Explain important terms like diversification and asset classes in simple language.
2. **Clarify the Process:** Ensure clients understand the entire process before discussing specific programs.

Build Trust

- Spend time thoroughly explaining key points.
- Use tools like the investment viewfinder to actively involve clients in decision-making.

Figure 18.3   Empowerment: What Does It Really Mean?

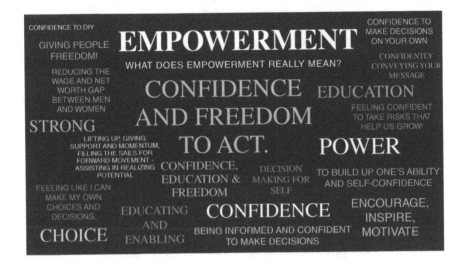

Emotional Connection to Money

Recognize the emotional aspect of money for many women. Emphasize key investment goals that resonate personally:

- **College Savings:** Highlight the importance of saving for children's or grandchildren's education.
- **Retirement Planning:** Discuss the significance of being prepared for retirement, especially for maintaining lifestyle without a spouse.
- **Social Security:** Provide detailed information on benefits and employer plan options.
- **Philanthropy:** Explain charitable giving options, such as gift annuities and donor-advised funds.

Risk Management

Women are often more risk-averse than men. When discussing risk with women, be sure to do the following:

- Explain the necessity of taking calculated risks for long-term growth.
- Discuss the drawbacks of keeping too much cash and the benefits of a diversified portfolio. Remember the cash hoarders we discussed earlier.

Respect Personal Networks

Women value and trust their personal networks. Build strong, trust-based relationships:

- Cover key points thoroughly and provide education.
- Ensure both spouses are equally involved in financial discussions when applicable.
- Don't assume early in the relationship she will introduce you around to her friends. You must earn that trust over time.

Women as Referral Sources

Women can be powerful referral sources if addressed correctly. Authentic conversation leads to positive word-of-mouth, much like the viral spread depicted in the 1980s Faberge Organic Shampoo commercial. Women share their positive experiences widely, helping to build a strong client base through their social networks. According to the NY Life research, over a lifetime, women will make 26 referrals to a financial advisor on average compared with 11 by the typical male clients. That is *more than double!*

By understanding these communication preferences and tailoring your approach, you can effectively support your female clients, helping them feel confident and informed in their financial decisions.

Solution

Implement a communication strategy that emphasizes empathy, education, and empowerment tailored to the unique perspectives and needs of female clients. This includes understanding their long-term goals, values, and risk tolerance, using clear and inclusive language, and building trust through consistent, values-driven advice.

Questions for Financial Advisors to Ask Themselves

1. **Understanding Client Needs**
   - How well do I understand the unique financial goals and concerns of my female clients?
   - Do I regularly ask my female clients about their long-term objectives and the broader impact they wish to achieve with their investments?

2. **Communication Style**
   - Am I using clear, descriptive language that aligns with the preferences of my female clients?
   - Do I incorporate empathy and active listening into my interactions with female clients?

3. **Values and Investment Strategies**
   - How often do I discuss values-based investing options, such as ESG investments, with my female clients?
   - Do I explain the beliefs and criteria guiding investment choices rather than focusing solely on complex analysis?

4. **Education and Empowerment**
   - Am I providing educational resources that help my female clients feel informed and confident in their financial decisions?
   - How do I empower my female clients to take an active role in their financial planning?

KEY TAKEAWAYS

1. **Empathy Is Key:** Build trust by listening and addressing women's unique financial concerns with empathy.
2. **Different Decision-making Styles:** Women prioritize broader societal impact before personal goals, unlike men who focus inward.
3. **Values-driven Investing:** Women prefer investments that reflect values, like ESG, which aligns with their focus on sustainability and ethics.
4. **Share Your Why:** Women value trust and connection over technical knowledge; sharing personal stories builds rapport.
5. **The Three Es:** Effective communication with women requires Empathy, Education, and Empowerment.
6. **Educational Engagement:** Simplify financial concepts and clearly explain key topics like retirement and risk management.
7. **Women as Referrers:** Women are powerful referral sources when they feel empowered and respected.

NOTE

1. Nuveen. (2023). Heirs likely to retain family's financial advisor if relationship is established early. *PR Newswire*. Available at: https://www.prnewswire.com/news-releases/heirs-likely-to-retain-familys-financial-advisor-if-relationship-is-established-early-301815941.html.

CHAPTER NINETEEN

BUILDING DEEPER CONNECTIONS AND TRUST THROUGH SOCIAL MEDIA

Social media isn't just about broadcasting messages; it's about creating conversations. Engaging with female clients through social media means listening to their needs and responding with genuine value.

–Randi Zuckerberg

PROBLEM

Many financial advisors struggle to effectively leverage social media to connect with female clients, missing out on opportunities to build deeper relationships, establish trust, and engage with clients in a meaningful way. This can result in a lack of visibility, reduced client engagement, and missed opportunities for client acquisition and retention.

In today's digital age, social media is a transformative tool for financial professionals aiming to connect with female clients, build deeper relationships, and establish lasting trust. Here's how you can effectively harness social media to foster these connections. Women want to know who you are and what you stand for. I feel privileged to be able to participate in my clients' lives via social media. I am connected with all of them. I get to see birthdays, vacations, and celebrations in real time rather than having to wait for a meeting. And they get to participate in my life as well. It keeps us connected.

Choosing the Right Platforms

Select social media platforms where your target audience is most active:

- **LinkedIn:** Ideal for professional networking and sharing insightful industry content
- **Facebook:** Great for community building and engaging in discussions
- **Instagram:** Useful for sharing visually appealing content and personal stories
- **X (Twitter):** Effective for sharing quick updates and participating in trending conversations
- **TikTok:** An emerging platform for short, engaging video content, especially popular among younger demographics.

Share Valuable Content

Create and share content that resonates with your female clients' Interests and needs:

- **Educational Posts:** Share articles, infographics, and videos about financial planning, investment strategies, and money management.
- **Inspirational Stories:** Highlight success stories of female investors and entrepreneurs.

- **Tips and Advice:** Offer practical financial tips tailored to women at different life stages.

Engage Authentically: Engage with your audience in a genuine and authentic manner.

- **Respond Promptly:** Answer questions and comments quickly to show that you value their engagement.
- **Personalize Interactions:** Use names and personalize responses to make your audience feel valued.
- **Show Empathy:** Recognize and respect the unique challenges women may face, offering supportive, empathetic advice.

Build Community: Create a sense of community where female clients feel supported and connected.

- **Host Live Sessions:** Organize live Q&A sessions, webinars, and workshops on relevant financial topics.
- **Create Groups:** Form private groups or forums on platforms like Facebook or LinkedIn for discussions.
- **Encourage Discussions:** Start conversations on relevant topics and encourage your audience to share their thoughts and experiences.

Showcase Expertise and Credibility: Establish your credibility as a trusted financial advisor.

Share Success Stories: Post testimonials and case studies from female clients. This is the new SEC testimonial rule.

What are the new SEC rules on testimonials?

With the rule update, you're now welcome to use testimonials if you meet certain disclosure requirements. The SEC writes: Advertisements must clearly and prominently disclose whether the person giving the testimonial or endorsement (the "promoter") is a client and whether the promoter is compensated (Aug 1, 2023). Women are incredible referral sources. I know I keep sharing this information, but I can't overemphasize this enough.

- **Post Regular Updates:** Keep your audience informed about the latest financial trends, news, and insights.
- **Feature Collaborations:** Partner with influencers, industry experts, and organizations focused on women's financial empowerment.

Use Visual Content: Engage audiences more effectively with visual content.

- **Infographics:** Simplify complex financial concepts with infographics. My favorite one I did was comparing shoes to asset classes.
- **Videos:** Share short videos offering tips, explaining financial concepts, or highlighting client success stories.
- **Images:** Post images of events, client meetings (with permission), and behind-the-scenes looks at your work.

Running Targeted Campaigns

Use targeted advertising to reach a specific demographic of female clients. Tailor campaigns to address their specific needs and interests. I have never done this, but I hear from others that it works.

Monitoring and Adapting

Regularly monitor your social media analytics to understand what content resonates most with your female audience. Adapt your strategy based on these insights to continually improve your engagement and connection efforts. I know this is more than most of us as advisors do, but there are many firms that can help: Samantha Russell at FMG, Candice Carlton at FICOMM, or Snappy Kraken to list a few names.

MY JOURNEY WITH MEDIA AND SOCIAL MEDIA[1]

Throughout my career, I've utilized various media channels to build my brand and connect with clients. Starting with traditional media in 2002, I was quoted in newspapers and magazines and appeared on TV and radio. Social media became a significant part of my strategy during the financial crisis of 2008–2009 when I joined Facebook. Over the years, I've expanded my presence to LinkedIn, X (Twitter), Instagram, and I really disliked if TikTok is banned.

Early Days: Traditional Media

When I first started my practice, I relied heavily on traditional media. I was frequently quoted in newspapers and magazines and appeared more often on TV than on the radio. These channels helped me establish my credibility and grow my brand professionally.

Transition to Social Media

I began using social media during the financial crisis of 2008–2009. Initially, I joined Facebook to reconnect with friends and relieve stress, but I soon started sharing work-related content, like publications and TV appearances. In 2010, I joined LinkedIn, back when it was more of a job-hunting site, and today I have nearly 10,500 followers. I joined Twitter in 2014 right before my book release in 2015 because my agent advised it. It took longer to get on Instagram, but I finally did in 2019 and became active in 2023. I also joined TikTok in 2023.

The Power of Connecting

Social media allows me to tell the world who I am, what I do, and what I stand for. It helps maintain visibility and build a pipeline of new clients.

Throughout my career, I've been the first person my clients call when they retire, experience a sudden-money event, or reach other milestones. With social media, I can participate in my clients' lives in real-time, enhancing our connection beyond formal meetings.

Lessons from a Hiatus

A hiatus from social and traditional media can significantly impact visibility and influence. During my time at Goldman Sachs, strict compliance rules limited my social media activity, leading to isolation and loss of momentum. My ranking in the Investopedia Top 100 Advisors dropped from the top 10 to completely off the list. Since rejoining social media, I'm back on the list but not yet in the top 10.

Understanding the Media Landscape

Media spans traditional channels (print and broadcast) and digital platforms (websites, podcasts, and social media). Digital media is accessible and effective for advisors looking to build a bridge to their clients. If you don't have contacts in traditional media or a big budget, digital media allows for experimentation without a huge investment. Hiring a marketing firm specializing in digital media may also be worthwhile after determining your goals.

Using Media to Build Client Relationships

Social media is a natural medium for me as a connector. It allows me to stay informed about my clients' lives and keep them updated about mine. This two-way street enhances the client-advisor relationship beyond formal meetings. For example, I use social media to get new clients and stay in front of existing clients. I share personal and professional updates, blending both worlds seamlessly.

Expanding Digital Outreach

In addition to social media, I use my website to generate leads and offer complimentary consultations. Although I haven't started my podcast, I've been a guest on many. Each digital platform serves a unique purpose in my overall strategy.

Understanding Platform Demographics

Different platforms attract different demographics. For example, nearly 80% of millennials and Gen Z have sought financial advice via social media, and 50% reported financial gains based on such advice. According to a study by fintech firm Advisor360°, half of wealthy investors said they'd be more likely to engage an advisor who uses YouTube, followed by Facebook and LinkedIn. Even 36% of older Gen X and younger boomers responded similarly. However, only Gen Z and younger millennials view Instagram as an advisor advantage.

Tips for Each Platform

- **LinkedIn:** Share thought leadership content and connect with professionals. Avoid immediate sales pitches from new connections. I dislike any sales pitch unless someone is trying to hire me.
- **Facebook:** Blend personal and professional content. Static pictures often perform better than videos or stories.

- **Instagram:** Use for visually appealing content, including pictures and video reels.
- **X (Twitter):** Share quick updates and engage in conversations, though engagement has changed since recent platform updates.
- **TikTok:** Still learning the platform but aiming to talk about money and financial literacy. It is my least favorite and a chore for me to post and share on it!
- **YouTube:** Host and link videos for broader content sharing.

Verification and Security

Getting verified on social media platforms is crucial for protecting your identity and credibility. My experience with a cloned Instagram account highlights the importance of verification to prevent misuse of your profile. I had someone pretend to be me and sell crypto and nefarious trading strategies. Luckily I was informed by almost everyone the imposter contacted. As soon as I would report them, they would pop up again with another version of my name. I had to get an attorney and spend thousands of dollars to contact the legal department of Instagram. It is much less expensive to get yourself verified. I am not saying someone will not try but at least you will have more protection.

My friend Reshell Smith said, "Social media plays a crucial role in my business, serving as a platform to connect and communicate with current and potential clients. It helps me understand the mindset of my target audience, particularly the many divorcees I work with. Through social media, I can engage directly with these women, addressing their questions and providing solutions to their unique situations. Although the advice shared isn't specific, it often helps them make informed decisions. As a divorcee myself, they can relate to my experiences. I often share my successes and challenges. This approach not only allows me to offer valuable guidance but also builds trust, makes me more relatable, and fosters deeper connections. All of these qualities are essential for supporting my clients through their financial journeys."

Leveraging social media effectively can help financial professionals connect with female clients, build deeper relationships, and establish lasting trust. By choosing the right platforms, sharing valuable content, engaging authentically, building a community, showcasing expertise, using visual content, running targeted campaigns, and monitoring and adapting strategies, financial advisors can enhance their engagement with female clients in meaningful ways.

Solution

Financial advisors can harness the power of social media to build deeper connections and trust with female clients by selecting the right platforms, sharing valuable and relevant content, engaging authentically, building a supportive community, showcasing their expertise, and using visual content effectively. This approach involves understanding the unique needs and preferences of female clients and tailoring social media strategies to meet these needs.

Questions for Financial Advisors to Ask Themselves

Choosing the Right Platforms

1. Which social media platforms are most popular among my female clients?
2. How can I tailor my content to suit the specific features and audience of each platform (e.g., LinkedIn for professional content, Instagram for personal stories)?

Sharing Valuable Content

1. What type of content resonates most with my female clients (e.g., educational posts, inspirational stories)?
2. How can I ensure that my content addresses the specific financial needs and interests of women at different life stages?

Engaging Authentically

1. Am I responding promptly and personally to comments and questions from my female clients on social media?
2. How can I demonstrate empathy and understanding of the unique challenges faced by women in my social media interactions?

Building Community

1. What steps can I take to create a sense of community among my female clients on social media (e.g., hosting live Q&A sessions, creating private groups)?
2. How can I encourage meaningful discussions and interactions within my social media community?

Showcasing Expertise and Credibility

1. How can I use testimonials and success stories from female clients to build trust and credibility on social media?
2. What kind of regular updates and collaborations can I share to establish myself as a trusted advisor?

Using Visual Content

1. How can I use visual content (e.g., infographics, videos, images) to make complex financial concepts more accessible and engaging for my female clients?
2. What types of visual content have received the most positive feedback from my audience?

Running Targeted Campaigns

1. How can I use targeted advertising to reach and engage a specific demographic of female clients?
2. What specific needs and interests should I address in my targeted social media campaigns?

Monitoring and Adapting

1. What tools and metrics can I use to monitor the effectiveness of my social media strategy with female clients?
2. How can I adapt my social media approach based on the feedback and analytics to continually improve engagement and connection efforts?

Verification and Security

1. Have I taken steps to verify my social media accounts to protect my identity and credibility?
2. What measures can I implement to safeguard my social media presence from potential misuse or impersonation?

Personal Reflection and Adaptation

1. How can I share my own experiences and stories on social media to build relatability and trust with my female clients?
2. What lessons have I learned from my own social media journey, and how can I apply these to improve my connection with clients?

KEY TAKEAWAYS

1. **Choose the Right Platforms:** Use platforms where female clients are most active, like LinkedIn, Instagram, and Facebook, to maximize engagement.

2. **Share Valuable Content:** Tailor posts to address women's financial needs through educational material, success stories, and practical advice.

3. **Engage Authentically:** Personalize interactions, show empathy, and respond promptly to foster deeper connections.

4. **Build Community:** Encourage discussions, host live sessions, and create groups to nurture a supportive online space.

5. **Showcase Expertise:** Use testimonials and case studies to build credibility and trust, leveraging the new SEC testimonial rule.

6. **Leverage Visual Content:** Simplify complex topics using infographics, videos, and images to enhance understanding and engagement.

7. **Monitor and Adapt:** Track social media performance and adjust strategies based on analytics to improve connection with female clients.

8. **Ensure Security:** Verify social media accounts to protect your identity and credibility against potential misuse.

NOTE

1. This section was originally published with Rethinking 65.

CHAPTER TWENTY

HOW I CHARGE CLIENTS

Clients want to pay for financial advice the way they pay for other professional services. They want clarity, transparency, and to know they're getting value for their money. The more you align your fees with the value you provide, the better the relationship you'll build.

–Michael Kitces

PROBLEM

Many financial advisors struggle to communicate and justify their fee structures to clients, leading to misunderstandings, mistrust, and potential loss of business. Clients often perceive fees as unclear or excessive, particularly when compared to "free" advice from other brokers.

I started my career as a fee-only financial advisor because I always believed in this model. I really wanted to be paid for my advice like an attorney and I never wanted to simply give away this advice or sell products. It never made sense to me.[1]

The president of a very large broker-dealer once told me that I was ahead of my time for thinking this way. I disagreed. I just wanted to be paid hourly, or a flat fee for a financial plan, or a retainer fee or a percentage of AUM–or some combination of the above.

Consultative selling is much harder that commission selling but much more rewarding to me. This view hasn't always been well received by potential clients–until I explain it to them.

PRODUCTIVE INTRODUCTIONS

When I first started in the business, I competed with male brokers who told clients everything was free. Instead, I told my clients, "Here is my pre-meeting paperwork (homework). You have to complete this and then I do a comprehensive financial plan that I charge a flat fee for."

The initial meeting is always complimentary. I decide if I want to work with them and if they are a fit. I send them the quote and price after the meeting but give them a range during the meeting. I tell them I will scope the fees after we meet, and I see what their net worth or income is.

I always felt, "How can I give advice without knowing everything?" It is almost like going to a doctor and only telling them part of the story. It should be a full disclosure relationship.

So many men I have worked with over the years clashed with me on this. They said you should be doing it for free, and I said, "*No*, I am not giving away my advice and financial plan on a hope and a prayer that the clients will want to work with me." I wanted to be paid to prospect. Also, I needed to know if I wanted to work with the person as much as they were interviewing me.

NEXT STEPS

Once I start working with clients, I charge everyone a flat fee in Year 1. My first-year fee, which includes my comprehensive financial plan and one year of advice, runs between $2,500 and $10,000. I calculate it on a scale based on income or assets. Most of the time, potential clients fall within the same band. I use my judgment or split the difference.

For example, if a younger client is earning a high salary, they may be in the $4,000 band for income but in the $2,500 band for net worth. Accordingly, I would charge $3,250. Or for a retired individual with a lower income (that might put them in my $3,000 range) and a higher net worth (says, closer to my $6,000 fee), I would charge $4,500.

I always spend a lot of time in Year 1 with a new client. It's a very labor-intensive time that includes multiple meetings and lots of background work to analyze current investments, insurance coverage, 401(k) plans, various documents, etc. If I charged by the hour, I might even lose money on this client, but it's worth it to me to get to know their situation.

NOTHING VALUABLE IS FREE

When some clients replied, "I am getting it free from XYZ broker," I would say, "If you believe the advice you are getting for free is more valuable than my conflict-free advice, then take it." Nothing valuable is free. I also asked them to bring me the other broker's recommendations so I could review them. In most cases, these recommendations were for loaded mutual funds or high expense variable annuities.

Most people don't read prospectuses or even know where to look, so I found myself educating clients about this "free advice" they'd received elsewhere.

For example, I let them know that with these funds other brokers recommended, they'd be paying a 5% front-load fee, a 1.5% ongoing management fee, and sometimes also get charged on the way out. All of this is not easy to see on the statements.

I highlight these fees in the prospectus and give it to my potential clients or clients. They'd respond that the other brokers never told them this, and I would say, "They don't have to. All they have to do is give this to you or send it in the mail."

SELECTING THE RIGHT FEE MODEL

Earlier, I mentioned that I'm interested in an assortment of payment models. After Year 1 of working with a client, we decide which model–retainer, AUM, or a combination–works best.

Here's a look at the pros and cons of each. As a female advocate, I also believe full disclosure of fees is better for all but especially for women. In my opinion the fiduciary model works so well for women because it lets them know the advisor is working in their best interest.

I never want any women to be taken advantage of or be so trusting that they are overcharged or put in products or investments they don't understand.

Retainer Fees

Most clients under retainer (a flat annual fee) do not have assets for me to manage directly but want advice on everything. They often have most of their assets invested in their business, 401(k) or other work retirement plan, family limited partnerships, or real estate. These clients usually have higher net worth and complex situations.

My flat fee includes ongoing financial planning as well as advice on assets I am not directly responsible for, such as 401(k) accounts and business assets. Sometimes I adjust my annual fee downward for a client after the first year because so much work is handled in Year 1.

Pros: We can give advice on all of it and charge a flat fee.

Cons: None for the client.

AUM Fees

These fees are for clients who decide they just want asset management services. They pay us to directly manage their assets under management. We are responsible for trading, performance reports, and picking and managing the managers.

Pros: We are on the same side of the table as the client. If their assets grow, so does our fee.

Cons: When the market falls like it did in 2022, our revenue goes down and is tied to the market no matter how good our recommendations are.

Combined-financial Planning Plus Asset Management Fees

This fee structure is for clients for whom we do a bit of everything. We provide them with an ongoing financial plan, give and update advice every year, and take direct responsibility for their investments. As with clients who select the AUM-only model, we monitor and report on their performance, trade, pick and monitor their investments, and make sure their asset allocation is correct.

Pros: We get to help on both fronts, and it matters. The price is usually lower for clients who use both services. We get to make the most impact here. For example, one client wasn't paying us for advice, just portfolio management. They were very happy with the return and started overspending. The next thing we knew, the client filed for bankruptcy. They said, "If you were telling us what to do and how much to spend and holding us accountable, this never would have happened."

Cons: It will cost a little more because it is worth it!

Thoughts on Hourly Fees

I rarely charge hourly fees because I think the flat fee is more effective. If I charged clients for the amount of time that it takes to get to know them intimately during that first year, most people would not want to pay it. If people only want to pay for advice on an hourly basis, I refer them to the Garret Financial Network, which charges hourly fees. Some of my friends are advisors on that network.

We keep track of what our clients pay us by using our portfolio accounting software and old-fashioned spreadsheets. Once a year, we send out hard-copy invoices for retainer fees and follow up on them.

My favorite saying from my grandmother was, "Don't be pennywise and pound foolish." My other favorite from my dad was, "You only cry once when you buy quality." The message advisors need to convey to clients is this: Using the right advisor with the right pricing model will make you rich, keep you rich, or make you richer!

Solution

Financial advisors can address this issue by adopting transparent, value-aligned fee structures that clearly demonstrate the benefits and value of their services. By offering a range of fee models, such as flat fees, retainers, and AUM fees, and by educating clients about these options, advisors can build stronger, trust-based relationships.

Questions for Financial Advisors to Ask Themselves

Selecting the Right Fee Model

1. What fee models (hourly, flat fee, retainer, AUM, or a combination) align best with the services I provide and the needs of my clients?
2. How can I clearly explain the pros and cons of each fee model to my clients?

Transparency and Communication

1. Am I providing full disclosure of my fees and how they are calculated to my clients?
2. How can I better communicate the value of my services in relation to the fees charged?
3. What strategies can I use to ensure clients understand the long-term benefits of paying for quality financial advice?

Client Onboarding and Education

1. Do I offer a complimentary initial meeting to assess potential clients' needs and explain my fee structure?
2. How can I educate potential clients about the drawbacks of "free" advice and the hidden costs associated with it?

Assessing Client Fit

1. How can I determine if a potential client is a good fit for my services during the initial meeting?
2. What criteria do I use to decide whether to offer a flat fee, retainer, or AUM model after the first year of service?

Value Alignment

1. How can I align my fees with the value I provide to ensure clients feel they are getting their money's worth?
2. What additional value-added services can I offer to justify my fees and enhance client satisfaction?

Monitoring and Adjusting Fees

1. How do I assess and adjust my fees based on the complexity and needs of each client's situation?
2. What processes do I have in place to review and adjust my fee structures periodically to ensure they remain fair and competitive?

Handling Objections

1. How do I handle objections from clients who compare my fees to "free" advice from other brokers?
2. What information and examples can I provide to demonstrate the long-term benefits and value of my services?

Fee Collection and Management

1. What systems do I have in place to track and manage fee collection efficiently?
2. How can I ensure that my invoicing process is clear, timely, and professional?

Building Trust and Credibility

1. How can I use client testimonials and success stories to build trust and credibility around my fee structures?
2. What measures can I take to ensure my fee transparency aligns with my overall brand and professional values?

KEY TAKEAWAYS

1. **Clarity and Transparency Are Crucial:** Clients want clear, upfront information about fees. The more transparent you are with your fee structure, the more trust and stronger relationships you build with clients.

2. **Value-driven Fee Models:** Aligning fees with the value provided helps clients see the worth of paying for professional advice, as opposed to relying on "free" advice from brokers, which often hides costs.

3. **Tailored Fee Structures:** Offering a variety of fee models (e.g., flat fee, AUM, retainer) allows advisors to tailor their services to each client's financial situation and needs, promoting flexibility and fairness.

4. **Education Is Key:** Advisors must educate clients on the hidden costs of "free" advice, highlighting the real benefits of paying for conflict-free, fiduciary-based advice that serves their best interest.

5. **Client Onboarding Strategy:** A complimentary initial meeting helps assess client fit and needs, after which the fee structure can be tailored. This allows advisors to build a relationship before discussing specific pricing.

6. **First Year of Service:** Advisors often spend the most time with clients in the first year, so charging a flat fee during this period helps account for the significant effort involved in understanding their financial picture.

7. **Handling Objections:** Educating clients about the value of your services and exposing the true costs of "free" alternatives builds trust and helps overcome objections to paying for advice.

8. **Fee Review and Adjustments:** Advisors should periodically review their fees to ensure they remain aligned with the complexity of the

client's needs, adjusting where necessary to reflect the value being provided.

9. **Building Trust Through Quality:** Demonstrating the long-term benefits of paying for professional advice helps clients appreciate the value of quality services, as highlighted by quotes from family wisdom like, "Don't be pennywise and pound foolish."

10. **Tracking and Invoicing:** Having systems in place for tracking and managing fees, including regular invoicing, ensures transparency and professionalism, strengthen the advisor-client relationship.

NOTE

1. A version of this chapter was originally published in Rethinking 65.

CHAPTER TWENTY-ONE

CASE STUDIES AND WHAT WOMEN NEED IN FINANCIAL SERVICES

Women's purchasing decisions are deeply personal and often driven by a desire for empowerment, self-expression, and authenticity.

–Cindy Gallop

CLIENT CASE STUDIES

My case studies are from my own experience as well as a little help from my friends. Bridget Venus Grimes, CFP® is president of WealthChoice, a wealth management firm for women executives, and cofounder of the SEC-registered investment advisor Equita Financial Network, a community of women-led financial planning firms. Bridget is a CFP Board Ambassador. She authored the best-selling book *Corner Office Choices: The Executive Woman's Guide to Financial Freedom* and has written countless articles for major US media channels. Following are some of Bridget Grimes' case studies:

1. **Jayda, business executive**

   Jayda is the CEO of a mid-sized, profitable, and privately held company. She is in her mid-50s and the breadwinner of her family. Her children are grown, and her husband is retired.

   Her need

   Jayda had no idea if they were financially on track. As a CEO, she was too busy to spend time with her personal finances. She didn't have a relationship with the broker her husband had been working with. She had no clarity about their financial situation or how they were invested. She wanted to know if they were financially okay. She also was considering selling her company but had no idea how much she'd need to sell it for to replace her lifestyle long into the future.

   Jayda wanted clarity around their finances and to know that they had a plan to continue the same quality of life into the future. She wanted a partner and a guide she could trust who she knew had her best interests at heart. She wanted someone who looked like her, and someone with whom she could relate and trust.

   How we helped

   We started with a deep dive into her personal and financial life as we do with all clients. We reviewed every investment and found no strategy around her retirement goals, and expensive, poor performing products. There was not nearly enough savings, and she was not on track to retire with a similar lifestyle. We created one investment strategy so every dollar they had was working best and was invested for growth; we consolidated accounts, and we divested of investments that were expensive and poor performing.

Selling the business would be a major part of funding her retirement, so we strategized around the business sale. We created a strategic team of a new CPA and business attorney that we are an active part of the process. We reviewed the business insurance and retirement account investment options that were costing the company a significant amount of money, which ate into business profit.

For her personal life, we also created a new team of strategic CPAs for collaborative tax strategy, an insurance team to analyze and review personal insurance needs. We partnered with an actuary for analysis on specific products they had been sold, and we collaborated with their estate attorney on legacy planning and current estate documents.

Because she was a high earner, we implemented several tax savings strategies, including tax loss harvesting on investment accounts, maximizing all retirement account contributions, and working closely with the CPA on tax options for business sale proceeds.

Where are we now?
We've significantly increased investment performance and net worth. There is a clear plan to retire with a similar quality of life, we have a defined legacy plan, we have a strategy around lowering taxes, and most of all, Jayda knows where she is financially and trusts us to guide her.

2. Rebecca, retired attorney
Rebecca is a newly retired attorney partner in her late 50s. She worked for years as a respected attorney at an American Law Top 100 firm. She is a single woman in California.

Her need
Rebecca wanted to be financially able to choose to stop working in the high pressure, long-hours job of attorney partner at age 55 to

pursue other interests. Rebecca wanted a plan to be on track to replace her income then. She wanted to know that her investments were working best to provide this retirement option for her.

How we helped

Because Rebecca relied on what she earned and what she saved to retire, her income drove her success. Her success in her role as attorney partner directly affected her financial success. For many years working together, we collaborated on annual compensation. Rebecca had an annual review at which compensation was addressed. We encouraged her to advocate for herself in an industry that is notorious for not paying women fairly.

We created a custom investment portfolio, which included managing her 401k while she was employed. This account was by far her largest asset and the growth of this was critical to funding her retirement. We were able to invest this for her as a self-directed account, which our portfolio and trading team could oversee. We opened trust accounts to help Rebecca save and invest well above what her retirement funds would allow. We had an aggressive savings strategy. Frequent check-ins on where Rebecca was in terms of reaching her goals kept her motivated. We employed tax strategies to lower taxable income so Rebecca kept more of what she earned and could invest more.

Where are we now?

Rebecca retired at her target date of age 55. She is pursuing other interests, consulting with several companies, working on her own schedule. She is several years into "retirement," and we are focused on helping her stay on track financially now that savings has stopped and her portfolio is poised to provide for her living expenses now. Tax strategy continues to be important to save as much of her income as possible.

3. Anne, tech exec

Anne is 40 and a mid-level exec in a publicly held tech company. Like many of our tech clients, she has moved around tech companies as opportunities arise. She is a single woman who lives with her partner in San Francisco.

Her need

Anne wants the option to retire at age 50 with a similar quality of life. She'd like to have the option to provide some amount of financial support to her mother if she needs it. Because a fair amount of her compensation is from stock awards, she wanted a strategy around these. These stock awards also necessitate a tax strategy, so she wanted a plan around managing taxes.

How we helped

For each company Anne worked at, we created a strategy around her stock awards. These tend to be RSUs, so we track the grants, vesting schedule, and employ a strategy to sell the shares and reinvest the proceeds in her portfolio. We introduced Anne to and collaborated with a CPA who is strategic and will advise on cash to be set aside for upcoming taxes every time shares vest. In some cases, the companies Anne has worked for have gone public, so we have created a strategy around divesting the shares and any tax implications.

Anne has a pretty aggressive goal of retiring at a young age with a high cost of living. To reach this goal, we have helped her determine how much she needs to save annually over and above what she is saving in retirement accounts. We opened trust accounts that she contributes to, and we created a customized investment strategy that is growth focused for her. We have frequent check-ins so that she knows where she is in terms of reaching her goal.

When Anne stops work, we know that Roth conversions will lower her taxes over time, which means increased income. Because she plans to retire young, there will be many years for her investments to grow, and tax-free growth will generously add to her income. We'll create a strategy of how we convert her pretax investments to Roth once she lowers her income at retirement, but we are able to see now through scenarios what that might look like.

Many years ago, Anne became quite ill and went from short-term to long-term disability. We helped her navigate this period by working with her employer on benefits, and then Social Security. Understandably, she chose to lower the amount of growth in her investments at that time to be much more conservative. Once she was well and comfortable with taking more risk in life, we revisited her portfolio and repositioned it for growth.

Where are we now?

We are 10 years away from Anne's target retirement age, and she is on track for this goal. To make sure this happens, we are helping with accountability in savings, reducing taxes so that there is more money to save, and pursuing an ongoing stock awards strategy. Once she retires, we plan to implement a Roth conversion strategy so there will be lower taxes and ultimately higher income over the course of her life.

4. **Lisa, C-suite executive**

Lisa is the breadwinner in her early 40s, married, and a C-suite executive at a publicly held company. In the 15 years that she has been working with us she has changed industries, married, had children, and moved states. She has also moved up in management over time to a very senior role in her company.

Her need

She wants to have the option to stop work and transition to a lower stress job in an industry of her choosing, but she wants to make sure her family continues with their current quality of life long into the future. She wants to fully fund her children's education, travel with her spouse annually, and have a strategy to help her minimize taxes as a high earner.

How we helped

For Lisa, having the ability to get off the hamster wheel of executive life when she wants is a priority. This has been the case since we first started working with her 15 years ago. Once we determined how much her cost of living was, we could determine how much money she would need to save and invest. Then we helped her choose where it was best for her to put this money. We made sure she contributed the maximum to her 401k annually. However, we also know that to replace her income in retirement will take more savings than that. For this reason, Lisa saves in investment accounts that are invested with the goal of funding her retirement. Her spouse also saves for retirement, and we have one portfolio strategy that is the same across all accounts–those we manage for them and those at their employers. We review those accounts at their employers periodically to make sure they are on track with our strategy.

Lisa has two children, a three-year-old and one-year-old. She and her spouse have decided they'd like to pay for four years of an in-state college. Our software allows us to track current tuition and room and board for their preferred college, so we have a good idea of the cost of college for both children. We've identified how much Lisa can afford to save monthly towards this and have opened 529 accounts for both children.

When extra income has been received in the form of a bonus or stock awards, which Lisa receives, we discuss where this money should go. We check in on their goals to see if anything has changed. Over the years they've had new goals like home renovations, new homes, moving, new cars, so we reassess where best to deploy the money during the year.

Tax strategy is a priority for Lisa. We review all employer benefits to make sure Lisa is leveraging all tax savings benefits that will lower her taxes as a high earner. Our firm helps provide Lisa tax savings with tax-free investments and tax-loss harvesting. We have a close relationship with Lisa's CPA so that we discuss potential tax bills and make sure enough money is set aside for those, especially when stock awards vest.

Where are we now?

Lisa is financially on track to stop funding retirement now because of the savings and investing she has done over the years. Her children are on track for college to be funded. Most importantly, Lisa has peace of mind from knowing that, should she pivot to another industry or a lower paying job, she is financially secure. And by having a tax strategy, she knows she is keeping more of what she and her spouse makes so that they have the options they want around career and life.

RITA CHENG'S STORY: THE IMPORTANCE OF DISCUSSING LONG-TERM CARE

Marguerita (Rita) M. Cheng is the CEO at Blue Ocean Global Wealth. She is a past spokesperson for the AARP Financial Freedom Campaign and a regular columnist for Investopedia & Kiplinger. She is a CFP® professional, a Chartered Retirement Planning Counselor℠, a Retirement Income

Certified Professional®, and a Certified Divorce Financial Analyst. As a CFP Board Ambassador, Rita helps educate the public, policymakers, and media about the benefits of competent, ethical financial planning. The following is about her experience in her own words.

One of the key aspects of serving women in financial planning is understanding the topic of caregiving. This was a significant lesson I learned after the birth of my son when I approached my parents about long-term care planning.

INITIATING THE CONVERSATION

As financial advisors, we need to be aware that caregiving and long-term care are often on our clients' minds, even if they find it difficult to discuss. This topic requires courage, patience, and empathy. We must approach it in a way that encourages meaningful action without overwhelming or intimidating our clients.

USING LIFE EVENTS AS CONVERSATION STARTERS

I used the births of my children to encourage my parents to update their estate plan. My daughter was born in 1996 and my son in 1998. At that time, my youngest sister was 22. I told my parents, "All of us, your three daughters, are over 21 now. It's a good time to update your estate plan."

My mom responded positively, and I gave my parents small tasks to start the process. They updated their advanced medical directives and created financial power of attorney documents. It's crucial to give clients manageable steps and acknowledge their progress.

ADDRESSING LONG-TERM CARE DIRECTLY

When discussing long-term care, I said to my parents, "I know how excited you are about being grandparents. I'm thinking about saving for retirement and college, but I'm also concerned about ensuring high-quality care in the event of a long-term care need. It's important to plan now while you're healthy and active, so you have choice and control over your care."

My mom initially responded, "Isn't that for old people?" She was 54, and my dad was 68 and in great health. I explained, "We're having this conversation now because you're young and healthy. It would be inappropriate for me to decide what you want. I want you to be included in the process and have control over your future care."

IMPLEMENTING LONG-TERM CARE INSURANCE

In 2000, I purchased a 5% compound long-term care policy for my mom and a 5% simple policy for my dad, considering their 14-year age difference. The compound policy was more robust but expensive, while the simple policy was cheaper but still provided essential coverage.

OVERCOMING INSURANCE AVERSION

After my dad passed away, my mom remarried. Her new husband was initially insurance averse. It took three meetings to address his concerns. I explained, "When Dad got sick, we had long-term care insurance that provided case managers and caregivers. This support was invaluable. I want to ensure we can extend the same level of care to you."

He eventually understood the importance, and although his policy isn't as comprehensive as my mom's, some protection is better than none.

ADDRESSING REMARRIAGE AND ESTATE PLANNING

Remarrying later in life raises important questions about beneficiaries and living arrangements. I encouraged my mom's husband to establish a life estate to protect my mom's interests. It's essential to consider the motivations behind people's decisions and ensure their future security.

ENSURING FINANCIAL STABILITY

My dad chose a 100% survivor pension benefit option and deferred his Social Security benefits until age 70 to provide my mom with a larger benefit. This decision exemplifies the importance of proactive planning for long-term security.

TAKEAWAYS FOR ADVISORS

- **Use life events** to initiate conversations about long-term care.
- **Provide manageable tasks** to help clients start the planning process.
- **Emphasize choice and control** to make clients feel empowered.
- **Address insurance aversion** with patience and clear examples of its benefits.
- **Consider the implications of remarriage** and ensure estate planning protects all parties involved.

By understanding and addressing the unique challenges women face in caregiving and long-term care planning, we can help them achieve financial stability and peace of mind.

Chloe Moore, CFP®, is the founder of Financial Staples, a virtual, fee-only financial planning firm based in Atlanta, Georgia, and serving clients nationwide. Her firm is dedicated to serving tech employees who are entrepreneurial-minded, philanthropic, and purpose-driven. Chloe believes that money is an emotional topic, and it impacts many aspects of our lives. She enjoys helping clients unpack their money history and discover how they can use money to support a life that is most meaningful to them. You can learn more about her at financialstaples.com. Following is a story of one of her clients.

TIFFANY, TENDER OFFER AT A PRIVATE COMPANY[1]

- Age 39, single with no children
- Approximately $1,400,000 in vested restricted stock unit (RSUs) (before taxes)

- $350,000 on-target earnings (base salary + quarterly cash bonuses)
- Emergency fund (6 months) and short-term savings goals funded
- Owns home w/mortgage, no other debt
- Around $400,000 in investments outside of company stock (brokerage, 401[k], and IRA rollover)

Key Decisions

- How much tax to withhold on RSUs when they vest (had a choice between 22% and 37%)?
  - Total income including RSUs put her marginal tax rate at 37%.
  - She preferred withholding shares instead of paying a big tax bill.
  - She decided to withhold 37%.
- How many shares to sell during the tender offer?
  - She had the ability to sell up to 100% of her vested shares.
  - She still had approximately $200,000 in unvested shares and would continue to receive additional grants annually.
  - The value of her total RSUs represented 80% of her investment assets.
  - The tender price equaled the vest price, so selling created no additional tax impact.
  - She decided to sell all vested shares.
- What to do with the proceeds (approximately $750,000 after taxes)?
  - Analysis: How I added value as a financial planner.
    - Calculated amount needed to achieve early retirement goals and how much could be gifted to charity without impacting those goals
    - Developed plan to manage cash flow (including bonuses) and decided on a target amount to invest annually
    - Incorporated a mega backdoor Roth into her retirement savings strategy

- Introduced her to a CPA and worked with them to estimate the tax savings from charitable donations
- Decisions
  - Gifted $250,000 to a donor-advised fund (DAF), which reduced tax bill by approximately $100,000
  - Invested remaining $500,000 in a diversified portfolio (plus around $100,000 tax refund the following spring)

With her current investments and regular contributions from cash flow, Tiffany is now on track to become work optional between ages 50 and 55! This plan gave her the confidence to spend more annually on "splurges" like vacations, conveniences to buy back her time, and a fun token to celebrate her hard work. It's been fun to see her transition her mindset from saving aggressively to splurging on things that bring her joy.

TAKEAWAYS

1. Working with a financial planner helped Tiffany understand her goals, create a strategy for how to navigate this tender offer, and develop a long-term plan to reach both her short- and long-term goals. This was a life-changing windfall that came with many critical decisions. Having the expertise of a financial planner and CPA to help her understand her situation and options as she made these important decisions proved to be very valuable.

2. Being "good" with money goes beyond saving and living a frugal lifestyle. If you take pride in living below your means and investing aggressively, it may be hard to also spend money, even on things you value. Once you reach your goal of financial freedom or you're well on your way, most people don't magically change their habits and start enjoying life more. As you work hard to build the habits of

saving and investing, don't forget to include the habit of treating yourself along the way. It's all about finding a balance between living in the present and saving responsibly for your future. After all, life is short. Don't wait for some day in the future to live it.

EILEEN SHOVLIN'S STORY

Eileen Shovlin joined Crump Life Insurance Services in 2016 and currently serves as director of business development. She is responsible for forging relationships with fee-only and fee-based RIAs, broker-dealers, employee benefits firms and large property and casualty (P&C) agencies for Crump sales channels nationwide. She has more than 28 years of experience in both the insurance industry as a regional vice president, brokerage sales director, and marketing director. She is a dedicated salesperson with a reputation for consummate professionalism and exemplary ethics. This is her story in her own words.

When I was 27 years old, I was involved in a very serious car accident. Although I was in the financial services industry, I had no will and no life insurance.

I walked away from being hit by a box truck (doing about 55 miles an hour) with stitches in my face, memory loss, and overall body pain. It was a wakeup call to put together a plan for my son. I am a single mom and a solo mom and had nothing in place for him if something happened to me.

I met with an advisor who suggested some term life insurance as well as some permanent life insurance term for the income replacement for my son until he reached 25 and permanent insurance that could double up as both income replacement for him as well as cash value that would build up in a variable product that I could use to supplement his 529 plan. If not needed for my son's college tuition, I'd also have that available to me for retirement income.

Fast forward to age 32, and I was diagnosed with a blood clot in my brain. I spent a week in the intensive care unit and then the stroke floor until they figured out how to treat me. When in the hospital, there was a lot less stress and anxiety because my planning was in place and if something happened everything was already taken care of.

Thankfully, I'm still walking this planet and two years ago decided to update my financial plan. My son turned 25, and I was now looking at my retirement (specifically on extended care planning). Three of my four grandparents suffered from dementia or Alzheimer's, and my parents were getting to an older age. Looking at the cost of healthcare and long-term care, I wanted to make sure that I had something in place again to take that burden off my shoulders and make sure my son would not need to worry about paying for any of my care.

I was able to exchange the cash value in the variable life insurance policy and split it between a paid-up life insurance policy of approximately $600,000 that I can use either for charitable bequest or as a legacy asset. I have no worries of any future premiums, and it's guaranteed to last to age 129 with no future payment.

I took the other half of the cash value, about $100,000, and used it as a single pay into a long-term care policy. Based on a hypothetical return of 6% (as this is on a variable chassis), I will have approximately $1,000,000 at age 84 to use for my long-term care. This money will come out tax free and will be a wonderful supplement to paying for any home health care, assisted living, or long-term care that I might need.

DIVORCEES AND WIDOWS

Lindsey Lewis, a Chartered Financial Consultant' (ChFC'), MBA, and CFP® Professional, is a dedicated advocate for diverse women in the financial services industry. With experience as a senior financial advisor at a leading broker-dealer, she is trailblazing her role as managing director and chair of the American College Center for Women in Financial Services. Passionate about modernizing the industry, she collaborates with firms to develop strategies that attract and retain diverse talent.

As we learned throughout this book, not all clients are divorcées or widows, but many women fall into those buckets. When working as a senior financial advisor, Lindsey, experienced what many financial professionals experience, working with women post-divorce. What was fascinating about these two client cases for Lindsey was that both women experienced "gray divorce," meaning the separation happened near or during retirement years. One of her clients got divorced at 80! Now this is where being a "therapist" for clients comes into play.

Lindsey's female client aged 80 got divorced from male client aged 85. Her client had never utilized technology and did not have any idea how her money was being invested. Her previous spouse stated that she was in "conservative investments that should take care of her throughout her life." This female client's portfolio of nearly $1M was invested completely in the S&P 500. With her RMDs and charitable contribution desires, this was a misalignment on many levels. Additionally, in the divorce, the female spouse was still paying the expensive memory care facility cost, and he did not chip in on the expenses.

This is where empathy paired with applied financial knowledge comes into play. Based on an investment analysis and the client's risk tolerance level, Lindsey wanted to dive into correcting the investment allocation. This client, however, was more concerned about her charitable contributions and paying her bills. This is where there was time spent understanding the client and her needs. Lindsey listened and worked through three phone calls before the client was ready to change her allocation. Had Lindsey "bulldozed" through the recommendations, she would have missed the opportunity to partner with this client.

As it relates to empathy, Lindsey also shared about a client who got divorced around age 60. Her previous spouse and she were just married under 10 years. After their divorce, she began working at a state-run agency. This client did not realize that she was not paying into Social Security. Because she had worked on and off, personally she had not acquired enough quarters to qualify for her own Social Security benefit. The state-run pension would not kick in until 20 years of working, and because her previous marriage did not meet the 10-year rule for Social Security, she essentially was in a position where she would never be able to retire. Lindsey and this client sat in that room together and just cried. It was devastating for them. There were no quick remedies, loopholes, or answers in that moment that could subside their grief.

Even though qualified financial professionals possess technical answers and best practices, the reality is that without the appropriate runway, it can be challenging or nearly impossible to implement these strategies effectively. Some days, our role extends beyond financial expertise, requiring us to exercise our therapy skills and express empathy and sympathy. This underscores the critical importance of competent, applicable, and quality financial advice for women *early* and *regularly*. Ensuring that women are informed and prepared can prevent such heartbreaking situations and provide them with the financial security they deserve.

LAZETTA RAINEY BRAXTON'S STORY

Lazetta Rainey Braxton, MBA, CFP® is a high-impact, solution-oriented chief executive with a proven track record of building successful entrepreneurial ventures, driving innovation, and navigating the complexity of diversity in the financial services industry. As a qualified financial and human capital strategist, she possesses significant experience with RIA start-ups, brand positioning, and media engagement as in her roles as founder and managing principal of The Real Wealth Coterie, a wealth management and RIA firm, and of Lazetta & Associates, a business consulting firm. Here, she tells of her experience:

At The Real Wealth Coterie, we guide clients in aligning their mission, mind, and money. We anchor our guidance in the belief that you are your biggest asset. Human capital–your education, expertise, experience, and essence–elevates your access to income and its transformation into wealth. The ownership and management of human capital hold significant meaning to me as one of the few Black, female-owned registered investment advisor (RIA) firms.

As a descendant of enslaved people in the United States, my ancestors appeared as line items on slave owners' balance sheets and were insured as assets. My distant grandmothers' birthed children of slave owners through force and not choice, with their heirs disregarded as beneficiaries of the largesse built by my Black ancestors.

Fast forward to 2024, Black women who work at White male-dominated institutions continue to lag in pay, earning only $0.63 for every $1 a White man earns. The deficient earning power across centuries stiffens our ability to turn income into wealth and live the life and legacy we desire and deserve.

My decision to earn my Certified Financial Planner® designation and empower households with knowing, owning, and navigating their worth through financial planning allows me to work with a broad spectrum of people with aligned visions and values. In this exercise, I will highlight how I guide clients in unleashing their human capital as valued professionals on their *Real Wealth* journey.

UNLEASHING HUMAN CAPITAL THROUGH FINANCIAL PLANNING

Knowing and strategically positioning our worth in today's workplace requires unrelenting confidence and knowledge of corporate tactics and personal finance. Corporations seek to maximize their profits, and employees seek to maximize their compensation. The inherent conflict of interest demands that each party position themselves for an optimal win-win situation. As a fiduciary, I represent my clients' best interests in protecting and advancing their economic circumstances.

The *Real Wealth* journey introduces career planning in the second meeting, the Envision Meeting. During this meeting, we ask our onboarding clients whether they enjoy their jobs and the reasons behind their answers. Their answers provide insight into the investment and potential trajectory of their human capital. We listen for workplace conditions that offer support, pay equity, promotion, and advancement. We gauge their initiative to test their market value by entertaining recruiters and job opportunities.

When we devise their financial plan, we incorporate the qualitative data from the Envision Meeting and research quantitative data on comparable salary and compensation using databases such as Salary.com and Monster.com and job listing websites such as Indeed and LinkedIn. The client's length of employment with their current employer may also indicate the competitiveness of their current compensation package.

One of our clients demonstrated strong loyalty to her employer despite the questionable workplace culture and volatile line of business. She preferred comfortable chaos over consequential change. Her 15+ year tenure proved compensative stagnation with a material gap relative to market rate packages for her experience and expertise.

The quantitative projection in their financial plan indicated that the couple would need additional income to realize their goals. This observation strengthened our recommendation to explore new job opportunities aligned with their values and goals. We provided our salary negotiation spreadsheet detailing aspects of position, compensation, and benefits compared to new job opportunities. The one-page visualization assisted the client with a clear understanding of her current situation and room for advancement.

The client also engaged a career coach to assist with the "mind" aspect of embracing change. We invited her to share updates as a collaborative process with alliance partners to guide our mutual client in achieving her goal. We also invited her CPA to share tax implications of various benefit opportunities such as bonuses, RSUs, and deferred compensation. When the desired job opportunities arose, we had a role-play session that empowered her to incorporate salary negotiation and market research into the negotiation process in her own way. We invited an employment attorney to assist with successfully negotiating a total compensation 39% higher than her previous position. To add icing on the cake, she joined a more supportive work environment.

The client acknowledged that I stretched her limiting beliefs about her value and worth. While she recognized that I held her to her vision and values, she often felt uncomfortable working through being true to herself during our meetings. She and her spouse experienced great relief with the career planning outcome. This pivotal step allows them to experience a new level of *Real Wealth*.

As trusted partners in the financial planning experience, clients look to us to provide holistic approaches to defining and building their wealth and securing their legacy. Investing in oneself can be the playbook for the approach to investing in a broader portfolio of assets. Guiding clients in assessing risk and reward in their own lives empowers them to screen future investment opportunities with care and confidence.

MY CLIENT CASE STUDIES

Client type: Breadwinner and business owner

This client is a very high earner. Her husband stays home to take care of the kids. She owns her own successful firm.

Challenge: She has no time! Between running her firm and being a mom, financial planning and financial decisions are *not* top of mind. They are on the bottom of the list, but she still worries about finances and knows she should be doing more. She also thinks she is overpaying in taxes and hasn't even thought about college for her kids. She has a 401(k) but not sure if she is in the right investments. She hates budgeting or being told to spend less. They are worried about their aging parents. She is also comfortable delegating.

Solution: She needs a female advocate. Step one is to work with her and her husband to establish a financial plan baseline, get all her goals down and see where she is toward retirements, cash flow, taxes, college, investments, and estate goals. I reviewed her taxes, and because she is self-employed, she can set up a cash balance in conjunction with her current 401(k) at work. This will save her over $100,000 a year in taxes while funding retirement, which is 10–20 years away. We can establish 529s for the kids and got them on auto-deductions so they can set it and forget it. We can use behavioral finance to understand goals and risk tolerances and rebalance to be aligned with her values. We can do baseline estate planning so she has documents in place if something happens to her. We will make sure her insurance life, health, and long-term care is what they need. Finally we will meet with them twice a year for check-ins and monitor their performance along the way.

Feedback: My client says she can sleep at night now. She doesn't worry anymore about finances because she knows, thanks to me, she has all her ducks in a row. Saving her time and money on her taxes are just another benefit to our relationship.

Client type: Early retiree

Challenge: My client, who is also the primary breadwinner, got offered an early retirement buyout from her firm where she worked for more than 25 years. She was 55. She came to me to evaluate her options. She lived in the

Northeast but wanted to move to Florida. Her dream was to build a new home. Her husband was on the same page. They were a blended family, and each had children from a previous marriage. Her health was not great, and she rarely had time to exercise with her demanding job.

Solution: We had to really get to know our clients and do a financial plan for them. The biggest hurdle was finding out if she should take the buyout offer. The answer was yes. Then we had to figure out how to get her dream retirement home in Florida. She retired, moved to Florida, and her life changed overnight. Her health significantly improved. She takes walks in nature daily and says she has to pinch herself. We figured out estate planning for the two of them, which is important with a blended family. We want to make sure no children get disinherited. We manage her and her husband's investments according to how comfortable they are with the market.

Client feedback: Cary is phenomenal. She clearly cares about her clients and consistently takes time to understand our goals and priorities. Her in-depth industry knowledge has ensured that our money has been well managed and her regular updates regarding our personalized portfolio strategies keep us well-informed. She is the perfect mix of honest and supportive. She is a huge part of making our retirement dreams come true and we are so grateful for her.

Client type: Recipient of an unexpected inheritance

My client's dad passed away unexpectedly. He was a child of the Holocaust. He never spent anything, and no one, including the family, knew he had any money. He died with an eight-figure estate. My client never worked with an advisor and wanted to be true to her dad and honor his estate, but she also saw the value of working with professionals, CFPs, CPAs, and attorneys (which her dad never did). Due to his life history, he believed no one should know your business.

Challenge: Because her father had never worked with anyone, the flow of the estate was a bit of a mess. Beneficiaries did not necessarily match the will, taxation of specific assets were not optimal, intentions may not have met precise objectives, all matched with the grief of his widow who had difficulty making financial decisions on how to proceed and moving forward.

Solution: We began by assessing the full family wealth picture, not only for our client, but also her mother, measuring both the family's common objectives as well as our client's and her mother's. Eventually, the client's mother also became my client, and we worked integrally with her other advisors, both accountant and estate attorney, to start organizing the pieces of the puzzle, in a tax efficient manner, updating beneficiaries to match the family's intended risk tolerance and wealth distribution to the second generation, and beyond.

Client feedback: Cary makes financial advising personable, family centered, and classy: all things hard to find in services today, which lean to automation and generic AI prompts, impersonal teams, etc. The fact that Cary doesn't give up the true purpose of her profession makes her a champion. I applaud Cary for doing this, through all the layers and realities of womanhood and life in professionalism.

Client type: Recent divorcee

My client never worked. She was a stay-at-home mom and was very happy to take care of her husband and the children.

Challenge: She put her career on hold to support her family. She was upset and never expected this to happen to her. She was scared and felt she had lost her identity. On the precipice of this upending change, she was not sleeping or eating and didn't know what to do.

Solution: I was able to work with her as a female advocate. In this role, I was more than an advisor: I was a friend, confidant, and supporter. We worked together to figure out what she wanted her new life to look like. The silver lining was that due to my own divorce, I understood what she was going through. I went to mediations with her and advised her on what we should ask for. We discussed whether to sell the house and figured out what she needed to support herself. I taught her about investing and how to live off the portfolio she received in her settlement.

Client feedback: I would not have been able to make it through that dark time in my life without Cary. She made me stronger and the woman I am today.

Client type: Her husband and son died in an unexpected accident

My client was overwhelmed with grief after losing the love of her life and her child at the same time. She and her husband owned a business together, and he usually handled all the finances. She was understandably overcome by all the decisions she had to make. She didn't know who to trust but she knew wouldn't stay with her husband's advisor.

Challenge: She was untrusting and had to bring a family member to every meeting just to make sure she didn't miss anything. We had to get her set up to dissolve the business and real estate and to move, set up her financial accounts for her to pay her bills, and make sure her remaining child was her beneficiary.

Solution: We began with basic financial education while she was still grieving. We met regularly and made sure she was comfortable with everything we did. We did financial planning, investment management, and set her up with a new CPA and estate attorney. She became stronger and more educated. We set her up to live comfortably off her portfolio so she didn't have to worry about money.

Client feedback: I value my relationship with Cary. She was there with me during a very dark time, and she is a friend first. She always gives me wise counsel, and I am empowered now to understand everything I need to know about my finances.

NOTE

1. A tender offer often occurs when an investor *proposes buying shares from every shareholder of a publicly traded company for a certain price* at a certain time.

CHAPTER TWENTY-TWO

STORYTELLING AND SELLING HELP

Storytelling is the new marketing. It's about creating an emotional connection with your audience and making them feel a part of your brand's journey.

–Bernadette Jiwa

Storytelling is vital in the financial services industry for numerous and varied reasons.

1. **Builds Trust and Rapport**
   - **Personal Connection:** Storytelling allows women to build personal connections with clients, establishing trust and rapport. Clients often respond positively to narratives that humanize the advisor and create a shared experience.
   - **Relatability:** Stories help make complex financial concepts more relatable and understandable, enhancing clients' comfort and confidence in their financial decisions.

2. **Differentiates in a Competitive Market**
   - **Unique Perspective:** Women can use storytelling to highlight their unique perspectives and experiences, differentiating themselves from competitors. This personal touch can be a compelling factor for clients.
   - **Brand Building:** Crafting a distinctive personal brand through storytelling resonates emotionally with clients, fostering loyalty and long-term relationships.
3. **Overcomes Stereotypes and Bias**
   - **Challenging Norms:** In a male-dominated industry, storytelling enables women to challenge stereotypes and demonstrate their expertise in an engaging manner.
   - **Empowerment:** Sharing stories of success and resilience can inspire other women, promoting a more inclusive and supportive financial environment.
4. **Simplifies Complex Information**
   - **Narrative Structure:** Financial services can be complex. Storytelling simplifies these concepts, making them more accessible and easier to understand.
   - **Illustrative Examples:** Real-life examples and anecdotes illustrate financial principles, strategies, and outcomes, making information more tangible and relevant to clients.
5. **Creates Emotional Engagement**
   - **Emotional Connection:** Decisions are based on emotions as much as logic. Storytelling allows women to connect with clients emotionally, making their advice and services more compelling and memorable.
   - **Trust and Empathy:** Stories that convey empathy and understanding build deeper trust and rapport, crucial in financial

advisory roles where clients need to feel secure about sharing personal financial information.

6. **Serves as an Educational Tool**
   - **Learning Through Stories:** Clients often learn better through stories than abstract concepts or statistics. Women can use storytelling to educate clients on financial strategies and their impacts.
   - **Engagement and Retention:** Engaging stories help clients retain information better, leading to informed decision-making and greater satisfaction with advisory services.

7. **Nurtures Advocacy and Influence**
   - **Advocacy:** Storytelling helps women advocate for their clients' best interests, explaining recommendations persuasively and convincingly.
   - **Influence:** Compelling narratives influence clients' financial behaviors and attitudes, encouraging more prudent and proactive financial management.

KEY ATTRIBUTES FOR CLIENT RELATIONSHIPS

Based on the NY Life Women's Foundational Study, successful client relationships with women hinge on five attributes:

- Empathy
- Financial wellness
- Alignment
- Communication
- Education

SUGGESTED DOS AND DON'TS

Do

- **Listen:** Pay close attention to the client's needs, concerns, and preferences.
- **Empathize:** Show genuine empathy to make clients feel comfortable, heard, and seen.
- **Observe body language:** Interpret nonverbal cues to understand client's feelings and reactions.
- **Tell Stories:** Use relatable anecdotes and personal experiences to illustrate points and connect with clients.

Don't

- **Ignore her:** Always acknowledge and validate the client's input and feelings.
- **Make her feel silly:** Avoid making clients feel foolish for not understanding complex financial concepts.
- **Use jargon:** Use clear, straightforward language instead of industry jargon that might confuse the client.
- **Mansplain:** Avoid patronizing explanations; ensure communication is respectful and considerate.

Fostering Trust and Transparency

Trust and transparency are crucial in building and maintaining relationships with female clients. Financial professionals should strive to do the following:

- **Communicate clearly:** Use clear, jargon-free language to explain investment options, risks, and strategies. Ensure clients fully understand their financial plans and feel confident in their decisions.
- **Be accessible:** Make yourself available to answer questions, provide guidance, and address concerns promptly. Establishing open lines of communication fosters trust and demonstrates your commitment to your clients' success.
- **Show empathy:** Recognize and respect the unique challenges and experiences that women may face in their financial journeys. Approach each client with empathy and understanding, offering support and encouragement along the way.

Events to Attract Female Clients

Attracting women as clients in financial services can be achieved through targeted events that address their unique needs and preferences. Based on the NY Life research, married breadwinners have an 81% likelihood of participating in these events. Following are several ideas for events that can help:

- **Educational Workshops and Seminars:** Focus on financial literacy, investment strategies, retirement planning, and tax planning.
- **Networking and Community Building:** Create opportunities for women to connect with peers and mentors in the financial industry.
- **Specialized Events:** Offer workshops for entrepreneurs, family financial planning, and women's wealth management.
- **Experiential Events:** Host financial planning boot camps, investment clubs, and retreats focusing on financial wellness.
- **Digital and Virtual Events:** Provide accessible financial education through webinars, online courses, and podcast series.
- **Partnerships and Collaborations:** Collaborate with women's organizations and sponsor events to reach a wider audience.

- **Personalized Financial Planning Sessions:** Offer one-on-one consultations and small group advising to provide tailored advice.
- **Themed Events:** Organize themed events such as brunch and learns, spa parties, travel experiences, and more to engage and educate clients in a relaxed setting. Following is a list of ideas:
  - **Financial Fitness Challenges:** Organize challenges that motivate women to achieve specific financial goals.
  - **Brunch and Learn (or Lunch and Learn):** Combine social elements with educational content in a relaxed setting.
  - **Spa Parties:** These are my favorite. I've done these for clients, friends, and future clients. I've rented the entire spa a few times and I've done it in my home and made every room in the house a spa room.
  - **Travel Experiences**
  - **Paint and Pour**
  - **Fraud Prevention:** Teach women useful information; I would even do it to protect them from the "Tinder Swindler" romance scams.
  - **Health and Wealth Combined:** I used to do presentations with a female cardiologist, and it was fantastic.
  - **Women, Wealth, and Wine:** These are evening events for socializing and having an educational speaker. You could also bring in a sommelier.
  - **Fashion and Finance:** I've seen fashion shows or partnering with local women's clothing stores. High-end boutiques work well because they can host in the store.
  - **Beauty and Finance:** This is similar to the spa events with makeovers and products and makeup. It can also be a local store. You can also partner with a plastic surgeon or cosmetic dermatologist.
  - **Valentine's Lunch for Your Clients Without a Sweetheart:** I love this one.

- **Art Show or Shows:** These work even better if your client is an artist.

By integrating storytelling into their practice and organizing events tailored to women's needs, financial advisors can build stronger relationships, foster trust, and differentiate themselves in a competitive market.

Questions for Financial Advisors to Ask Themselves

1. How can I integrate storytelling into my practice to build stronger client relationships?
2. What unique experiences and perspectives can I share to differentiate myself from competitors?
3. How can I use storytelling to simplify complex financial concepts for my clients?
4. In what ways can I create emotional connections with my clients through storytelling?
5. How can I ensure my communication is empathetic, clear, and jargon-free?
6. What types of events can I organize to attract and engage female clients?
7. How can I foster trust and transparency with my clients through storytelling and open communication?

Connection, Authenticity, and Partnership

- *For Clients:* "What does a genuine and trusted partnership with a financial advisor look like to you?"
- *For Advisors:* "How can I build authentic connections with my female clients that foster trust and collaboration?"

Storytelling

- *For Clients:* "Would you be open to sharing your financial journey or any personal experiences that have shaped your money mindset?"
- *For Advisors:* "Am I creating an environment where my female clients feel comfortable telling their stories?"

Communication Style

- *For Clients:* "Do you prefer discussing financial plans in a more detailed and personal way? How can I better align my communication with your needs?"
- *For Advisors:* "Am I actively listening to the emotional cues and detailed stories my female clients share?"

Defining Success

- *For Clients:* "What does financial success mean to you personally? Is it about peace of mind, freedom, or something else?"
- *For Advisors:* "Am I helping my female clients define and achieve success in a way that aligns with their values and peace of mind?"

Loyalty

- *For Clients:* "What qualities or values in a financial advisor are most important for building a long-term relationship?"
- *For Advisors:* "How can I demonstrate commitment and consistency to foster loyalty among my female clients?"

Perspective on Wealth

- *For Clients:* "How do you view wealth in terms of security, freedom, or life goals? What role does money play in your life beyond just financial gain?"
- *For Advisors:* "Am I focusing on the security and well-being aspects of wealth that many female clients prioritize?"

Philanthropy

- *For Clients:* "Are there causes or philanthropic goals that are important to you? How would you like your wealth to make a positive impact?"
- *For Advisors:* "Am I incorporating philanthropy and impact-driven strategies in my planning for clients who value giving back?"

KEY TAKEAWAYS

1. **Builds Trust and Rapport:** Storytelling humanizes advisors, fostering trust and making financial concepts more relatable.
2. **Differentiates in a Competitive Market:** Personal stories help women stand out and build strong personal brands.
3. **Overcomes Stereotypes:** Storytelling challenges industry biases and empowers women by sharing success and resilience.
4. **Simplifies Complex Information:** Narratives make financial concepts easier to understand through real-life examples.
5. **Creates Emotional Engagement:** Stories connect emotionally, making advice more memorable and building trust.

6. **Serves as an Educational Tool:** Clients learn better through engaging stories, leading to better decision-making.
7. **Nurtures Advocacy and Influence:** Storytelling helps advisors advocate persuasively and influence client behavior.
8. **Social Events for Women:** Women love events just for them. Use this as a great way to meet new clients and prospects and deepen the relationships with your current female clients.

CHAPTER TWENTY-THREE

MAKING THE INDUSTRY FEMALE-FRIENDLY

When women do better, economies do better.
–Christine Lagarde, former Managing Director of the
International Monetary Fund (IMF)

UNDERSTANDING THE NEED FOR CHANGE

This is a difficult nut to crack. I've often been told there is nothing wrong with the industry as it is. However, after reading this book, I hope you see the need for change. It's clear that many things need to change, and it's not just one issue. The industry is built by men, for men. Women are often an afterthought. It's nobody's fault, but it's a reality we need to address.

What is interesting is that when researching for this chapter, nothing specifically aimed at female clients came up. The focus was primarily on gender equity, gender equality, and bringing more women into leadership. While these are important, our industry faces additional hurdles because many women and girls don't even know what a financial planner is unless they have a personal connection to one. Societal issues influence how women are raised, taught math and money, and why they might think men will handle financial matters for them.

I put this query on LinkedIn: What are ways to make financial services more "female-friendly" for clients? I received hundreds of comments, with suggestions like *respect her, listen to her, see her, add a woman to your team, talk about health care, use stories, avoid technical jargon, create safe spaces, promote women to leadership positions, talk about emotions and feelings, create a community,* and *ask her what keeps her up at night. Care, spend more time with her.* Some people questioned why women should be treated differently.

WHERE MY GIRLS AT?

It starts with getting more women into the profession. How do we reach girls and plant seeds that this is a career? This is a problem for all of us. Girls are not adequately exposed to our profession, leading to the current gender imbalance, with only 23.6% of CFP° professionals being female. We must expand our efforts to reach female candidates at younger ages.

One significant challenge is raising awareness among women about this career path. Initiatives like the collaboration between Charles Schwab and Girl Scouts of the USA to modernize and relaunch the Girl Scouts' financial literacy badges are a good start. Additionally, events like the Girl Scouts National Convention in Orlando, known as Phenom by Girl Scouts, provide inspiring spaces for girls to explore financial careers.

The author and Reshell Smith, Orlando, FL, July 2023 at Girl Scout National Convention

MORE WOMEN IN KEY POSITIONS

Workforce diversity boosts performance. A BlackRock study from November 2023 titled "Lifting Global Growth by Investing in Women," highlights that gender lens investing significantly boosts financial performance and supports gender equality. Key findings include the following:

1. **Improved Financial Returns:** Companies with diverse workforces, particularly those with women in executive roles, outperform their peers by 1.6% in return on assets, resulting in an average outperformance of 29% per year. Portfolios of overweight companies

promoting women into senior roles performed 72 basis points better annually than the MSCI World Index over the past four years.

2. **Enhanced Start-up Performance:** Women-owned startups delivered twice the return per dollar invested compared to those founded by men between 2014 and 2022.

3. **Economic Impact:** Women's increasing purchasing power and financial capital are driving economic growth. McKinsey predicts that by 2030, more than two-thirds of US wealth will be held by women.

4. **Venture Capital Success:** Venture capital firms with a higher percentage of female partners achieve better returns and more profitable exits. A UN Women report indicated that firms with just 10% more female investing partners saw 1.5% higher fund returns and 9.7% more profitable exits.

5. **Gender Lens Investing Growth:** The market for gender lens equity funds and bonds is expanding, with significant assets under management and strong performance. These investments not only advance gender equality but also achieve robust financial results.

MAKE MONEY EQUAL CAMPAIGN

A Make Money Equal Campaign was commissioned as part of Starling Bank and Brunel University in London. In May 2021, they did a Summary Report: "Gendered Representation of Money in Visual Media, a Study." It states, "Our world is not only represented through images, but it is also shaped by them. They influence our self-perceptions of belonging and capacity, as well as how we judge others and behave towards them. Visual representation of money and how men and women use it are particularly important because money is so central to living a full and fair life."

This study concluded that women are portrayed as immature and unsophisticated when it comes to money. It cited outdated stereotypes of women as passive, inexperienced, or inept. It portrayed women as spenders and men as savers.

I had trouble finding a stock image for this book. I searched for an image of a confident female who was strong with money. What kept coming up was a woman in her 20s married to a sugar daddy in his 80s. A picture speaks 1,000 words. This bank teamed up with Lensi photography to create inclusive and empowered women with money photos. You can search for #makemoneyequal online for examples.

LEARNING FROM OTHER INDUSTRIES

Technology: The technology sector has seen initiatives aimed at increasing the representation and support of women. Companies like Google and Microsoft have launched various programs to support women in tech, including mentorship and career development programs. I was fortunate enough to speak to some female execs from Google. The first one was Diana Britt who said they set up employee resource groups (ERGs) for women, formal sponsorship programs, and mentor rings. They have strong male allies. Mary Gerhardt was the second woman I spoke to and a member of the Google Cloud Sales Organization; she said, "In my experience as a Googler, we are getting it right for gender equality."

Consumer Goods and Retail: These industries have increasingly focused on products and marketing strategies that resonate with female consumers. Brands like Procter & Gamble have launched empowering campaigns, such as "Like a Girl" By Always and "Share the Load" Take out by Ariel.

Automotive: The automotive industry is also making efforts to appeal to female buyers. Manufacturers are designing cars with features that cater to women's preferences and safety concerns, and dealerships are training staff to provide a more inclusive customer service experience. Campaigns like Audi's "Daughter" and Nissan's "She's Mercedes" are examples of this shift.

Health Care: The healthcare industry has increasingly recognized the importance of addressing women's specific health needs. Services tailored to women, such as the Cleveland Clinic's Women's Health Center and Johnson & Johnson's focus on women's health innovation, are becoming more prevalent.

BUILDING A SUPPORTIVE COMMUNITY

Creating a supportive community is crucial. A mastermind group formed after the release of "Where Are All the Women" led to a fantastic article in Rethinking 65 by Jeri Klein, highlighting female advisors' experiences. One is called, "Female Advisors Need More Pathways"; the other is called, "Female Rainmakers Reveal Secrets to Success." It's clear that support, mentorship, and community are essential for women to thrive in the financial services industry.

Questions for Financial Advisors to Ask Themselves

1. **Awareness and Understanding**
   - Do I understand the unique financial challenges and goals that women may face?
   - How can I improve my awareness of gender biases in financial planning?

2. **Client Engagement**
   - Am I actively listening to my female clients and addressing their specific concerns?
   - Do I create a safe and inclusive environment where women feel comfortable discussing their finances?
3. **Team Diversity**
   - Is my team diverse and representative of the clients we serve?
   - How can I ensure that women are included in decision-making processes within my practice?
4. **Education and Outreach**
   - What initiatives can I implement to educate young girls and women about financial planning careers?
   - How can I collaborate with organizations to promote financial literacy among women?
5. **Personal Reflection**
   - Am I challenging my own assumptions and stereotypes about women and money?
   - How can I become a more empathetic and supportive advisor for my female clients?

By asking these questions and acting, we can begin to make the financial services industry more inclusive and supportive for women, both as clients and professionals.

UNLOCKING THE FULL POTENTIAL

By understanding and addressing the distinct needs of female investors, financial professionals can unlock significant growth opportunities. Tailoring your approach to better serve women not only drives business success but also contributes to closing the gender wealth gap and promoting financial equality.

To reshape the financial services industry, we must engage with women throughout their lives, providing support and resources to enhance financial literacy and empower them as wealth creators and decision-makers. Closing the gender gap in financial services could unlock $700 billion in revenue and secure the future of women around the world.

Women's rising wealth presents a transformative opportunity for financial professionals. By leveraging research, embracing tailored strategies, and building authentic relationships, you can harness this demographic shift to achieve million-dollar success. Seize the moment and position yourself as a trusted advisor who champions the financial empowerment of women.

We're not where I want us to be. I hope that we can get there during my lifetime. That's my goal: to change the industry so it's better for women advisors, CFPs, employees, and clients. My hope is that reading this book opens your eyes, ears, and hearts and makes you the best advisor you can be for yourself and your clients—or even better, a better human being!

KEY TAKEAWAYS

1. **Recognizing the Need for Change:** The financial services industry was historically built for men, often overlooking the needs of women. A cultural shift is necessary to better serve female clients and create a more inclusive environment.

2. **Importance of Exposure:** Many women and girls lack awareness of financial planning careers. Initiatives to engage young women early and expose them to financial literacy are essential to balancing the gender disparity within the profession.

3. **Empathy and Engagement:** Advisors must focus on listening, respecting, and understanding female clients' unique needs.

Creating safe, inclusive spaces and avoiding jargon are key strategies to foster trust and long-term relationships.

4. **Promoting Women in Leadership:** Greater diversity, especially in leadership roles, enhances company performance. Research shows that firms with more women in executive positions achieve better financial outcomes and growth.

5. **Gender Lens Investing:** Investments that prioritize gender equality deliver strong financial returns. Supporting women-owned start-ups and investing in gender-diverse companies leads to improved profitability and economic growth.

6. **Changing Stereotypes in Media:** Visual representation in media shapes societal perceptions. Campaigns like Starling Bank's #MakeMoneyEqual challenge outdated portrayals of women in financial roles, promoting more empowered, accurate imagery.

7. **Learning from Other Industries:** Sectors like technology, consumer goods, and healthcare have launched successful initiatives to support women, offering valuable lessons for financial services to adopt.

8. **Building a Supportive Community:** Mentorship, networking, and collaborative communities are crucial for women to thrive in the financial services industry. Creating pathways for female professionals strengthens the industry's diversity and success.

9. **Asking the Right Questions:** Financial advisors must reflect on their practices by asking if they're actively engaging with female clients, promoting diversity, and challenging biases within their teams.

10. **Unlocking Women's Wealth Potential:** By addressing the distinct financial needs of women, the industry can close the gender wealth gap and unlock immense business opportunities, securing growth and success for both advisors and clients.

RESOURCES

Empowering Female Anthems: Songs That Inspire and Uplift

Music has a unique power to inspire, uplift, and empower. For women, songs that celebrate strength, independence, and resilience can be particularly motivating. Here are some of the most empowering female anthems that you should add to your playlist today, in no particular order!

1. *"Run the World (Girls)" by Beyoncé*
   This powerhouse anthem from Queen Bey is all about female empowerment. With its infectious beat and bold lyrics, "Run the World (Girls)" celebrates the strength, resilience, and power of women everywhere. It's the perfect song to boost your confidence and remind you that you can conquer anything.

2. *"Fight Song" by Rachel Platten*
   Rachel Platten's "Fight Song" is an emotional and powerful declaration of inner strength. This song became an anthem for many who

needed a reminder that their voice matters and that they have the strength to overcome any obstacle.

3. *"Roar" by Katy Perry*

Katy Perry's "Roar" is a triumphant anthem about finding your voice and standing up for yourself. The empowering lyrics and upbeat melody make it a perfect song to lift your spirits and remind you of your inner power.

4. *"Stronger (What Doesn't Kill You)" by Kelly Clarkson*

Kelly Clarkson's hit song "Stronger" is all about resilience and coming back stronger after facing challenges. With its catchy chorus and motivational message, it's an ideal anthem for anyone going through tough times.

5. *"Girl on Fire" by Alicia Keys*

Alicia Keys' "Girl on Fire" is a celebration of powerful, unstoppable women. With its soulful melody and empowering lyrics, this song is perfect for when you need a reminder of your own strength and potential.

6. *"Confident" by Demi Lovato*

Demi Lovato's "Confident" is a bold anthem about owning who you are and embracing your confidence. Its powerful beat and assertive lyrics make it a great song to play when you need a boost of self-assurance.

7. *"Respect" by Aretha Franklin*

Aretha Franklin's classic "Respect" is a timeless anthem for women's empowerment. This song demands respect and asserts the importance of self-worth and dignity. It's an essential addition to any empowering playlist.

8. *"Survivor" by Destiny's Child*

"Survivor" by Destiny's Child is a powerful song about overcoming hardships and emerging stronger. Its fierce lyrics and upbeat tempo make it a great motivational anthem for anyone facing challenges.

9. **"Unstoppable" by Sia**

Sia's "Unstoppable" is an empowering song about resilience and strength. With its uplifting lyrics and powerful chorus, it's perfect for when you need a reminder that you can handle anything life throws your way.

10. **"Born This Way" by Lady Gaga**

Lady Gaga's "Born This Way" is a celebration of individuality and self-acceptance. Its inclusive message and danceable beat make it a fantastic anthem for embracing who you are and celebrating your uniqueness.

11. **"Just a Girl" by No Doubt**

Gwen Stefani's "Just a Girl" addresses the limitations and stereotypes placed on women with a mix of sarcasm and defiance. This punk-pop anthem is perfect for when you want to challenge the status quo and assert your independence.

12. **"Man! I Feel Like a Woman!" by Shania Twain**

Shania Twain's "Man! I Feel Like a Woman!" is a fun and celebratory song about female empowerment. Its catchy chorus and upbeat tempo make it a feel-good anthem for embracing womanhood and having fun.

13. **"Brave" by Sara Bareilles**

Sara Bareilles' "Brave" encourages listeners to speak their truth and be themselves without fear. Its uplifting message and catchy melody make it a perfect anthem for anyone needing a boost of courage.

14. **"Express Yourself" by Madonna**

Madonna's "Express Yourself" is all about self-expression and empowerment. Its energetic beat and bold lyrics encourage listeners to be true to themselves and demand what they deserve.

15. **"Good as Hell" by Lizzo**

   Lizzo's "Good as Hell" is an anthem of self-love and confidence. Its positive vibes and empowering lyrics make it a perfect song to lift your spirits and remind you of your worth.

   These empowering female anthems are more than just songs—they're declarations of strength, independence, and resilience. Whether you need a confidence boost, a reminder of your worth, or just some feel-good vibes, these songs will inspire and uplift you. Add them to your playlist and let their powerful messages motivate you to be the best version of yourself.

16. **"The Man" by Taylor Swift**

   "The Man" by Taylor Swift is a feminist anthem from her 2019 album *Lover*. In this song, Swift explores gender double standards by imagining how her career and personal life would be viewed differently if she were a man. The lyrics criticize the disparities in how society treats successful men versus successful women, addressing issues like how women are judged more harshly for their ambition, relationships, and decisions. Swift uses the song to challenge how men are often praised for behaviors for which women are criticized, such as being assertive or career-driven.

   The song's central message is that, if she were a man, she would be celebrated for her success and confidence rather than facing scrutiny and judgment. Swift uses the lyrics and a powerful music video to highlight how societal expectations and biases still affect how women are perceived in the workplace, media, and relationships.

17. **"Sit Still, Look Pretty" by Daya**

   "Sit Still, Look Pretty" is a 2016 pop song by Daya that challenges traditional gender roles and expectations placed on women. In the song, Daya rejects the notion that women should simply be passive, decorative figures, waiting for a man to provide for them. Instead, she asserts that women are capable of achieving their own dreams and ambitions without relying on a prince or any man to give them a fulfilling life.

The song's empowering message promotes independence and self-sufficiency, encouraging women to focus on their goals and refuse to conform to societal pressures to "sit still" and "look pretty." Its catchy, upbeat rhythm and feminist themes resonated with audiences, making it a popular anthem for female empowerment.

Worthy Nonprofits Helping Women

Savvy Ladies

Savvy Ladies champions the advancement of self-reliant, financially educated women, helping reduce gender, economic, and racial disparities in financial education. Savvy Ladies' mission is to equip and empower women to take control of their finances by providing a professional network of support and guidance, offering free financial professionals and educational programming to help women make informed and confident financial decisions. The Savvy Ladies Free Financial Helpline, the organization's primary free financial educational resource, provides easy access to financial education to all women across the United States and enables women to be matched 1:1 with a Savvy Ladies pro bono financial professional to answer their financial questions, creating pathways to financial advancement, building financial confidence, and promoting financial well-being.

CFP Board Center for Financial Planning

The Center is an initiative of CFP Board to create a more diverse and sustainable financial planning profession so that every American has access to competent and ethical financial planning advice. I am a benefactor of this organization and have spent time on the development committee. My focus, bringing women into the profession.

Women's Leadership Alliance

The Women's Leadership Alliance (WLA) is a 501(c)(3) nonprofit organization founded by a group of leading female financial planning professionals from around the country. The alliance seeks to attract more women into the financial planning industry and to provide impactful resources and empowering support to women financial planning professionals. We are dedicated to changing the conversation regarding women and the field of financial advisory services and strive to significantly increase the ranks of women within this dynamic and meaningful profession.

Rock the Street, Wall Street

We bring the M in STEM to diverse high school girls, offering financial and investment mathematics that support an inspired path from high school and college to their first roles on Wall Street. Our aim is to provide high quality education to break barriers and foster inclusivity in the capital markets and financial workforce, dedicated to empowering young women with equal footing.

BLatinX Internship, Inc.

BLX Internship's mission is to increase awareness and access to the financial planning profession for systematically excluded communities and create opportunities, resources, scholarships, and a community for aspiring financial planners. Their summer internship program provides an entry point to the profession for Black and Latinx individuals. It also provides hiring resources and a talent pipeline to financial planning firms who want more diverse team members. To learn more, please visit blxinternship.org.

Women Moving Millions

Women Moving Millions (WMM) believes that if women step into their leadership and make big bold investments, we can accelerate progress to realize gender equality to support this vision and mission. WMM creates transformational learning opportunities where members can build a supportive peer network and grow within their philanthropy and leadership by leveraging the collective resources, expertise, and influence of the community. Working in partnerships with frontline movement leaders, we believe can build a more equitable world for all.

Amplified Planning, The Externship

Although not a nonprofit, the Externship is an eight-week virtual program for aspiring financial planners and those seeking CFP certification. Held every summer, the Externship is designed to highlight the many ways that financial planning can be done! Externs have access to real client meetings, financial planning technology, *and* trainings/sessions with some of the profession's top experts. They can also network and learn from other aspiring planners and current professionals via Externship forums and live learning calls! Those who complete the Externship in full can earn 500 CFP Board Standard Pathway hours by submitting their certificate of completion. This eight-week summer Externship has become a standard in the profession and boasts more than 3,000 alumni! For more info, go to amplifiedplanning.com/externship.

ACKNOWLEDGEMENTS

Thank you to Judith Newlin from Wiley. Thank you to Rethinking 65 Jerilyn Klein, Dorothy Hinchcliff, Kathleen Kingsbury, Carolyn Mcclanahan, Bridget Grimes, Jessica Bellucci, Chloe Moore, Willow, Lacy Garcia, Eileen Shovlin, Rita Cheng, Theresa Gralinski, Lindsay Lewis, Suzanne Siracuse, Reshell Smith, Barnaby and Alison Reidel, Marie Campion Rich Westhelle, and all my clients who let me fulfill my life's purpose.

AUTHOR BIO

Cary Carbonaro is an award-winning Certified Financial Planner™ professional with more than 25 years of experience and currently serves as Managing Wealth Advisor and Women and Wealth Ambassador for Ashton Thomas. She leads a multimillion-dollar financial planning practice, specializing in empowering women to overcome financial challenges and increase their financial literacy.

Cary's extensive career includes leadership roles at ACM Wealth, Goldman Sachs where she was Vice President and Head of Office, and United Capital where she founded and led the Women's Leadership division. At United Capital, she earned titles such as Diamond Office Winner, Managing Director, Partner, FinLife Coach, and MVP Managing Director.

Cary is the author of the bestselling book, *The Money Queen's Guide: For Women Who Want to Build Wealth and Banish Fear*.

She serves as a CFP® Board Ambassador, representing the financial industry in the media, and has been honored six times on Investopedia's Top 100 Financial Advisors list. In 2016, she was awarded the prestigious Investment News Women to Watch. In 2024, Cary was appointed as the sole female member of the Nasdaq Advisor Council. She has also endowed a scholarship at the State University of New York at Cortland for Women in Business, where she was the founding president of Sigma Delta Tau sorority.

Cary is the founding president of the Women's Giving Alliance, a giving circle in the South Lake Community Foundation, and a member of the Benefactors Circle at the Center for Financial Planning, where she advocates for advancing women in the financial industry.

Cary's knowledge and expertise are highly sought after, and she frequently appears as a commentator on local and national television news channels. She has spoken around the world on financial literacy, with a focus on advocating for women and guiding them to financial empowerment.

TAKEAWAYS

We've covered a lot of ground in this book, but here are some quick reference takeaways:

What Keeps Women Up at Night

- Bag Lady Fear (Not Having Enough Money)
- Healthcare Costs
- Fear of Raising Entitled Children
- Anxiety About Work
- Fear of Success (Higher we climb, the more we get judged)
  - Marianne Williamson said it best: "Our deepest fear is not that we are inadequate. Our deepest fear is that we are powerful beyond measure. It is our light, not our darkness that most frightens us."

Cary's "To Be" List for Financial Planners Working with Women

- Be sensitive.
- Be transparent.
- Be empathetic.

- Be present. (See and hear her.)
- Be a teacher.

What We Can Do

"People don't care how much you know until they know you care." — Theodore Roosevelt

- Plant Seeds for the Future to Girls
- Change the Language
- Bring More Women into Leadership
- Create a Nonjudgmental Environment (where women can be seen, heard, and safe)
- Use Money Stories and Behavioral Finance
- Tie Financial Goals to Dreams and Experiences, Not Numbers
- Don't Use Jargon
- Be Empathetic
- Acknowledge Unconscious Bias
- Help Women Save Time
- Talk About Feelings; Money Is Emotional; Create a Community
- Use Visualization Techniques for Visual Learners
- Have Women on Your Team
- Talk About Health and Menopause
- Understand Fears and Bag Lady Fear
- Understand Women's Risk Tolerance May Be Different and Why
- Study Other Industry Case Studies and How They Changed
- Look Through a Female Gender Lens (and ask a woman if you can't see it)
- Highlight Women Employees and Clients
- Give Women Spaces and Opportunities to Gather and Collaborate
- Take the Quiz to See If Your Practice Is Female-Friendly
- Invest in Professional Development

- Support a More Collaborative, Rather Than Competitive, Approach to Working with Clients
- Be Patient; Women May Take Longer
- Make It a Win-win Collaboration
- Respect HER, Your Clients, Employees, and Women in Your Life

INDEX

Note: Page numbers followed by *f* refer to figures.

O

OECD (Organization for
Economic Cooperation and
Development), 119
Oprah Winfrey Foundation, 252
Oprah's Angel Network, 252
Orlich, Shanna, 182
Orullian, LaRae, 87
Overconfidence, 169. *See also*
Confidence

P

Patronizing attitudes, 50, 63, 204, 342
Pay equity, 27–28, 90, 111–112, 332.
See also Gender pay gap
Perfectionism, 313
Perry, Katy, 360
Personal connections, 34, 56, 58, 200,
203–204, 339, 350
Personal networks, 288
Pew Research Center, 40, 102
Phenom by Girl Scouts, 350, 351*f*
Philanthropy, 233–234, 249–261.
See also Legacy planning
Pink washing, 122
Platten, Rachel, 359
Pooled income funds, 255
Pre-retiree clients, 227
Pregnancy Discrimination Act, 85
PriceMetrix, 32
Private foundations, 254
Procter & Gamble, 353
Product design, 50, 51, 61

Property and casualty (P&C)
agencies, 327
Property ownership (for women),
37, 75, 81
Property rights, 80–82, 95
PwC (PricewaterhouseCoopers), 112

Q

Quad A (Association of African
American Advisors), 85
Qualified charitable distributions
(QCDs), 255

R

Racial bias, 142. *See also* Bias
Radical candor, 271
The Real Wealth Coterie, 330–331
Reddit, 112
Referral Sources, 57, 288–289
Registered investments advisors
(RIAs), 14, 17, 210,
327, 330–331
Remote work, 91, 92, 92
Representation. *See also*
Underrepresentation
advocacy for, 132, 136, 137
awareness of gender, 70
of Black and Hispanic women, 41
cultural, 42
diverse, 108, 144, 157
of female entrepreneurs, 39
of female financial advisors, 33
and gender disparities, 43, 89, 93